# Alex in Wonderland

Alex King is an antidote to the twentieth century blues; a storyteller without peer; one of the few free souls left.

*Mine Enemy Grows Older* is the King in book form: his salt, his warmth, his capacity for coping. It's the explosive autobiography of the last of the unself-conscious nonconformists and it's setting the country on its ear.

## S. J. PERELMAN *calls it uproarious*

"For sheer gusto—or rough-woven gusto which I happen to prefer—I haven't read anything in years that touches *Mine Enemy Grows Older*. Uproarious, anarchic, and loaded with explosive anecdote, his book has wit and abrasive honesty."

## GEORGE S. KAUFMAN *is fascinated by it*

"It's gay and bouncy, and sad and fascinating. You'll get no neutral opinions on it. Me, I had a whale of a time with it."

## GROUCHO MARX *is ecstatic*

"I read the whole thing in two nights. To give you an idea of how insular my existence is, I had never heard of Mr. King. If you see him, please tell him from me that his book is sheer ecstasy."

## CHAS. ADDAMS *reads it non-stop*

"I've just finished *Mine Enemy*. I never stopped, and I know I'll read it again. It's just great. King has known people I think I've invented."

---

THIS IS A REPRINT OF THE HARDCOVER EDITION
ORIGINALLY PUBLISHED BY SIMON AND SCHUSTER.

## Other SIGNET Books You Will Enjoy

**A Child of the Century** *by Ben Hecht*
Packed with sex, laughter and entertainment, the memoirs of a famous Chicago writer who led many lives.                    (#T1212—75¢)

**Too Much, Too Soon**
                                    *by Diana Barrymore & Gerold Frank*
A glamorous actress's candid account of her shocking descent into alcoholism and her courageous comeback.                    (#D1490—50¢)

**The Intimate Henry Miller** *by Henry Miller*
Challenging essays and unorthodox opinions of the controversial author of *Tropic of Cancer*, collected and made available for the first time to a wide audience.                    (#D1653—50¢)

**Safe Conduct** *by Boris Pasternak*
The memorable autobiography, short stories and poems of one of the greatest writers of our time.
                                    (#D1669—50¢)

To Our Readers: We welcome your request for our free catalog of SIGNET and MENTOR Books. If your dealer does not have the books you want, you may order them by mail enclosing the list price plus 5¢ a copy to cover mailing. The New American Library of World Literature, Inc., 501 Madison Avenue, New York 22, N. Y.

# Mine Enemy
# Grows Older

## ALEXANDER KING

 A SIGNET BOOK

Published by THE NEW AMERICAN LIBRARY

*To My Margie*

*All the characters
in this book are real people,
with the possible exception of*

THE AUTHOR

FIRST PRINTING, FEBRUARY, 1960

*SIGNET BOOKS are published by
The New American Library of World Literature, Inc.
501 Madison Avenue, New York 22, N. Y.*

PRINTED IN THE UNITED STATES OF AMERICA

# CHAPTER ONE

IN A SUN-DRENCHED April world when I was only fifteen years old, I had a date to take a pretty girl to the Museum of Art. When we reached the bus stop she got on ahead of me and, because the step was rather high, she disclosed her whole leg and even a piece of an innocently coquettish garter.

Remember, this was some forty years ago. It gave me quite a jolt. A very pleasant jolt, I must say. So, the minute we were seated side by side in the bus, I wondered why in the hell I was taking this rosebud to a dopey museum, of all places.

"How about going to Nepera Park?" I said.

"Aren't we going to the museum?" she asked.

"Yes, but it's such a beautiful day, we can talk about art in Yonkers," I said. "Besides, I know all about Rembrandt anyway."

"You just paid the fare," she said.

"Oh, that's all right," I said. "It's worth it."

It was.

The only reason I have for offering this banal biographical tidbit is that in its own way it is a kind of parable of much that happened to me in the next forty years. Heaven knows I've often carried high and noble purpose in my heart, but, somewhere along the line, I would suddenly glimpse an aspect of some greater urgency and it would unexpectedly change my course. I would leave the well-paved highway of my purposeful intentions and wind up under shadowy ferns among mystical beetle tracks.

The diversions which sent me wandering were not always the legs of youthful seduction. Not a bit of it. Once a playful wind blew a scrap of paper up against me, and on it, quite by accident, was charted the new direction of my life for the following five years.

And why am I bothering to tell all this at this particular time? Well, it all began last year in the office of Dr. Alfred Berenson, a famous genito-urinary specialist in New York City. The doctor was showing me some X-ray photographs of my ravaged interior. The first look I had at the pictures of my kidneys was even more shocking than the first view I ever had of my profile. The blotched and speckled pelvic region seemed like a sinister lunar landscape.

"You've got about six cubic inches of one kidney left," said the doctor, "and even that little piece is full of stones. You need an emergency operation. Better get to the hospital day after tomorrow."

"I'm not so enthusiastic about an operation," I said.

"You haven't got a chance without it," said the doctor.

"And with it?"

"You've got a pretty good chance."

"Just pretty good?"

"Pretty good, pretty good."

And that was that. This conversation took place sixteen months ago on Park Avenue in a room full of auction-room furniture and false friendliness. This Dr. Berenson was the last of a series I had consulted. The most alarming one was a Dr. Vintner. Raoul Vintner. That first name deceived me for a while. He was a surgeon and looked at the world through bloodshot eyes. I had almost decided to let him operate on me, but, corny and sentimental as I am, I wanted to reach a purely human level of sympathy and understanding with him first. I wanted him to like me. There you have it.

I'm like an ancient iguana full of splenetic wrinkles. I wanted this character to respond to my personal charm. I covered him with the slime of my amiability until he looked web-footed. I got no response. Don't misunderstand. I didn't expect him to talk about Babylonian mosaics or Balinese dancing. I just wanted him to emerge for a moment from behind his surgical tools and to give me a reassuring, human wink. No soap.

I finally decided that Dr. Raoul Vintner had become the victim of his own constant occupation and preoccupation. As I looked at him sitting behind his tooled-leather ambuscade I became convinced of it. This squat, ovoid, red-faced man, permanently submerged in his urinous misgivings and speculations, had finally himself turned into a kidney.

I decided to test my theory on the spot.

"How is it possible," I asked, "that such a little piece of kidney has been able to keep me alive all these years?"

He opened his pink eyes and a charming, a beatific, smile spread across his ventricular face.

"My dear boy," he said, "the kidney is a truly *marvelous* organ."

So I had at least knocked a human reaction out of him. I suppose I should have let him carve me up after that. After all, he had the best credentials.

But I left him as I'd left all the others because—well, because I'm terribly dated and full of anachronistic notions. I might as well confess now that today in my latter fifties I still have my appendix, my tonsils and my adenoids.

Like a pterodactyl.

Also, I really haven't much faith in medicine. I know they've made great progress, especially in surgery, but I'm leery of doctors just the same. I'm particularly prejudiced against specialists. When you're sent to them they don't know you and they don't want to know you. They make an efficient chart of that small territory of your afflicted carcass which comes under their jurisdiction and they don't care a hoot in hell about what has broken loose in the adjacent county. The ulcer man is busy with his ulcer routine, the eye-and-ear man will go down as far as the throat, but the kidney man doesn't give a rap what goes on north of the bladder.

For my money they can all drop dead of their specialty.

At any rate, all these doctors agreed that unless I was operated on pretty pronto I would die of uremic shock. The last one I consulted was particularly urgent and persuasive. That was sixteen months ago, but when I sat down to write these pages I still hadn't parted from my ossified giblets.

To tell the truth, the news about my pebbly drainage system was indeed shocking but not altogether unexpected. I had known for some thirty years that I had some gravel deposits in my right kidney. Luckily everybody has two kidneys and I was shrewdly banking on my healthy spare.

Upon close examination it turned out, however, that my left kidney had never functioned at all. In fact, it was unanimously agreed that this *marvelous* organ had probably died early in my childhood shortly after I'd suffered an attack of scarlet fever. That siege of scarlet fever brings to my mind the first doctor I had ever known and in whom I did believe, implicitly.

His name was Dr. Tschurchentaler. Ah! Now, there was a man, a friend, a physician. He was six feet four inches tall and had an enormous red beard. Dr. Tschurchentaler wore a silk hat and a fur-lined coat on all occasions. He moved in a penumbra of carbolic acid and other potent antiseptics, and half an hour after he was gone the place would still reek with reassuring odors.

He was not just a man, or a doctor. He was Medicine; he was Science itself. He was never concerned with just a single afflicted organ. He thumped and pummeled until both he and the patient were breathless and exhausted. He had never heard of Sigmund Freud, but he was, nevertheless, fully aware of possible psychic complications. This good man had brought me into the world, had pulled off the job successfully although I emerged as an underdone seven-month calamity, weighing less than a good-sized broiler. He knew my insides as familiarly as the insides of his beaver gloves.

So you see, I too believed in doctors once. I believed in Dr. Tschurchentaler—and in my beautiful all-forgiving mother, and in a couple of other people . . .

Although the other people didn't stand up so well.

## CHAPTER TWO

SINCE IT APPEARS that I am doomed, and because I leave eight grandsons, some of whom I have never laid eyes on, I have decided to write down a sort of record of my life. I want my grandchildren, later on, to have an inkling at least of some of my hopes, my struggles and my meanderings.

It is particularly difficult for me to do this because it appears that my life didn't happen in any logical time sequence at all. Also, I have a very accurate but willful memory that has granted me a few truly benign lapses.

I can remember clearly the looks of a little girl who stood at Deutsch-Altenburg on the shores of the Danube some fifty years ago. I can plainly see her throwing chunks of stale bread to a large, fungus-covered carp, and I would risk my soul on the assertion that there were caraway seeds in that loaf of bread.

Even so, I often have trouble remembering my current telephone number, and somewhere since the twenties I have definitely mislaid a couple of decades.

Nonetheless, the highlights of my memory do form a thrilling galaxy, and I stand in its radiance with my fragment of calcified kidney, hoping to live long enough to finish this page, this chapter and, if heaven is kind to me, even this book.

So, for a very bad beginning, I must confess that very early in life I decided to become an artist. I was only fourteen then, and I couldn't speak English, because I had just come over from Vienna with my harmless, elderly parents.

I suppose I might as well level with you altogether. This art business is not just going to crop up from time to time; I'm afraid it is going to form the funny, the grotesque and the bitter bias of my whole story.

I also have some pleasant promises to make. This biographical audit contains no whimsical or eccentric relatives. I was the sort of little boy who never snuggled up to the resilient bosoms of warm-breasted aunts. My golden tresses were never trapped in the pince-nez chains of adoring grand-mothers. I haven't a single memory of any relative on either side of my family who merits reanimation at my hands. I must say I never missed them.

All I can tell you is that when I landed in New York I loathed it on sight. I loathed it with a fierce and relentless passion that seemed unappeasable. The Nedick's orange stands, the United Cigar stores—everything everywhere within sight was an unmitigated series of eyesores to me. Ten years later I went on a visit to Europe and I nearly died of homesickness for New York. In Vienna I had a sudden vision of the Plaza at noon and Riverside Drive at sundown, and my heart laughed in my breast with the knowledge that I was free to return to them at will.

But all this is beside the point. We are here concerned with art and the artist, God help him.

I must tell you that I knew even as an adolescent that if there was one thing America could do exquisitely without, it was another artist. This wasn't a mere suspicion. I felt the truth of it in the very depth of my consciousness. Forty years have passed since then and, for my money, the conditions are quite unchanged.

There will be objections to this from various sources, of course, and my answer to them is "Horse manure!"

I know all about the tremendous interest in art and music that is currently sweeping the country. "Horse manure, my friends, horse manure!"

I see the Renoir and Utrillo prints on people's walls. I also notice the bright honeymoon couples who rise from their mattresses and, when they come up for air, go hand in hand through Greenwich Village in search of masterpieces.

I make you a free present of these connoisseurs. You can have them—them and their plywood furniture and their Mexican candlesticks—and if you are very lucky you might even lose them in some movie house where *Lust for Life* is permanently on view.

In fact, now that all America has finally become aware of poor, self-mutilated Van Gogh, I feel like a phony because I still have both my ears.

No, my friends, that isn't how it's done. Art needs a proper climate. The average Frenchman is no more artistic than the average American, that's for sure. But the French climate is good for art, because in France an artist isn't expected to earn as much as a stockbroker. He is justified in his existence even if he is just a *little* artist. He doesn't have to be Picasso. He counts as a necessary human factor although he hasn't reached the very top.

Joyce Cary, in his fine book *The Horse's Mouth,* writes about an old artist who's had an awful deal in life. A young friend commiserates with him. "England doesn't deserve to have artists," says the youngster indignantly. "I know she doesn't," says the old painter, "but whether she deserves them or not, she's going to get them, just the same."

So, America got me, whether she deserved it or not.

But I'm probably misleading you. I sound like someone who sat in a dusty garret, scratching his head in a cloud of dandruff, while the world passed him by. It was nothing like that. I had a lot of jobs to do. Some of them were amusing and some of them even paid a lot of money. It stands to reason that in so rich a country a few fat crumbs were bound to fall off the tables for the likes of me, too. In due time I'll tell you about some of these crumbs that fell to my lot.

But at this point I want to reassure my grandchildren. My story is by no means a dreary recitative of artistic frustration. For nearly twenty-five years I stopped painting altogether and busied myself with other matters. I was, during that time, managing editor of *Stage* magazine, scorekeeper for the Chemung County Baseball League, associate editor on *Life,* assistant to Frank Crowninshield on *Vanity Fair,* and editor-in-chief for *Americana.*

Also, during that time, I was twice in prison, three times in a hospital and four times married. I've written movies, television serials and ten legitimate plays. I wrote articles for *Vogue,* profiles for *The New Yorker,* and once I read my own three-act play in a Broadway theater to an audience that sat crowded cheek by cheek to the exit doors. What's more, I got wonderful reviews from all the first-string critics.

I didn't begin that way. You see, since I couldn't make a decent living as a painter, I became a book illustrator. It certainly was congenial and logical work for a chronic reader like myself.

In my twenties and my thirties I illustrated sixty-four books, mostly special limited editions of the classics. I also did the plays of Eugene O'Neill, and the Limited Editions Club issued its first book, a *Gulliver's Travels,* with my illustrations. They printed three others later on.

So what am I bitching about? The fact that I was mostly paid for a small facet of my capacity, same fragmentary or fraudulent sliver of my real self and hardly ever for what I could truly and wholly deliver. I find it typical, for instance, that I, who am so adroitly multilingual, have never done a single translation from the German. I once did make a translation of the love books of Ovid, but of course I don't know any Latin.

That was one of the crumbs that fell to my lot. It had quite a bit of salt on it and I will tell you all about it later on as this speckled history unravels.

# CHAPTER THREE

AND WHAT WAS that rancorous palaver about art just a little while ago?

I think I had better establish a couple of basic axioms so I can proceed with at least a reasonably coherent bias.

Let's begin right off with the biggest nubbin of confusion and ask, What is Art?

Twelve hundred years ago a nameless Chinese said, "Art is the creation of absolute order in an area of spiritual exertion."

And what does the artist do?

More recently—that is to say, about seven hundred years ago—an equally anonymous Hindu said, "The artist takes a deep breath of blind assurance from some unimaginable source of certitude and thereupon makes his utterance."

I quote these aliens because they both make a lot of sense and not because I'm overwhelmingly impressed with the wisdom of the East. The wisdom of the East is too frequently spiked with mysticism, and I'm as suspicious of mysticism as I am of psychoanalysis.

But these two lads, the Chinese and the Hindu, had their fingers on the pulse, and I go along with them all the way.

I will make a little plainer what these two heathen gentlemen are saying specifically to me. They are telling me that there is no art to a Hamburger, nor to a Frankfurter, despite the fact that these masterpieces are concocted with a great deal of artifice and know-how. Nor is there any art in preventing underarm embarrassment, nor in helping anybody toward crotch security.

In fact, it is a lot easier to say what art is *Not* than what it *Is*.

You see, dear grandchildren, we live in a world in which a good many people feel that if they could only have spared the time they might have become quite proficient at writing plays or poems. It just happened that they were busy with more important things, like adulterating marmalade, or polluting the rivers of their native states with the waste products of their hairpin factories. Even so, a few of these creators can still turn out some mighty snappy slogans, and some of their jingles have been known to amaze and delight their advertising staffs.

11

I might as well tell you something really unpleasant: The basic ingredient of art is *talent*. And I'm going to top it off with a still greater heresy: When I say talent, I don't mean a talent for making money! So there it is.

I do hope you, my grandsons, at least will go on reading these subversive pages and give me a chance to explain my seemingly antisocial attitude.

You see, boys, we Americans are the kindliest and most generous people in the world, but we are fiendishly avid for experience. We have an insatiable appetite for multiplying our sensations. We don't like to miss anything. Just take a look at your fellow citizens. They've got their nice homes full of wonderful gadgets, and their slick air-conditioned cars are loaded with raging horsepower, but still they're not quite happy.

They've got a funny feeling that those artist fellers, and them show people, are having some kind of a ball that excludes them. So they start hankerin'—the women particularly—and, before you know it, they've got some kind of a society or club going where art is perpetrated in some form or another.

And you'll say, "All this is admirable. Why not?"

Oh, I suppose it is harmless enough. In the end it only winds up in a little culture snobbery and a collection of Grandma Moses Christmas cards. Nobody is hurt.

Nevertheless, let me tell you something. I indicated a little while ago I had given up painting for twenty-five years—remember? Well, I started again three years ago and I even had a one-man show in New York recently. You want to know why I went back to it again? Because I was alarmed by the fact that Churchill and Eisenhower had taken up painting. Like an old retired Army horse, I heard the phantom bugles blowing. If those two characters were attracting attention with their oafish daubs, it was high time to run to the colors. I began to paint again just to restore order. I couldn't let the old girl down. The poor thing was having a bad enough time, with her rear end to the wind and a ninety-mile gale blowing. After all, I didn't butt into the Suez Canal or disarmament crises. I left that to the politicians, although I could hardly have made a greater mess of it than they did.

In short, I'm against any trampling mass participation where even the sages and the saints have tiptoed at their peril.

But isn't art being encouraged more than it used to be?

It sure is. But you see, talent is a weird substance. It is an absolutely unjust and undemocratic commodity. It has a willful tendency to settle on the most unworthy brows. It comes, unreasonably, to strange pimply girls who have never been even within semaphore distance of glamour. It comes to lisping Southern fairies who act like probationers from a booby hatch.

I know it isn't fair. But there you have it.

Clean-cut people from nice families who take courses in poetry and playwriting, and who seem in every way suitably equipped to serve as nesting places for the damned thing, just simply can't seem to attract it. It's enough to make a body wonder whether those antiperspiration creams really do as much for you as the advertisements say.

But art is certainly very much encouraged, isn't it? It always was. Remember, there was Maecenas and Lorenzo the Magnificent and, of course, there was Otto H. Kahn. He encouraged me.

I met him in 1926. I was introduced to him by Horace Liveright, a fascinating monster who eventually plays quite a role in my little saga.

Otto Kahn was a famous banker who in his spare time helped to finance the Metropolitan Opera Company. Also, he gave quite a bit of help to painters and sculptors whose work happened to appeal to him. (Also to poets, like Hart Crane.)

The first time I saw him was, very briefly, in the Liveright waiting room. The second time happened up in Horace's private office, late one December afternoon.

On first impact, Mr. Kahn's coloring seemed deliberately theatrical. His hair, which he parted in the middle, was pure white, as was his beautifully groomed and waxed mustache. But his eyebrows were two astonishing patches of black caracul. He was small, like a bullfinch, and his clear, hypnotic stare, his tiny well-shod feet, and his quick emphatic movements gave him a sprightly, birdlike quality.

Although he had been in the country most of his life, I noticed that he still had a strong German accent.

He told me he had been looking at my pictures for half an hour before I arrived.

"You ought to go abroad for a while," he said. "You should see what is happening in the art world of Paris and Italy."

I couldn't have agreed with anybody more. But, although I was just a youngster myself, I had already acquired a wife and two children. I pointed out to Mr. Kahn that I was a husband and a father, of sorts, and that I couldn't find it in my heart at the moment to abandon those three dependents.

He stared rather stonily at me as I confessed my domestic felicity to him. He slowly turned his back on me and had another sampling of my pictures. After a while he came around to me again. He gave me a tiny commiserative smile.

"You come to my office," he said, "and we'll have a talk about it." And that was the end of my first meeting with him.

So, the following day I went down to his banking establishment, which was Kuhn, Loeb and Company in lower Manhattan.

When I entered his office I realized not only how rich he was, but how rich he had always been. This office of his was a tiny room containing a diminutive desk and two authentic Renaissance chairs. We sat practically knee to knee during the whole interview, which lasted less than thirty seconds. He began at once without any preliminaries.

"I have decided to take care of you for a year, in France," he said. "Later on we will see."

"And when do you think I ought to go abroad?" I said.

"If I were you," he said, "I would go tomorrow."

Upon this we shook hands and I left.

I couldn't get rid of our furniture that fast, but we sailed eight days later, on the *Rochambeau*. My wife was a little distressed and both my kids were coughing like crazy, but we were on the high seas by Christmas.

That was Otto H. Kahn. May the earth rest lightly on his generous heart. You will search in vain for his like today. He saw my work and approved it. We met face to face. He sized me up. He made up his mind. And that was the end of it.

I can also tell you that he was one of the few rich people I have ever met who could tell a funny story with point and with grace. (Generally the rich don't really bother, because people are going to laugh, anyway.)

You can tell by the foregoing account that the nature of patronage has altered a good deal since 1926.

Recall that I filled out no application blanks in sextuplicate; I made no solemn avowal of my mendicant-student intentions; I furnished no proof to establish the worthiness of my grandparents.

And yet, I received a substantial sum of money in advance, without the donor ever asserting his ethical ascendancy over me. I didn't have a beggarly stipend doled out to me as if I were a shiftless nomadic pauper. And, finally, no member of my family had to furnish a urinalysis or a blood smear to prove that we were free from syphilis or leprosy.

You can see that I have at last worked myself into the awkward position where I am compelled to deduce that those were the good old days.

## CHAPTER FOUR

I'M SITTING UNDER some ancient elms in a tiny hamlet up in Maine. The weather is painfully lovely for an ailing man.

I think it must have been on such a day surely that the holy

14

anchorite in his wilderness suddenly recalled the great beauty of Thais. And it must have been this same kind of day when poor pale Queen Mélisande dropped her fateful wedding ring into the green stillness of the shadowy lake.

And what do I recall on such a day? My drug addiction.

It seems that in the biographical bird's-eye view I offered a few pages ago, I did not mention that from 1945 to 1954 I was addicted to drugs. That is one of my mislaid decades. My not mentioning it before was no mere oversight; I just couldn't make a casual, statistical reference to anything so devastatingly significant to my whole existence. I'm afraid that those nine years require a good deal of explaining. I will be only too glad to explain as much of it as I can, but I myself have never quite fathomed the full implications of that morbid interregnum.

I originally became addicted through the help of regular medical practitioners who prescribed morphine to relieve my kidney pains.

I must say I liked morphine from the start. It performed a sort of minor miracle for me. It made me graciously tolerant of every form of human imbecility, including my own. It lifted from my mind every worry, every heartache, and every form of urgency. I never had any bodily pains, and for nine years I didn't have a single cold. Drug addiction is, in all probability, the secret cure for the common cold. Although it is a drastic cure, I can testify that it works.

You have no hangover after drugs, you just have to have more drugs. An addict can do beautifully without women. He is not necessarily impotent, he just doesn't need them. His euphoria is so complete he can do fine without seductive titivations. He has only one anxiety—that he will run short of his poison.

Otherwise he is abreast of any contingency. Suppose the phone bill is overdue, the rent unpaid, and his wife threatens to leave him. The addict can liquidate such difficulties with a smile of sweet understanding.

So, what is wrong with drug addiction? First of all, it is illegal. It is safer for you to renege on your income tax than to get mixed up with drugs. Uncle Sam is bound to get you sooner or later and then there is heaven and hell to pay. Geography, too, is against you. You can be an addict in Bangkok in perfect safety, but the U.S.A. is definitely out. So, if you can make a living in Siam, go ahead and move into your tropical snowstorm with Santa Claus!

The second reason why addiction is taboo is that it makes you absolutely uncompetitive. You can't survive without cheating or stealing because you're certainly not going to work. Let's face it, we are living in a world which is not only highly competitive but which admires strenuousness for its own sake. So you can't afford to tune out. If you want to lie down blissfully on a wet cement floor and pass your time just thinking about lovely things, you'll have to get yourself a transfer to Thailand. And you'd better go in a hurry, before some United Nations subcommittee on narcotics catches up with that shady corner. (I'm sure their consulate will solemnly assert that you can't get drugs there even now, but they are most thoroughly misinformed.)

Let's agree, then, that narcotics are definitely un-American. It must be obvious by now that the nine years of my addiction must have had certain nightmarish overtones. I certainly had to tell lies from the very beginning, since no doctor would prescribe my constantly increasing dosages. So I went to twenty doctors for my needed prescriptions, which is illegal even if you are sick. Fortunately, I ran into a few practitioners who charged me ten or fifteen dollars a visit and gave me two prescriptions a week, knowing perfectly well that I was hooked.

I must tell you about one of these crocodiles I got to know 'way back in the beginnings of my addiction, many, many morphine tablets ago. He lived out in Staten Island somewhere, and I can't quite make up my mind about his name. It was either Harbinger or Spring. At any rate, I know it held some sort of promise for me.

He was a little bit of a wrinkled body, like an overdone baked apple that has been left on the window to cool. I think his practice had reduced itself to his doling out prescriptions to dope addicts. He had no car, and he never went out on calls. His clients were sure to come to his lair although it took half an hour by ferry and twenty minutes by bus to get to him.

(Incidentally, I once took a plane to Chicago just to cash one prescription that a visiting Chicago doctor had given me.)

At any rate, my Dr. Harbinger, or Spring, was type-cast to play the apothecary in *Romeo and Juliet*. His unkempt eyebrows made little thatched roofs over his colorless eyes. His clothes were much too large for him, as if a son of his, a substantial citizen somewhere, had endowed him with his cast-off wardrobe.

This medical barnacle used to charge me thirty dollars for two prescriptions, and in the year and a half that I had been going to him he had never once asked what ailed me. So everything was cool between us. We understood each other. We were a couple of scoundrels and words were only going to becloud the issue.

But I am incorrigibly curious about people, and sometimes

16

I felt I would have liked to know him better. I didn't expect to be pals with him or think that he would reduce his bitter tariff because of any greater familiarity between us. I understood the rules. We had a desperate silent deal on, and we were both stoically waiting to get busted by the narcotics squad. But even so, he was some kind of a man, wasn't he? He wasn't the Iron Maiden or a cuckoo clock.

Then, quite unexpectedly, one day he copped out to me.

"I have a bum ticker," he said. "They gave me up three years ago."

I recall that in my hallucinated state my first surprise was to discover that he had a heart at all. He not only had one, but it was even on the fritz.

So that was his secret. He just sat there hour after hour, day after day, listening to its erratic gurglings.

"You'll outlive us all," I said. "Yessir! You'll bury the lot of us."

"I might at that," he admitted. "Yes, I fooled them, going on three years now."

I wondered who "them" was. The medical profession? The dark powers that rule the world? The common decencies? I never quite decided. And that was the extent of our utmost intimacy.

One nasty fall day in 1947 I had run myself sick and breathless trying to chisel the thirty dollars that I needed for his fee. At last an old schoolmate, a stanch collector of books I had illustrated, was deeply flattered when I asked him for fifty dollars.

It was four-thirty in the afternoon when I hit the ferry down at the Battery. I hadn't had a fix in eight hours and I was sweating like a hunk of rancid pork. Finally we landed on the island and I got on the bus. I've never had such a bus ride in my life. Something was wrong with the carburetor, and every ten revolutions of the wheels a crazy explosion would rock the old cracker barrel. My coat collar was pasted behind my dripping ears and each combustion mishap in the expiring engine was duplicated in my demoralized circulatory system.

At last I got off. I tottered down the street with the wind freezing the sweat under my clothes, my teeth chattering, and my burning eyes out of focus. Even so, I could see there was a mob in front of the doctor's house. What had happened? Had he finally got pinched?

Then I saw the wreath on the doorpost, and I knew the worst. The son-of-a-bitch had died on me. I was suddenly overwhelmed by such a feeling of despair, I began to bawl.

People started to notice me and moved respectfully aside to make room for my grief. Obviously I was the chief

17

mourner, since nobody else was crying. Kindly, dark-shawled women put consoling arms around me. The undertaker led me to the first black limousine.

I was too feeble to protest. I just let it all happen and kept on leaking at most of my apertures. But when I was plumped in the car I realized with horror that I was on my way to some far-off cemetery. God knows where they bury people in Staten Island. I was just about to hurl myself out the door when I saw another unconsolable weeper in the far corner of the limousine.

Even in my miserable condition I instantly spotted him for a sick junkie. He was in better shape than I, but he was also slopping over with grief.

And then in the midst of my agony the grotesque humor of the situation hit me. I took out my handkerchief and started to clean myself up. I even smiled at the junkie.

He was a blue-eyed overgrown baby, with astonishingly well-groomed fingernails. He had straight sandy hair and a three-day growth of silky stubble on his jowls.

"How far to the cemetery?" I asked him.

"Never mind," he said. "Give me yer hankercher and help me outa here."

Since drug addicts are all members of a secret brotherhood, the Brotherhood of the Most Desperate Need, I handed him my kerchief.

"How will we get away from here?" I said.

"I got a jalopy down the street," he said. "We'll tell 'em we're gonna get his brother from St. Louis that's comin' over on the six o'clock ferry."

Well, we somehow pulled it off. We made it back to New York. We even made it up to the Bronx, where my new-found friend knew another croaker who wrote scrip for junkies. We forked over our money, whereupon that scientist and healer forthwith issued us the precious documents.

Half an hour later we were safe in a cafeteria that was reeking of latrinal antiseptics, and here, in this altogether fitting shrine, we toasted the memory of our departed bene-factor from Staten Island.

And why not? After all, who had wept most copiously at his passing? Who had suffered the greatest loss? And who would miss him most sincerely, now that his bum ticker had finally run down?

✳

# CHAPTER FIVE

I NEVER BOUGHT heroin, so I never had any real dealings with the underworld. I just dealt with the nether world. Hundreds of druggists in all the five boroughs were fully aware of my addiction but they kept their mouths shut because I was compelled to be a good customer. Morphine is a very cheap drug if you buy it legitimately; they could charge me only a dollar and a half for twenty tablets. But I didn't dare hand in just my prescription, for fear they might call the narcotics squad. They pretended that I was kosher because they could unload great quantities of hair tonic, shaving lotion, face powder, cough medicine, sanitary napkins, and God knows what else on me. I would later drop their loathsome garbage into the nearest trash can, because whatever room I happened to occupy was already cluttered with their hideous decoctions.

These rooms I lived in merit a saga in themselves. For seven out of the nine years of my opium hegira, I was not married. I lived in strange theatrical hotels in the West Forties, in rooming houses on Sixth and Eighth avenues, and sometimes I just slept in Turkish baths.

One flea bag in the West Forties, the Hotel Minnetonka, left a particularly lurid shadow in my memory.

The night clerk at this caravanserai was an ectoplasm called Pheeny. I imagine Pheeny was an endearing diminutive for phenobarbital. He was also a junkie and occasionally supplied me with a fix. At a price, of course.

He was a homo and, like most pansies, had few of the virtues of men, and all the little weaknesses of women. He came originally from Georgia, which in itself is no laughing matter. Pheeny was, above all else, a bewildering clearing house for general misinformation.

A description of his appearance is not so simple, because he had phases, like the moon. Sometimes he was plump, and then again he seemed haggard. On all occasions his skin looked like melting paraffin. He also fancied an elaborately curled black toupee which had no connection whatever with his face. It was the sort of hairpiece that, in my childhood, used to grace wax effigies in barbershop windows. Pheeny's pudgy, dimpled hands constantly fluttered about his person like a couple of demented bats, but I think his eyes were his most winsome feature; one of them was brown, the other a frozen, forget-me-not blue.

When I first met him he had already been at his post for fifteen incredible years, and I made a great hit with him because, on moving in, I presented him with my whole floating pharmacy of beauty crap.

Most of the hotels in that neighborhood look as if they had come down in the world, and they probably have. Not the Minnetonka. That hostelry was originally conceived as a horror and has so maintained itself through the years. I suspect it has even improved a little, since it has a certain soothing, gray-green, dirt patina that cannot be inaugurated, it has to accrue. In the lobby, which smells like a neglected men's room, there are four ossified palms, whose roots are permanently embedded in cigarette butts.

I moved into the Minnetonka in November, but my neighbors all had their doors wide open. Next to me, on my left, there lived an altogether ball-less wonder, who was something of a dandy. An Edwardian dandy. He was only a little over four feet tall and all his lacking size seemed to have gone into the construction of his head, which was alarming. His two little hands could just barely touch each other, and he also featured that burlesque seaman's gait so common among dwarfs. He was pop-eyed and froggy-faced and his hair had the texture of steel wool, and, for reasons best known to himself, he had dyed this fungoid excrescence a bright yellow.

He was called Wimpy. His real name was Humphrey Engelbert, and he told me his cradle had been a theatrical trunk. I used to marvel at his wardrobe and couldn't imagine where he had garnered all those dated outfits. He would pop up with checkered frock coats, gray derbies, double-breasted vests, and he even had some pearl-button shoes with suède uppers. Later I learned that his people had once been theatrical costumers, and that over the years he had lifted these doodads out of their files.

I also found out his quite unusual means of livelihood.

Wimpy owned two aristocratic Russian wolfhounds that slept under his bed most of the day. But at night they blossomed out in the lobby, brushed and feathery, with rhinestone collars and lizard-skin leads. Wimpy would pilot these disdainful Romanovs down the street, and half an hour later he would return without them. It was a nightly routine. When I got to know him I asked him about it.

"What happens to the grand dukes?" I said. "Do they perform somewhere?"

"No sir," said Wimpy, "they're real class. They're top dogs, that's what they are. Royalty, that's them. They just get paid for looking snooty." Then he laughed like an apoplectic foetus.

"How come?" I said. "Do they pose for a photographer? Or model for radiator caps? Or what?"

Wimpy doubled up in an absolute colic of hilarity. His eyes hung out so far you could have knocked them off with a stick. He was guttural and speechless with triumphant enjoyment. At last he subsided, wiped his eyes with a lace-trimmed handkerchief, and cleared his throat, as one about to shed great illumination.

"I rent them to a couple of hookers," he said. "They can make a classier deal that way. Get it? The marks get a bang out of all that ice, and the payoff is heavier all around."

Very freely translated, his information amounted to this: He was acquainted with a couple of prostitutes who were, obviously, ladies of vision. They would walk these dogs in select neighborhoods, around the Plaza for instance, and the results were easily predictable. Even on harmless occasions, dogs are facile conversation pieces. As pickup media they are practically irreplaceable. But these hounds attracted no mere traveling salesmen or unemployed saxophone players. As Wimpy had accurately phrased it, they had class. The increase in dividends that accrued due to the borzoi snob appeal paid off very handsomely all around.

"You're pretty cute," I said. "How did you figure out this racket of yours?"

"It's no racket," said Wimpy. He was suddenly sober and a little pained. "There's overhead, ain't there? And wear and tear. And those beasts eat like I slaughtered the overlap from my racing stables. Sometimes when the season is slack I run myself bare-assed keeping those hounds in trim. If those tarts don't give them a workout, I got to exercise them myself. I'm short of breath, and they're powerful brutes. They drag me around like a wet rag."

"I suppose it isn't all gravy," I admitted.

"All gravy! Why, just look at their outfits. Last year four stones fell out of their collars and I had a hell of a time replacing them. Twice a year I have to get them plucked or they shed their fuzz all over the suckers. Believe me, this thing takes a lot of managing, a lot of managing."

He waggled his head like the top executive at General Motors who has to do every damned thing himself.

Wimpy exemplified the sad truth that every form of human endeavor entails endless hazards and hardships. Viewed superficially, he had a neat little stunt going. In the light of his explanation, he would have been just as well off on the stock market, or, better still, in the advertising business. I think he was ideally suited for the advertising business. He displayed

21

an acute awareness for the special nuances in the field of public relations, and his Edwardian outfits would have given a much needed touch of color to the alcoholic bleakness of Madison Avenue.

Before the sun finally sets behind Wimpy, I'd like to disclose one more jewel of information he offered me. It concerned the ambiguous activities of our night clerk.

"That Pheeny is plenty unusual," Wimpy said. "You know what he collects? He collects the old jock straps from wrestlers. Can you imagine? He's got about fifty of 'em. That's a hell of a way to lay out your dough, ain't it? I think that guy's got an unhealthy hobby."

I agreed with him, without qualification. Privately I thought that Krafft-Ebing would surely have doted on Pheeny and would gladly have given him a featured place in *Psychopathia Sexualis*.

After a while I came to know some twenty people who lived at the Minnetonka, but I will report to you about just one more. She was a girl who lived across the hall from me, who was called Panama.

That name of hers puzzled me for quite a while. She had never been to Panama, she didn't own a Panama hat, so how come? Later I found out she had spent nineteen of her thirty-three years in foundling homes, jails and reformatories, so I jumped to a long-distance conclusion. I decided that somebody along her rocky trail, some prison wit, some penitentiary Veblen, had figured out that in the course of her untidy life, mostly as a public charge, she had cost the U.S. Government as much as the Panama Canal.

I may have been wrong, but my deduction stilled my amazement.

At the time I met her, Panama was a quasi waitress in some waffle-and-cruller joint on Broadway. Everyone knows that waitresses are rarely single. With their tidy uniforms, their friendly smiles, their arms loaded with food, they project a facile domesticity, an instant wifely charm. Particularly to lonely men. So they have an easy time getting husbands.

Of course, there are exceptions. Panama was an exception. She never had a proposal, only propositions. Which could have been all right, too, because secretly Panama had the ambition to become a prostitute. She never made that, either. She had no sales resistance worth a damn and fell in with the most unpromising prospects.

She hadn't a shred of talent for being a whore. I used to bawl her out about it. I told her that a real hooker who expects to make something of herself has to keep her head. It was no use. Panama would get seriously involved with every passing tramp who tumbled her. I told her she couldn't afford to go overboard with all her clients. "That's not the way to run a business," I said. "Imagine if every mouse-trap manufacturer stood crying, sincerely, behind every mouse trap he sold and then hung around long enough for the customer to try it out, until it got busted. Figure it out yourself," I said. "If he got emotional about every one of his goddamned mouse traps, where the hell would *he* wind up?"

Panama agreed with me, but there was no improvement. Not while I knew her, anyway. She wasn't a bad-looking doll, either. She had a nice figure, and like most American girls she dressed cleverly. She wore her dark-brown hair in a page-boy bob, and, despite all her experiences, her large, dark eyes still looked trustingly at the world. She didn't have much of a chin, and her nose and her mouth were of the standard-brand, native variety.

Her hands were her real hang-up. She felt very self-conscious about them. Poor thing, she had worked in too many jail laundries and kitchens and those hands bore the visible marks left by those bitter years.

One evening she came into my room, and she again had that feverish, bridal look in her eyes.

"I've got a new boy friend," she told me.

As if I didn't know it.

"Yeah, he's real cute. I think he knows you."

"What's his name?" I asked.

"George," she said. "He's a real steady type. He eats a real breakfast. Oatmeal, a couple of eggs with sausage, three cups of coffee, and he leaves a quarter."

"Sounds like he's doing all right," I said. "What makes you think he knows me?"

"Oh, he asked about you. Not anything special, just what you're doing now, and stuff."

My heart skipped three beats.

"What did you tell him?"

"Nothing. I just said you were good people and real neighborly."

"I'm sorry, Panama," I said, "but I have to go out on a date. I'll talk to you later, when I get back."

Her expression dimmed with disappointment. She wanted to talk to me some more about the dietary habits of the new follower. I got her out of the room at last, and tottered onto my bed. The sweat started to pour down my back and for a moment I thought I was going to black out.

This George was a cop. I was sure of it. After all, the narcotics business, the legit end of it, is just a matter of bookkeeping. The squad checks on all the prescriptions in the drugstores and my name had certainly turned up a few thousand times.

23

I had to get out, and fast. (Luckily, my rent was square.) Once they were hep to you they never gave up. That's what they get paid for. It was a most inconvenient time for me to get out of town. Besides, where could I go? I had no money, I needed prescriptions, I had to have junk.

To steady myself I took a couple of shots right away. I had enough stuff to last me another day. But I really knew better. Under pressure, I was bound to take three times my usual amount. That's the way it is with junkies. Just to make sure I wouldn't get too rattled on the way out, I took another dose.

I threw my few shirts and socks into a bag and took one more look around the room. A big flying cockroach, who had probably come to New York on a banana boat, scooted through the open window just as I closed the door.

In the hall I wiped the sweat off my face again. Maybe the bastard was already waiting for me downstairs. I had to chance it.

It was ten o'clock and Pheeny was on duty. In my terrible state I decided to confide in him.

"The bulls are after me," I told him.

"You sure?" he said.

"Yes. Some guy buzzed Panama about me."

"Panama wouldn't rap to a bull," he said. "She'd spot him a mile off."

"Not the feds," I said. "They don't look so much like bulls. Some of those government cops are skinny bastards with fancy shoes."

"Maybe you're right. Where you gonna go?"

"I don't know, Pheeny, I just don't know."

"I'll tell you what," said Pheeny. "If you're smart you'll beat them to the draw. Go down for a cure, to Lexington, to the narcotic hospital in Kentucky. Check in as a volunteer, and you can leave any time you feel like it."

"How much does it cost?"

"Not a dime. Greatest place in the world for junkies. Like a country club. Golf, tennis—the works!"

"How much is the fare?" I asked.

"Last time I was down there, I flew. It was around forty bucks. And you can go by bus, for fifteen."

"You talked me into it," I said. "You have any stuff around?"

"Just a little tea," he said.

He meant marihuana, which is about as useful to an addict as creamed ladyfingers.

"No thanks," I said. "I'll just have to make it cold."

We shook hands like two preoccupied ghosts who are already late for their haunting.

I went to the Y.M.C.A. on Twenty-third Street, took another shot and went to bed.

It was most inconvenient for me to leave town just then. Most inconvenient. I had submitted a cover drawing up at *The American Mercury* and they had practically accepted it. But there were complications. The editor, Charles Angoff, a real nice guy, had accepted it. But the publisher, a man called Spivak who still flourishes on television, just couldn't make up his mind.

The people at the *Mercury* used to have cover caricatures made regularly by Al Hirschfeld. But Al had gone abroad and they were buying drawings from free-lancers. I hadn't made a drawing in nearly fifteen years, and, besides, to draw caricatures is a highly specialized skill, which I don't possess.

But I'd heard in some cafeteria that they paid a hundred and fifty dollars a throw, so I went up for a try. Angoff, who knew my book illustrations, was very helpful. They needed a picture of former Vice-President Wallace, and Chi Angoff arranged an interview for me. I would have preferred to make my drawing just from photographs, but the interview had been arranged, so I went. Of course it was a waste of time. Wallace looked exactly like his photographs.

I met him at a broadcasting station where he was going to give a talk. He was terse and decisive, like a good many unstable people with whom stubbornness passes for will power. But he posed for me amiably enough. I cut it all as short as possible because Wallace had started to talk to someone about astrology, and astrology is another subject that gives me the willies. I wondered how a man who had reached such eminence in the world could go for such drivel, but then I recalled that he was a corn breeder, a chicken breeder, a stockbreeder—a farmer, in short. And farmers always fall back on the old almanac, even if they become Vice-Presidents.

So I submitted my drawing to Chi Angoff, who accepted it. But I still hadn't been paid. Also, the Minnetonka was the only address the *Mercury* had for me. I'd have to go there in the morning.

And that's what I did. I had only six tablets of morphine left when I got to the office. Six tablets was enough for two shots. I told Chi I was leaving town and could use the cover money. He was a real sweetheart about it. He went right inside to talk to the publisher.

After a while the publisher himself emerged, tousled-headed, full of creative preoccupation, busy impersonating himself.

He gave me a quick flash of the magazine's future, which, obviously, didn't include me; he mentioned some encouraging circulation figures, indicated his own extracurricular interests and enthusiasms, and it suddenly became clear to me that he was about to leave us, to brood more constructively, I suppose, in his own editorial eyrie.

It was then that the terrible tide of my anxiety flooded my good manners, my tact and my caution, and I heard myself screaming, "Don't you budge out of this room, you hear?"

Now, this publisher might easily have been a match for me alone, but he was no match for me and ten grains of morphine. I still recall poor Angoff floating myopically in the background, as I blew an absolute tornado of maledictions about his employer's ears.

I haven't the vaguest idea what I actually said. But my desperate need came to desperate articulation. I must have bawled at the top of my lungs, too, because the office was a tomb of silence when I finally shut up.

I left the *Mercury* offices fifteen minutes later with a check for a hundred and fifty dollars in my pocket. What is more, it was endorsed on the back, so I could cash it at their bank.

I've bothered to tell this gruesome little episode in such detail not because the publisher was any sort of villain; he probably forgot the whole thing two days later. I've told it because the circumstances and the people's attitudes were typical. The publisher represented an archetype whose like you will run into often enough in life, only most of the time nobody makes a fuss. If you were a publisher, *you* might not act any differently yourself.

At any rate, I had collected, and at noon I hopped on a plane to Lexington. Later it proved that the cops had really been breathing down my neck and I had gotten away just in time.

## CHAPTER SIX

IF PETRONIUS, Dante, Rabelais and Heine could have combined their forces they might have done justice to what goes on in the Federal Narcotics Hospital, in Lexington, Kentucky. I will harness all my own poor powers to give you at least an inkling, but, as the French say, even the most beautiful woman cannot give more than she has.

Pheeny had, of course, exaggerated. It was not exactly a country club; it was, and is, predominantly a federal prison, with certain hospital overtones. For some unimaginable appeasement of purely verbal protocol, all the prisoners, including the ones who are serving fifteen years, are called "patients" by the staff. The staff is called "Hacks!" and "Croakers" by the patients. The croakers are the doctors.

Let me say at once that I found no individual villains among the people who were employed there. The real bane of the place lies in its undefined character and status.

In ordinary prisons there are certain established routines which penologists have found empirically workable. In hospitals the patients might be considered nuisances (by the working staff), but they are not considered criminals. Well, in Lexington you are both. I've thought a good deal about it and it is nobody's fault. It is one of those unsolvable problems that modern life has puked up, and I haven't many important suggestions for improvements.

First I would like to tell of my arrival and reception.

The hospital itself is not too unattractive. It comprises a series of low, Federal-style brick buildings, situated among spacious lawns in the undulant Kentucky countryside. The old-time prisoners later told me that the windows were barred to keep people from breaking in. These were not the only bars. At every outlet from floor to floor, and at regular intervals along the miles of corridors, there were barred gates which were locked most of the time. The turnkeys who took charge of these barriers, in fact most of the men and women who worked in the institution, were people recruited from around the Kentucky countryside. Only the doctors were not. They were rigged out in military uniforms and, according to seniority, wore stripes on their sleeves.

When I arrived I was registered, stripped, bathed, and examined by a friendly young medic. His carefully prescribed routine required him to search earnestly in my rectum for possible concealed narcotics, which process was known locally as getting a finger wave.

By the time he got through with me I was so shaky I could barely stand up. I hadn't had a shot in seven hours.

"You'll get a shot upstairs," the doctor said. "You'll get regular help for a few days."

"How many days?" I asked.

"As long as we think you need it. Don't worry, it won't be too bad."

I received pajamas, socks, a toothbrush, and a comb and went up to the floor where the new arrivals roosted.

I got a room to myself. An immaculate room with a night table, a chair and a bed with clean linen. It was certainly superior to anything in Bellevue Hospital, and to many private hospitals, for that matter. I had to wait for my shot

27

another hour and a half because medications were administered at clocked intervals. Meanwhile, I crawled into bed.

Then an orderly appeared and tucked me in. He turned out to be a Negro pansy with a wind-blown bob, and his name was Gertrude.

"I can tell you're from New York," he said. "I'm from Harlem myself. I'm doing five years. What did you knock over?"

"I'm a volunteer," I said apologetically.

"Oh, a winder," he said.

"How come a winder?" (It is pronounced to rhyme with "binder.")

" 'Cause you're just gonna wind in and out of here for the rest of your life, unless you get busted and do time like me."

"I hope not," I said. "How much do you still have left to do?"

"Most of it. I'm only here sixty-three days. But I'm taking a course in hair-styling from a boy from Chicago who'll be here almost as long as me. So my time is going pretty good."

Incidentally, it was male hair-styling he was studying.

Gertrude was a wonderful orderly. He had cool hands, a soft voice, gentle manners, and a sympathetic attitude. Wherever he is, probably doing time somewhere, may God bless Gertrude.

I had nearly a hundred dollars when I arrived, so I was able to get a carton of cigarettes from the commissary. (The system has changed since 1947. You have to wait a week now before you can start using your funds.) At any rate, I was able to give Gertrude a couple of packs. Now, let's get this straight: This dark flower was nice to people who had no cigarettes to give him, he was kind and helpful to slum rats and country lice who had never said "thank you" in all their lives. He was the best nurse I ever knew, and I am only paying an old debt by setting up this memorial to his humanity.

After Gertrude came the floor hack, who was in charge and dished out the medications. He wore a white uniform and was called a psychiatric aide. No one had ever been more unsuitably titled. They did have psychiatric aid down at Lexington, that is to say doctors who gave personal and group therapy. But the hacks who doled out the drugs were convinced, to a man, that psychiatry was altogether moonshine. So they were called psychiatric aides, on the same principle that makes Americans call a bald-headed man "Curly," or a six-and-a-half-footer "Shorty."

This particular hack wasn't a bad fellow. He was clumsy and circumstantial in his official imbecility, but that is understandable. Although only recently recruited from behind a cow's udder, he had been given a certain briefing in the rudiments of pharmacy. He was therefore a degree above the ordinary turnkey. These turnkeys, by the way, were pretty primitive types. A few of them looked just like swollen glands. But there was really no harm in them, either. Of course the inmates resented the hacks, the nurses, the doctors, the chaplain, the rabbi and the priest. But they would have resented anybody, except maybe a flock of chorus girls. I must go on record now and say emphatically that I never met such a bunch of ungrateful sons-of-bitches in my life, as those "patients" down in Lexington.

But back to my psychiatric aide in the reception ward. He was a friendly man but had been warned over and over again by his superiors not to allow anyone to take advantage of him. These admonitions, plus some hideous experiences with the riffraff he monitored, had curdled the milk of his kindness until it was just rancid yoghurt. Like so many country people who lead a natural, outdoor life, his features had hardly any definition. He gave me the impression of an underdone veal cutlet.

So there was the psychiatric aide. His name was Walt Bunchy, and he too was an archetype. Some of his colleagues were shorter, older, skinnier, but they all had the same factory trademark. They all resented us, although we were their means of a good livelihood. I didn't blame them. Here was a bunch of junkies, the lowest form of social outcasts, and yet they were being given a lot of expensive medical attention.

It was actually only a modicum of medical attention, because after the doctors have once liberated you from the toxic effects of your addiction the subsequent medical care is quite negligible. I'm not complaining. I know the difficulties of the management too well to pretend I could have done a much better job than they did.

We got shots four times a day and an additional barbiturate sedative at night. They gave us a synthetic horror called Dolofine, which was invented in Germany under the Nazis and named after the great Adolf! The ward physician, another polite and good-natured young man, who visited me every morning, told me that it was easier to get off Dolofine than regular opiates. I'm sure he was convinced of it. Everybody not addicted to drugs was convinced of it.

Day by day my dosages were decreased. I felt real discomfort and anxiety only about half an hour before each shot was administered. Sometimes the hack was late in dealing out the medications and this caused real suffering—pain in the knee joints, eyes out of focus, shortness of breath, palpitation,

29

sweat gushing out of every pore, and too many other calamities to list properly.

Some of the psychiatric aides deliberately delayed giving us our drugs, pretending not to notice the agony tottering around them. They enjoyed their power and wanted to savor it. They were farm boys and had suffered callous authority themselves. Also, like everybody else including most of the doctors and all of the nurses, both male and female, they had a moral ascendancy over all drug addicts.

This, I'm afraid, can't be helped. There was a great deal of mealymouthed talk at Lexington about drug addiction being an illness and not a crime. Nobody believed this, not even the patients. There existed an occasional saint among the physicians who honestly felt that the addict was primarily a psychiatric and not a criminal problem, and I met two such men down there. One of them has since been booted out.

The food was good, clean, and plentiful. Naturally, everybody bitched about it. Particularly such characters as had never eaten well, or steadily, on the outside. That's human nature for you, and you can have it.

After seven days they stopped giving me even Dolofine and I instantly caught a cold. This is a standard development, as is vomiting, diarrhea and sleeplessness.

I stayed thirty days in Lexington and I never slept more than half an hour a night. The nights of the recently weaned drug addict are a special horror, because even after a few minutes' sleep his pajamas and his sheets are soaked with cold sweat.

After my last shot I was moved to another floor, among people who had already recovered. I had a roommate now, a mild, sentimental character from Chicago called Manny. Every Monday we had inspection. A really tough inspection. The men on the corridor spent most of Sunday evening polishing their floors, their windows and their furniture. Manny, too, proceeded to disembowel our room in a frenzy of cleaning and I tried to help him, but I had to take time out for puking every few minutes. He was wonderful about it. Manny had a certain resemblance to Groucho Marx and this, I think, had early conditioned him to be something of a comedian. With great perception he recognized that I saw other virtues in him, so he gave up trying to be funny for me.

He was a husband and father who had long ago lost his family along the drug route. For a living he played small character roles in summer theaters and road companies. He too was a volunteer, but he meant to stay for the full six-month cure.

After vomiting for about ten days I was so dehydrated that

30

I passed out in our room one day, so I was shipped back to the infirmary and to Gertrude. I was put to bed and given intravenous glucose, and I was sure that nobody in the whole world had ever been so deathly sick. I'll try to explain why it is so tough to cure a drug habit. When you take opiates in any but minute quantities, the body is shocked by these poisons and rejects them. That is normal. What is abnormal is to go on taking the stuff until the body is habituated to this toxic intrusion. The organism achieves this tolerance, finally, by altering the chemical constituency and balance of each of its billions of cells.

Now, then, when you go off drugs, the poor carcass has to re-establish its original chemical equilibrium, and as a result you become the battlefield of incalculable, painful syndromes. No bodily position of rest can be tolerated for more than a few moments. Even ordinary light becomes unendurably brilliant. With all this comes the return of all the unresolved psychic and other perplexities that were hushed and masked by the benign, banished poisons.

It is no laugh.

On the second night of my return to the infirmary Manny came to see me, and he brought along half a dozen friends. Such a wholesale visit was unheard of in the institution but my guests all turned out to be physicians. Also, they were drug addicts. During their stay in Lexington these doctors were expected to perform certain technical or routine duties in the wards, and to assist the regular medical staff wherever possible.

I discovered that there were quite a few inmate physicians in the institution, and I was told that comparatively few of them ever reverted to drugs again. The feds were very nice to them. No public fuss was made about an addicted doctor. After his cure he could quickly return to his practice and he didn't even lose his narcotics license. It was recognized, I suppose, that addiction was an occupational hazard with doctors.

The group Manny ushered into my room had an impressive medical record. Among them were heart specialists, distinguished gynecologists, a famous diagnostician, and one lost soul, an expert anesthetist, who was back for his eighth cure. This time he had not come back as a volunteer; he was serving a two-year term for forgery. He was a handsome man in his early forties, with grayish-blond, curly hair. His frozen eyes were flecked with green, and he had a surprisingly ruddy, outdoor color.

Since he had personally experienced my condition eight times, he naturally took charge. His name was Rex Starrett

31

and I found him urbane and poisonously witty. Also, he was a homosexual.

I seem to dwell overly much on the subject of homosexuality, but there is a good deal of it among addicts. Jews also seem very prone to addiction, which is strange because there are proportionately few Jewish alcoholics.

At any rate, Dr. Starrett gave me a thorough going-over, while his colleagues made appropriate remarks from the sidelines.

"You've got it bad, you poor kitten," said Dr. Starrett, "and I know only one thing that could give you any relief."

"And what is that?" I asked hopefully.

"A shot of morphine," said Dr. Starrett.

I didn't even smile. I was beyond smiling. I thought the whole bunch of them a lot of heartless bastards, and I turned my face to the wall.

Try to imagine the setting: six junkie doctors, like deflated braveries, squatting along the floor of my room; Manny hovering in the doorway, his soft-boiled eyes limpid with sympathy; I, flat on my back, with a needle in my arm, waiting for the inverted glucose bottle to pour its innocuous contents into my bewildered veins.

What were they all thinking about? Those doctors represented a lot of medical talent. Surely they knew much about the art of healing. And yet for themselves they had found only one potent anodyne, opium, the ancient painkiller that had been known even to the physicians of Nero.

*Is* there anything besides opium, I wondered.

Later, when they had left and the needle had been removed from my vein, I got up to go to the bathroom. On my window sill were seven oranges. Each of my visitors had left me his evening's dessert. I recognized this as a thoughtful and precious gesture, because fresh fruit came to us rarely and only as a very special treat. Then I suddenly remembered: It was Christmas Eve, 1947.

I heard some strange talk and met some strange people in the days that followed. I saw dreadful suffering and a great deal of kindness among the patients for each other. And I still couldn't sleep more than half an hour at night.

Two fellow patients along my corridor, Tony and Gino, used to come and sit on my bed and drop their ashes all over me. They were a couple of tough, swarthy kids from Chicago, Italian kids, excitable, warmhearted, and unpredictably callous. They had been nabbed for "pushing" junk but they were addicts as well. Just out of their teens, they had a rapid recovery and were full of plans for the outside; meanwhile they each had to do two years, of which they had served only six days.

"Right away we'll be in the street," said Tony, "and we'll be mixing it up again."

"Have you boys ever done any work?" I asked.

"Sure," said Tony. "We used to mix schmeck for Mike Malasino."

"Yeah!" said Gino. "That's how we got hooked, three years ago."

I remembered Manny telling me about these kids. They had worked for a big drug jobber, who, of course, adulterated the heroin with milk sugar and other crap. Nobody who uses drugs can ever lay his hands on pure heroin, that's certain. Tony and Gino had worked for a while mixing this mess and, by inhaling the poison for many months, had inadvertently saturated their systems with it. That's how they had become addicted.

"How long did you work for Mike?" I asked.

"Till we got hooked," said Tony.

"Mike can't use no junkies around the plant," said Gino. "They'd boost [steal] more than they'd pack."

They laughed immoderately over this.

"Are you going back on junk?" I asked them.

"I'm gonna joy-pop, just on weekends," said Tony.

"There's no such thing as just joy-popping," I said. "That's how every junkie gets started on his habit."

"We got something figgered," said Gino. "A guy from Michigan told us how we can get the stuff legit."

"How?" I said.

They looked furtively at each other, as if they had blurted out more than they had planned to.

"Aw, this guy King is a cool stud," Gino finally said. "We can cop out to him."

"All right," said Tony, "but keep it on ice."

"Who is this guy from Michigan?" I asked.

"He left yestiddy," said Tony. "He's an old hophead, older than you. He's lived the life a long time. He used to hit the pipe and he knew how to cook up paregoric and everything."

"Yeah!" said Gino. "He once did five years here, but this time he was a winder, so he cut out yestiddy."

"Sounds like a great guy," I said.

"He used C [cocaine]," said Tony, "and he told us how to make bennies out of sniffers."

Tony meant that their benefactor from Michigan had instructed them how to distill the Benzedrine out of medicated inhalers which could be bought without prescription in any drugstore.

"He was plenty hep," said Gino.

"Sounds like an all-round guy," I said. "And how did he aim for you to get the stuff legit?"

"It's easy," said Tony. "You just shoot some plain gasoline under your skin. Get it?"

"Not yet," I said. "Sounds like it would knock you on your can."

"Listen!" said Gino. "You're not shooting the gas for a bang, the gas is just the starter."

"Yeah," said Tony. "This guy told us that this gas is gonna give you cancer. A *small* cancer—get it? And with the cancer, the croakers gotta give you stuff, legit. Get it?"

"A small cancer?" I said. "How do you know it'll stay small?"

"Aw, go on!" Tony was disgusted by my pessimism. "Just under the skin. You ain't aimin' for your liver or your guts."

"That's what the guy told us," said Gino. "He beat it home so's he could do it himself. For a cancer, even a little cancer, the croakers gotta come across. That's the law, he said."

And here is my first suggestion for improvement at the hospital in Lexington: Don't mix the kids with the old-timers. It is even a mistake to mix the volunteers, who have the keys in their pockets, with men who are serving time. It is a great hardship for a prisoner to see the same people winding in and out, four or five times, while he is serving his long sentence. I understand some changes have since been made, the winders now have to stay a minimum of a few months; but the kids still sit cheek by jowl with chronic addicts. It is impossible to avoid this because the government is particularly niggardly in its funds for Lexington. This means that the management must get along with insufficient personnel and inadequate housing. When a young delinquent lands at the hospital he is greeted by a few hundred new drug connections and a couple of hundred old magicians, soothsayers, and alchemists.

There were about a thousand men and three hundred women at the institution in 1947, and a large number of these were young people. Since I'm neither a philanthropist nor a do-gooder, I have no theories about the problem of juvenile delinquency. I just know that Gino and Tony couldn't possibly have benefited by their two-year stay in Lexington.

Luckily, I didn't get addicted until I was forty-five years old. I had an active and a not altogether useless life in back of me. What happens to kids on the drug habit who have never done a decent day's work, who have never cared for or supported anybody, and who, after their cure, go right back into the same morass that spawned them is more than I care to speculate about.

I finally left the infirmary for good. I was wobbly on my

pins but my eyes slowly came back into focus and I was able to read again. They have a fine library in Lexington. However, the level of literacy among the inmates is very low and the most popular reading matter besides comics was a long, hideous poem called "This Is My Beloved," which was circulated in typewritten sheets among the jail cognoscenti. "The Ballad of Reading Gaol" was also highly favored, and the copy I saw was freely annotated in the margins by previous readers. "You said a mouthful" and "You were a good kid when you had it" were the sort of literary criticism that would have given a real fillip of delight to Oscar Wilde.

Now I became acquainted with the rest of the prison population, its sorrows, its delights and its privileges. There was a large auditorium where movies were shown on Saturday and where the inmate band performed quite often. That year they had one of the best jazz bands I've ever heard. I suppose it is common knowledge that jazz and drug addiction have more than a bowing acquaintance with each other, and yet the greatest jazz people are rarely addicts. Charlie Parker, Billie Holiday and a couple of others used stuff, but, by and large, the real top names keep clean.

But there is that in-between world of the not quite ace performers, the kings, queens and jacks of the jazz deck, who derive from drugs that lift of self-deception their frenzy seems to require. When they are off the stuff, they will freely confess that junk has never helped their playing one bit. It can't make them play high, it just makes them *think* high. Also, the life they lead is one of insidious pressure, of great nervous tension, of insufficient rest and unfounded joviality. Junk makes it all "cool." And once you're on it, it's tough to stay off.

Despite the good band, the fine library, and the plentiful commissary, I was pretty much depressed by the place. It really dragged me.

Then somebody suggested that I join the newly formed Addicts Anonymous. I am instinctively leery of joining anything. I never joined the Communist Party, the Automobile Club of America, or even the Camp Fire Girls, but I did go to one of the meetings of Addicts Anonymous. They were nice people, elderly people mostly, who had by their own testimony wrestled bravely with the dope demon. They had always lost. Most of them were chronic recidivists, and some cynics claimed you couldn't join unless you had been to Lexington at least six times. A good many inmate doctors belonged. Not the ablest, nor the brightest, but the oldest. The only exception was their chairman, a doctor in his mid-thirties. He housed along my corridor and it was he who had induced me to come. His name was Elmer Bishop.

There is a quasi-religious aura about these meetings which makes me uncomfortable. This is true about Alcoholics Anonymous as well. At any rate, I didn't go for it. I'm not happy when people confess their sins and trespasses out loud. I also had the feeling that some of these breast-beaters were enjoying themselves immensely as they resuscitated their pathetic crimes. After a while I had the idea that they were less concerned with repentance than with reliving their gruesome but nevertheless thrilling past adventures. Maybe I was off. But they dragged me, too. I wanted to jump up and say to them, "In Heaven's name, go out and get a shot of dope and stop *talking* so much about it."

I was probably wrong. I often am.

That evening Dr. Bishop, their chairman, came to visit with me. He would have been quite handsome, but his chin and his eyes were too wishy-washy. He looked as if someone had made a successful sketch of his head but had accidentally spilled some water under the eyebrows and below his mouth. He was fair-skinned, with straight blond hair, and any sudden emotional change sent a youthful flush of color to his face.

Dr. Bishop respected my misgivings about A.A. But, as I elaborated my objections to joining, the uncontrollable barometer of his telltale blood rose in his cheeks, indicating signs of distress. I suppose I should have shut my trap and let it all ride. In the end we shook hands, and, because he looked so much like a ripe pimento, I promised to give it another try some other time.

I never went back again, because the very next day, a little before sundown, something happened to settle my mind completely.

It was just about chowtime, and I wanted to ask Dr. Bishop something about my kidney stones. About a possible diet that might help me. Bishop was a genito-urinary specialist, but somehow I had never before thought of consulting him.

I opened the door to his room, and in the semidarkness I thought at first that he was out. His room was full of little domestic touches, such as hand-decorated lamp shades, ash trays he had hammered out of tin cans, and, most notably, three handsomely framed photographs of his demure wife and his sweet hypnotized-looking little daughters.

Then, as my eyes became accustomed to the sparse light, I suddenly saw him. He was kneeling beside his bed, with bowed head in an attitude of quiet reverence. I felt like a blundering ass and proceeded silently to back out of the room. I made it, too, without his having seen me.

But unfortunately for my soul's equilibrium, *I* had seen *him*. He had his sleeve rolled high up above his elbow. His eyes were closed in unmistakable ecstasy, while with his right hand he was giving himself an imaginary shot in the arm with a nonexistent hypodermic syringe.

I took a quick look at the shadowed faces of the three dependent women in his life and noiselessly closed the door behind me. What price salvation, now? I thought.

The following day I asked to be released from the institution.

I am one of those unfortunate people who don't believe that this life is just a curtain raiser, and that after it has closed I shall wake with heightened awareness to some purer form of existence.

Well, if this is the whole works, you would imagine I couldn't possibly spare any time for doodling. Nonetheless, I returned to Lexington three more times and spent, altogether, fourteen months within its walls.

The last two times I returned against my will, as a prisoner.

## CHAPTER SEVEN

Now, THEN, dear grandchildren, I must point out to you that other people besides me have written autobiographies. I earnestly suggest you give them a break; some of those works are of surpassing excellence.

Try Benvenuto Cellini, Marco Polo, Giacomo Casanova (I found those three cats tops), Goethe, Jean Jacques Rousseau, Laurence Sterne, Henry James, Henry Adams, William Butler Yeats, George Moore, Isadora Duncan, Karen Blixen, and Anita Makepiece Schlosser.

That last name is not so well known. In fact, on the chance of seeming immodest, I think I am the only man alive who has read her epic from cover to cover. Just a word about her.

I first ran into Anita Makepiece Schlosser in a tiny library up in Oswego, New York, about forty years ago. I happened to find myself in that particular forlorn corner of the earth because I had quarreled with my parents and cut myself adrift from all family ties. I'd had enough of it, I was going out into the world to find the legendary money-green pastures. Heaven knows, this is a common enough event, and it was high time it happened, since I was nearing my eighteenth birthday. What made my particular hegira a little less common was the fact that I took along with me my seventeen-year-old wife, who at that moment was about eight and a half months gone in her pregnancy.

We decided to run away to Oswego because we had a friend, Julian Greifer, who was immured there as a Hebrew teacher. Julian was a boy from New York. Short, dark-eyed, painfully reasonable and sentimental, he had fallen in love with a pretty doll called Adeline, who was slowly torturing him to death. So, by an extraordinary act of decisiveness—for a scholarly type—he had run off from his daily auto-da-fé and sought peace and forgetfulness in Siberia. It was only Oswego, but we were a literary crowd.

Because you children belong to a generation that is being reared on quickies, I'm not going to torture you with any unnecessary suspense. This tragic love affair had a happy ending. I saw Julian and Adeline about five years ago in Philadelphia, where they now have their home. Adeline is still pretty, and Julian is still scholarly. He is called Dr. Greifer, because he is a rabbi and an important factor in the community. Also, he is the father of a daughter who is now older than Julian was when he first enters this little history.

He enters it on the day, forty years ago, when I sent him a wire, "Arriving tomorrow."

And off we went. Not so simply, though. My little bride, who at that point had become all eyes and all belly, had nevertheless bought herself a new pair of sandals. Because they were made of some tough, unresilient material, we swapped shoes. I had small feet, but they weren't *that* small. At any rate, our miserable train was to leave on its sixteen-hour journey at some wee hour of the morning. Don't ask me why I picked that particular train. I do remember that if we had slept another night in our furnished room we would have had to pay another week's rent. *There* is probably the answer to the mystery of why we arrived at Grand Central Terminal four hours too early.

My darling, who had a knack of falling asleep on the slightest provocation, curled up on a bench in the waiting room and took off. I had her head in my lap, her shoes on my feet, and a book in my hand. The book was Max Stirner's *The Ego and His Own*.

I shall not trouble to describe the nightmarish voyage, the oversugared coffee, the melting paper cups, the bread sandwiches, the sticky Tootsie-Roll wrappers, the seats like correction booths, the stench, the dust-laden air. Let it suffice that we finally arrived at our destination like a couple of crushed paper napkins.

Julian was waiting for us at the station, moist-eyed and beaming. I had noticed on the train, some miles back, that the air was beginning to be filled with a penetrating odor of chocolate. When we got off it was even worse; we seemed to be stepping into a burnt chocolate soufflé.

38

"Does this stink go on all the time?" I asked Julian.

"Yes," he said, "but you'll get used to it."

"By that time we'll all have diabetes," I said. "I thought Hershey's was down in Pennsylvania."

"It is," said Julian. "Here they have the Oxheart Cherry factory. It's the town's chief industry."

It was. I had never believed, until then, that these chocolate-covered cherries were produced just by candy manufacturers. I thought the whole business was a secret frame-up sponsored by the dry-cleaning industry, because anytime you bit into one of these chocolate cherries a lot of the liquid goo was bound to run down the front of your suit. One bite and your clothes had to go straight to the dry cleaners.

Some day, a Congressional committee investigating such collusive matters may still prove that I had the real low-down about this, back in 1918.

Meanwhile, Julian installed us with a family called the Brombergs, with whom he himself was boarding. Of the Brombergs I remember only that they had a dog called Ponto, a balding St. Bernard who suffered from chronic flatulence and stank worse than chocolate.

Right the next day, after our arrival, I went down to the local Democratic paper to ask for a job. I wasn't altogether inexperienced. I had, for about four months, made sketches for the *Call*, a Socialist paper, and I'd sold some covers to a magazine called *Smart Set*. Most important of all, the New York *World* magazine section had reproduced several pages of my drawings. I took all these clippings along by way of salesmanship. I was received by a man who called himself the "owner-editor" and who seemed to have no other visible employees. He was an ancient gnome, with a head as bald as a Brancusi portrait, but compensatingly he had great wads of cotton growing out of both ears.

I told him I was a brilliant cartoonist, displayed my samples, and smirked at him expectantly.

"So you worked on the *World*," said the one-man newspaper staff.

"Yes," I said, "the New York *World!*"

"Ah," he said. "The *World*." Long pause. Big sigh. Finally, the memorable utterance:

"I used to know Horace Greeley." Another pause. A cough like a muted cymbal. "Yeah, knew him to speak to. Before your time, though."

I admitted it.

"How about a job?" I asked.

"Not now," he said, and he gave an experimental yawn.

"If not now, when?" I said.

"Not likely ever," he said. "Planning to stay long?"

"If I get a job," I said. "Is there another paper in town?"

"Yup. Republican, right across the way."

"Well," I said, picking up my clippings, "guess I'll try there."

"I wouldn't," he said.

"Why not?"

"I own that one too," he said.

He wasn't joking, he did.

So you see, dear children, the grass-roots press was in wonderful shape even when I was a kid.

My wife and I had only thirty dollars left at this pass, and I certainly had to bestir myself to make a living for us. Julian earned very little at his teaching job, but, until we had dropped in, he had merely been seeking a pittance to sustain himself in exile. We had brought the whiff of New York to his outpost and he had suddenly become discontented. He became freshly aware of the smell of chocolate cherries and the smell of Ponto. The time was ripe for a change for all of us. But we did remain two more weeks.

Well, then, it was during those two weeks that I meandered into the local public library and it was then that I first came upon the autobiography of Anita Makepiece Schlosser. It was a book of around seven hundred pages and, at first glance, frankly repulsive even to a booklover like me. But a born browser browses, so I opened the title page.

That's what got me, I counted 820 words on that title page, in twelve different sizes and fourteen different type styles. But, for me, the following was the *pièce de résistance*: "With portraits and one hundred and twenty engravings from designs by eminent artists, made expressly for this work."

And that was all. Not another word about who the hell these artists were or where they had been recruited from. But, as Joyce says, "now comes the hazel-hatchery part." I recognized in these designs the hands of some quite skillful practitioners. Unquestionably Birch and Kemble had done a good many of the original drawings. Not a name was signed. Finally I doped it out. The book was an edition limited to subscribers only. Anita Makepiece Schlosser obviously had dough and had paid for the publication. She had gotten the artists, at least a dozen of them, to make the illustrations, but she had refused to have anybody's name appear in the book, besides her own. A great gal.

The book was called *The Story of My Life*. And that's what it was. I read it in the next two days, and during dark periods of my own later life the memory of it helped to sustain me. Not the darkest periods, perhaps, as in Lexington, but in some twilight interludes between wives. Anita had a few things in common with me. She had married, had begotten some children, and had lived to see a few grandchildren. Frankly, the similarity peters out just about there, because the real critical high point of her life, as far as I could see, was a rained-out picnic.

She had a lot of friends, ministers of the gospel mostly, and she quoted a lot of their sermons. She also quoted heaps of poetry, the helpful type that is supposed to cheer you up when somebody has mislaid the dog, or a petticoat has been sucked into the open fireplace and blown up the chimney. There was quite a bit about love, too, mostly family love, as if all people were vaguely crippled and were somehow incomplete unless two or three other cripples were holding them up. Nowadays that's called Togetherness, I suppose.

In short, the book made quite a dent in me. I didn't know then what, specifically, I had found in it. I know now. I found in it what I had never before encountered, systematized boredom raised to the level of a poetic ideal. I've met a good deal of it since; remember, I was an editor on *Life* magazine for a couple of years.

So, now that I'm stuck with the remainder of my Oswego story, I might as well tell the rest of it.

After two more weeks of chocolate effluvium, we decided to try our luck in the nearby metropolis of Syracuse. That is to say, Julian and I were going alone, at first, to case the joint. The young prospective mother, who in eight and a half months of pregnancy had never once been examined by a doctor, remained at the Brombergs' with Ponto, the gas bomb.

Come to think about it, I haven't said very much about the little lady so far. She was, as I've told you, seventeen at the time, but she could easily have passed for three years younger. She had large gray eyes with lovely long lashes, a head full of dark curls that had never known the help of a hairdresser, and skin so inordinately fair it seemed artificial. I used to think of her as petite and piquante. English couldn't quite do justice to my feelings.

In short, dear tots, your grandmother was the same sweet little girl who, at the very beginning of this story, had gotten on and off the bus with me on that fateful April day and had gone with me up to Nepera Park instead of to the Metropolitan Museum of Art. You see, she must have made a lasting impression on me during that short excursion, since, less than three years later, I married her. As you all know, her name was Nettie.

Julian and I found Syracuse a lot closer to our tastes than Oswego. It was a college town with smart shops, delicatessen stores, and a traffic problem. It was almost as good as being in New York. There was just one question, and it was a leading one—how in hell were we going to make a living there?

Let me confess that I wasn't altogether planless. I've mentioned before that I once had contributed some drawings to a Socialist paper, the *Call*. Well, it seemed to me that in so large a town the *Call* might easily have circulated among the local Socialists, so, after sopping up the hustle-bustle for a while, we trickled over to Socialist headquarters.

And there we ran into a surprise.

It seems that the American Socialist Party had suffered a rift. At their last national convention, out in Chicago, there had been a split right down the middle, and now there were two Socialist parties. These two factions loathed each other with true fraternal venom, and I felt like Mr. Pickwick during the election in which he was suddenly confronted by the partisan fury of the Blues and the Reds.

Julian and I had, of course, been Socialists as children. We hadn't joined anything, but we liked to go to the Socialist headquarters down on Fourteenth Street. I suppose its cozy griminess appealed to us. We went there not because we understood or cared about dialectical materialism, but because they charged only a nickel for a game of pool and it was the only place in New York where girls were allowed to play. Besides, all the intelligent kids we knew hung out there. That was about the extent of our socialism.

So you see, we were not particularly qualified to understand the bitter intraparty schisms and shenanigans. Their fratricidal feud just threw us for a loss because it sounded like bad news. The Socialists didn't have very much money even when they were united, so how were they going to find use for us now, in their splintered condition?

It happened that the faction we encountered that afternoon was nominally under the guidance of a man called Crimmins. Dr. Joseph Crimmins, to be exact, and he happened to be present when Julian and I arrived. Recognizing that we were strangers, he introduced himself to us, and on hearing my name he fortunately remembered my drawings in the *Call*.

It is quite difficult for me to account for the strange effect this Crimmins man had on me. Now that I have grown old and shameless like a bedbug, I can at last admit that real goodness always had a tendency to floor me. It was not only rare and unexpected, it seemed even a little unfair. It caught me off balance.

Now, Dr. Joseph Crimmins was a truly good man. Later I discovered that even his socialism was merely a vain attempt to extend his own personal goodness to a doctrinaire movement. Unlike so many other party members, he did not believe that the world was going to be automatically improved by the logical application of a Marxian syllogism. I can only define

Only Julian seemed more and more depressed. I suppose my own happy married condition had started to drag him. He longed for love. More specifically, he longed for the love of Adeline.

I believe I have indicated that despite his congenital mildness Julian was a man of decisive character. His self-exile in Oswego proved that. Well, the time had become ripe for another powerful gesture.

One evening he sat down and wrote a ten-page letter to Adeline in New York. A week later Adeline got off the train in Syracuse and stepped into our welcoming arms. We were all enchanted. There was a barely perceptible smile of accomplishment on Julian's face that evening as we all sat down to dinner.

I never found out what the hell he put into that letter.

Anyway, now there were four of us. It was self-evident that Adeline was going to be no problem. She was a blond, curly-headed little beauty, with lively blue eyes, who was also an expert typist and stenographer. A couple of days after her arrival she got a job as secretary in a paint factory, and so we now proceeded to look around for a suitable dwelling for all of us because we had to have an additional room for Adeline. We finally found one, at the very tail end of a trolley line. We rented the top floor in the home of a widow, a Mrs. Parker, not only because it was spacious and clean but because from our windows we had a wonderful view of a nearby cemetery. We were all suckers for the beauty of the weeping willows that swished their theatrical drapes in the breeze across the way.

We tried, of course, to take most of our meals at home, but once in a while we blew ourselves to a served-up spread in a restaurant downtown. It was always the same place, the Schlesinger Brothers', where they had good grub and not too expensive. It was a cozy room with real table cloths and real napkins. Nobody had yet constructed tables from the waste products of coal tar, and chairs were not made out of stainless metals that would send a chill down your spine every time you leaned back. It was not a laboratory or a lavatory, it was a place where food was expected to be served and eaten.

And then one day, after we had finished our meal there, I had a brilliant idea. I decided that what that little restaurant needed to make it complete were some agreeable murals. At eighteen I must have been a pretty formidable time bomb, for I instantly tackled the elder Schlesinger about it. He was the front-office-executive type, while his brother usually hovered over the stoves.

This older brother, called Harry, was a short, balding Semite whose features were completely ravaged by the ceaseless battle between innate kindness and acquired avarice. Harry knew that I was some sort of an artist, so he was not too surprised by my proposal. Naturally, he felt no crying need for murals. Who does? But luckily for me some of my frenzies are catching, and Harry promised to talk it over with his brother Max. I must say I felt quite optimistic. After all, Harry was the hardheaded businessman of the outfit and he seemed at least willing to consider it. I'd met his brother fleetingly only once or twice. He looked like a bleached asparagus, limp and wet-handed, and it seemed to me that the accidents and occult mysteries of cooking were so much akin to the unpredictable happenings in the world of art that the younger Schlesinger might be quite predisposed to murals.

And I was right. His years in the kitchen had not left him unaffected. The brothers agreed, very tentatively, of course, that they might possibly go along with such a scatterbrained notion, provided the cost was within the scope of a practically bankrupt concern.

Since I was terribly anxious to paint murals they had an easy enough time with me. Before I give you the figures I want you to remember that I was to repaint the entire emporium, all but the ceiling and the floor. Their place hadn't been painted in a couple of years and they were planning to have a job done anyway, and the last time this had happened it had cost them around a thousand dollars.

So, it was agreed between us that I was to receive a hundred and fifty dollars in advance for expenses and an additional hundred and fifty when the job was completed, and that the four of us were to eat six meals a week at their tables for a period of two months. (Being religious Jews, they were closed Saturdays.) Nettie and my friends were, of course, present when these terms were ratified. The four of us shook hands all around, and we had our first free meal on the spot. The Schlesingers, like the Medicis, had a real sense of style and produced for this festivity an uncontracted bottle of raisin wine.

The next day I went out to Adeline's paint factory and laid in the necessary raw materials. Brushes and all, it ran to about fifty dollars, which meant a hundred dollars cash for the community exchequer. So far so good.

But now came a problem that had already confronted Giotto, Cimabue, Piero della Francesca, Michelangelo, Leonardo, and some lesser lights. What in hell was I going to paint? Mine was the biggest hang-up, not only because I had never before painted a mural but because my scope was practically unlimited. Those early Italians had a comparative cinch, as far as subject was concerned. The Church was their employer, so they couldn't possibly stray too far from the two Testaments. They might, by way of diversion, show the illumination or martyrdom of some saint, but the horizon of their interests was confined to the Biblical area.

I puzzled over my problem for a few days. I brooded about it at home, while my wife and my friends tiptoed considerately around my churning confusion. But one morning, as I was staring out the window, it suddenly came to me. There, across the way, was beauty in abundance, beauty that needed only the order of design to make it significant to all beholders.

I would paint the weeping willows.

Twenty minutes later I was down at Schlesinger's, atop a shaky ladder, laying in my first charcoal outlines. It took me two days to properly space the picturesque foliage. And then a new decision had to be made. What was most suitable to go with all the feathery wispiness? I mean, what human or animal factors, what architectural phenomena or vehicular devices would look logical in that subdued and moody atmosphere?

There was only one answer, the locale had to be China. It was a perfect solution. I had in the past spent many hours in libraries and museums poring over Chinese paintings and Japanese prints, so my memory was loaded with endless authentic Oriental details. I decided for China rather than Japan because I had never seen Japanese paintings, only the wonderful woodcuts of Hokusai, Hiroshige and Utamaro. These prints were much too decisive in color to serve as starting points for the plans I had. No, China would do fine, and China it was.

There was in the kitchen at the Schlesingers' a busboy called Irving, who was constantly in danger of being fired. The Schlesingers assured me that he was the worst busboy they had ever had and that only his status as a partial orphan and a full-time relative had served to maintain him in his post. It stands to reason that Irving the busboy really wanted to be an artist. Or a poet. Or something.

So, after his own chores had been wretchedly accomplished in the kitchen, he took to helping me. At first for nothing, but as his usefulness increased I raised him to a dollar a day. Irving certainly looked like an artist, like a sculptor anyway. He had a great abundance of tough black hair and a face full of aggressive pimples. He had fat sensuous lips, a thick nose, a cleft chin, and one black eyebrow straight across his forehead. His eyes were dark and full of persistent wonder, and, despite all the dishes in the kitchen, his hands were well-favored and looked intelligent.

It took me about a week to finish the first wall. It was a landscape out of Po Chü-i, an ancient Chinese poet who was my inspiration. Frail ladies, in costumes that shimmered like autumn leaves, were genuflecting before moss-covered idols. I guess I must have been a little influenced by the "Ode to a Grecian Urn," too, because I rendered a whole village in a state of eternal immobility. Mandarins of impressive demeanor and yet flimsy as kites passed in sedate discourse toward a sacred shrine. The top of a chaste pagoda hovered among the clouds. You can see I gave it the works.

Irving used to fill out the large, flat surfaces for me, and he showed undeniable control and even taste in these labors. He was bursting with sincerity, and puddles of earnest sweat accumulated all around him. It was August. The Schlesinger *frères* were completely flabbergasted by Irving's earnest craftsmanship and began to wonder whether he had not finally found his true métier. They were toying with the notion of apprenticing him to me permanently. Irving himself had certainly no intention of ever letting go of the four of us, and much to Nettie's disgust, he began to spend all of his leisure moments up at our house. This proved something of a hardship because he had taken to reading the books that Julian was still peddling, and their biased, didactic contents roused the loud voice of contention in Irving. But he was useful on the murals, so we all put up with him. After all, he was just a youngster. He was a whole year younger than any of us.

The second wall took only five days, and it was so much better than the first that I decided to do the first wall over again. Many years later Orozco told me that he had done the same thing in Mexico when he had had his own beginnings. At any rate, the work proceeded and the Schlesingers and their customers were obviously pleased. They didn't make a fuss about it, it wouldn't have been wise, or politic, or even businesslike, but their faces showed modest smirks of triumph when an occasional guest commented favorably on the proceedings.

And then, about five o'clock one morning, Nettie woke me and, in some distress but even greater embarrassment, told me that her bed had become soaking wet. She pleaded innocence of the whole shocking affair and from the height of my maturity I hastened to reassure her and to laugh her out of it. Before we had left New York, I had read a short compendium on childbirth and obstetrics. This book was specifically intended as a guide for sea captains and such, in case they should be suddenly confronted by an active case of human accouchement. That little Do-It-Yourself course had alerted me to the fact that the foetus was cushioned in its snug retreat by a protective water bag, and that this container was occasionally subject to untimely punctures. Whatever the hell it was, it was high time to get Nettie off to a hospital.

I quickly woke Julian and Adeline and told them that life,

the great mystery, was knocking at our portals. It was just a youthful euphemism, of course, because actually life had been its usual refined self and had thoroughly wet the bed.

Luckily the trolleys started going at six o'clock in the morning, and the four of us, frightened, creased, and yawning, crawled shakily aboard the first one out.

It was, of course, inevitable that the People's Hospital should be at a terminal point at the other end of the trolley line. It took us about half an hour to get out there, and poor Nettie suffered a couple of really bad spasms during that unbelievably endless ride.

Finally we landed. Two tired nurses, waiting to be relieved from night duty, roused themselves to kindliness and took Nettie off our hands. I mean they took her right inside, without asking her the names, the birthplaces, and the birth dates of all her grandparents. They didn't ask me for samples of spinal fluid and neither one of us was submitted to a third degree before the patient was put to bed. You know why? The People's Hospital was a twelve-room house, with a gable roof, a brick chimney and a picket fence. It had nine beds and a lovely sunporch, and nothing could have looked less clinical than its exterior. It was perfect.

Meanwhile, on our arrival, somebody had phoned Dr. Van Lengen. I saw him coming across the lawn in double trot. It did me good. I always enjoyed seeing him. Dr. Van Lengen looked like a six-and-a-half-foot Dutch tulip grower, and I was sure that that was just what his ancestors had been. He had their height, their weight, their complexion; he was derived straight out of a painting by Frans Hals, and I felt stronger and healthier for merely having him around.

He waved to us in passing and went inside to look after the patient. The three of us, stunned and superfluous, sat down on the front steps like a lot of unseasonably molting pigeons. We didn't say a word to one another. What was there to say? We were a bunch of dopey kids up against something real for a change.

Ten minutes later Dr. Van Lengen returned and, despite his clinical garb, seemed cheerful as a Dutchman on a cocoa box.

"You kids run along for a while," he said to Julian and Adeline. "Get yourselves some breakfast. This may take quite a few hours and it won't do anybody any good to have you hanging around."

So the two of them got up, shook hands with me, turned around, and toddled off into the morning mist. As I looked after them I gathered from their pathetic, childish backs a frightening image of my own forlorn condition.

What had I done? What had we both done? We were going

49

to have a child. And what kind of father was I? And Nettie was utterly dependent on me. Nettie and the baby, of course. How had I ever got into this monstrous predicament, anyway?

When I looked around, Dr. Van Lengen was gone. And then, suddenly, shatteringly, piercingly, a wild animal scream came out of the hospital. It was Nettie! But not *my* Nettie! It was not any Nettie I had ever known. No. It was all the poor bloody women on this earth who had ever screamed in childbirth since this silly ball had first started rolling.

I dashed down the steps, crossed the lawn, and began to walk quickly down the sleeping suburban street. It began to drizzle and my tears of shame and confusion mingled with the warm summer rain. A gaunt woman in a dust cap was sweeping her porch but she paused for a moment to look at me as I passed. I walked around those long country blocks three times. Each time I came by her house she stopped her work, and she always resumed it the second I hit the outer edge of her lawn. We seemed like two automatically interacting pieces in some primitive wooden toy. I wanted to get rid of her, so I marched off in another direction, my hands clenched in my pockets, my throat aching with unspent sobs. At last, when I reached the hospital again, I slowed down and tiptoed under the shelter of the porch.

There was silence now. The rain was stopping. It had just been a summer splash. It was the thirty-first of August.

I waited a long time, not daring to sit down. And then I heard someone coming along the corridor. I looked through the screen door.

It was Nettie, being wheeled past the main hallway. Her hair hung down over the edge of the surgical cart, her eyes were closed and her hands were folded across her breast.

But she was *flat!*

*She no longer had a belly!*

Then I saw Dr. Van Lengen walking through the corridor toward me. He was taking off his gloves. I quickly stepped out of sight because, God knows why, I didn't want him to catch me prying. I turned my back to the entrance, held on to one of the porch supports, and closed my eyes.

The screen door banged and Dr. Van Lengen stepped out on the porch. I felt his good, big hand on the back of my neck, but I made no move.

"Well, young man," he said, "you are now a father. The father of a fine son," he said.

I slowly turned around, and we shook hands, as men have always shaken hands on such occasions, slightly smug and superior because they don't have to suckle anybody.

"Thank you," I said. "I hope he'll grow up a good, strong man like you."

"He will," said Dr. Van Lengen. "The children of medium-sized immigrants generally grow much taller than their parents. Plenty of care, good food and lots of orange juice will do it. You better wait about half an hour until your wife wakes up. I gave her a sedative and she's sleeping now."

"Thanks," I said. "Is it all right for me to see the baby now?"

It is interesting that I said this. It shows that I had already become a social animal, ready to live up to certain established conventional procedures, because, as a matter of fact, I didn't care two cents about looking at that baby.

Good Dr. Van Lengen didn't suspect for a moment that I was just giving a traditional reading to my new role of fatherhood. He put his arm around my shoulder and shepherded me into the cool twilight of the little hospital.

A moment later a smiling nurse, who had probably seen innumerable movies of such buckeye situations, held up a small bundle for my inspection. In one end of a pale blue blanket there now appeared the wrinkled face of what seemed to me a prematurely born chimpanzee. I was staggered. I was absolutely staggered.

Luckily the doctor and the nurse were much better established and absorbed in their respective parts and gave no attention to the way I was fluffing my role. I realized, of course, that I had to live up to their decent, human expectations, and I proceeded to pull myself together. I am not by nature or character a hypocrite, but when an emergency arises I can be as convincing a phony as the occasion may require. So I came through with the proper sounds and grimaces, and I was finally released in my own custody until the little woman was ready to wake up.

Back on the porch I found Julian and Adeline, who had come back after breakfast just to take one more chance on a later news bulletin. They were grinning happily as I emerged because another nurse had already told them about the successful delivery. We kissed each other in silence, like decent people do who are vaguely ashamed at their inadequacy when a really shattering event has taken place.

In a little while we all went in to see Nettie. We embraced her, and the women wept, not only because it was habitual on such occasions but because they were both still children in their teens and they felt that we had all been touched by the shadowy wings of a great mystery.

But almost immediately the petty annoyances of everyday life crowded themselves in on us.

"We have no diapers," said Nettie. "We need clothes for the baby. You'll have to get me a bathrobe, too. I brought nothing along. Did you see the baby yet?"

"Yes," I said. "I saw him a little while ago. He's a fine-looking little chap."

This remark, that he was a fine-looking little chap, might have been passed unsuspiciously by a nurse, by a doctor, or even a psychiatrist, but my Nettie knew much better.

"Is there anything wrong?" she asked.

"No, the kid is fine," I said. "Normal. With one head and the usual number of features."

But Nettie was alarmed. She rang for the nurse.

"I'd like to see my baby," she said.

She had, in the last thirty seconds, become a complete mother. A mother from 'way back. When she asked for her child, it was the voice of Hagar asking for Ishmael in the wilderness. There obviously was no father present.

When the baby was brought in, everybody found it delightful. They made encouraging noises. Our friends were enchanted. The mother was proudly appeased. My fears had been for nothing.

And I realized once again what a terrible, what a bitterly lonely business it was to be afflicted with normal eyesight.

That evening, during supper, my friends went to work on me about calling up Nettie's mother in New York.

"You must admit she is a very good, kind woman," said Adeline.

"I think she ought to be notified," said Julian.

I would have done it, too, but there were drawbacks. Nettie's mother happened to be married to a truly monumental imbecile, whose outstanding character traits were mule-headedness and arrogance. Nettie also had a brother, a replica of the old man, who to the inherited gifts from his father had added his personal touch of street-corner boorishness. Father and son were both heavily overweight and they always appeared to me like a couple of landlocked whales. To hear either of these two people, even on a phone, was more than I could bear at that moment.

I was worried about our funds. In those days the hospitals generally kept a new mother for about two weeks, or at least ten days. I know things are different now. The mother gets off the delivery table, goes out into the back yard to bury the placenta, and then takes the wheel and drives the family home. But I figured that I would probably have to pay the hospital for about two weeks. It was a headache.

And then, on the very day when I was going to ask the Schlesingers for an advance on my next hundred and fifty dollars, an altogether unforeseen, soul-shattering calamity fell on me.

I feel that this interlude really merits some ominous mood music out of the more turbulent works of Richard Wagner, because, after all these years, I still get goose pimples thinking about it.

It was all brought about by a revolting busybody called Adolf Kimmel, who looked like a bald-headed anteater and was by profession a cigar salesman. I want you to know that, because of him, I execrated the name Adolf long before Hitler ever emerged from the mephitic swamps of Nazidom.

Well, anyway, this Kimmel character dropped into Schlesinger's one day to unload some of his urinous stogies. Generally on these visits he was in the habit of handing out some of his free samples to the help, and every time he appeared the place started to simmer like a New Jersey garbage dump. I can't stand cigars, either, since then.

As I'm saying, Kimmel arrived, handed around his Flora de Stinkos, and planted himself up front near the cash register.

"Painting the place, eh?" he said. "What is this stuff supposed to be, anyway?"

"They're muriels," said Harry Schlesinger. "Hand-painted muriels."

"Yeah, I see that," said Kimmel, "but who are these natives, those people in the bathrobes? And that house with the warped roof?"

"They are Chinese people," said Harry. "It's China a long time ago."

"I don't get it," said Kimmel.

I'd been listening to this whole dialogue from the top of my ladder and I thought it was time to butt in.

"What don't you get?" I asked. "Anybody with eyes can see what it is."

"I got eyes! I got eyes!" said Kimmel. "What I don't get is the meaning of it."

I came down from my ladder. I realized I was in for an argument about art. With a cigar salesman, no less. Such an argument would have bored the can off me even if the disputant had been Roger Fry, but Harry Schlesinger seemed to be getting uneasy and I thought I had better douse this stink bomb before he loused up my act.

"Chinese people," I said, "particularly in ancient times, dressed beautifully. They lived in beautiful surroundings, and their landscapes were trained by expert gardeners to make fine settings for them. Get it?"

"I admit all that," said Kimmel shoving his iron derby to the back of his skull. "I can see that they're very pretty people, and they're wearing very nice garments, and I have nothing against them."

"So what?" asked Harry.

"So this!" said Kimmel. "I'm asking you a plain fact. Is this, or is this not, a kosher Jewish restaurant? This *is* a Jewish

53

restaurant, and it's got a fine Jewish trade, it should only last a hundred and fifty years. And so I'm asking you this fact, what are Chinamen doing in a Jewish restaurant? That's all I want to know!"

He straightened his hat, shoved an eight-inch heater into his mouth, and looked at me as expectantly as a justice in the appellate court.

I realized, of course, that he was a numskull. But Harry and Max were no intellectuals either. Also, they were in the restaurant business, a notoriously mercurial form of enterprise. That's why so many Jews are attracted to it, it is a tremendously risky form of gambling. Every meal represents a hazardous hurdle. Let's say one day you've prepared five hundred plates of beef soup with marrow bones. That very day the customers may insist on pea soup with frankfurters. Or you have laid in a stock of two hundred portions of chicken livers. What happens? Everybody who comes into the joint has developed a bitter aversion to chicken livers but is suddenly possessed with a frenzied appetite for pickled herring. That's the restaurant business for you. And the people who run such a business are of more unstable temperament than oboe players.

What's the use of prolonging this painfully hideous story? Even as Kimmel had flung his undemocratic, racist challenge in my face, I felt an icy wind blowing premonitorily across the landscape of my hopes.

I began to splutter and defend myself. I was very young, very anxious, very worried, and, I'm afraid, finally very abusive.

After Kimmel had left and I had climbed back on my ladder, I was suffering my second really bad case of artistic frustration. The first had been very bitter, too, and, by a coincidence, it had also involved a Chinese theme. I'll get around to telling about that one later on.

But now I was in a real mess. The seed of doubt in the Schlesinger minds grew to jungle proportions. They consulted with fish peddlers, meat salesmen, laundry drivers and even inspectors from the gas and electric companies. The results, although confusing, were, in their totality, disastrous for China.

"Look here," Harry said to me one day, "I have the highest respect for your work. You're an able young man, I wish you everything good. You got a new baby, and you need the coupla dollars, so be reasonable."

"What do you want me to do?" I asked.

"It's like this," said Harry. "The people who understand the business tell me that every restaurant that features muriels has the kind of pictures that go with the place. A Mexican

54

restaurant has chili-con-carne-type pictures, a beer saloon has fat monks drinking out of beer mugs, and Chinese people belong in a chop-suey place."

I could see he had given it a lot of thought. He was genuinely convinced, and agitated. His walls were defaced; he had, in good faith, handed me a hundred and fifty dollars; and we had already eaten a lot of free meals. It was a real crisis.

"So what do you want me to do?" I said.

"I want to make a suggestion," he said. "Don't get angry, because my brother and I want to help you out."

"What's the suggestion?" I asked.

"It's just this. You're an artist and you'll know how to handle it. I don't know anything about your work, but I'm sure you can do it."

"Can do what?" I said.

"I think the best way out for everybody is if you change those people in your picture so they should look like Jews."

I had heard him all right, but he repeated it anyway. This scheme had been hatched out between him and Max and it had struck them as a Solomonic solution. We were each going to wind up with half a baby.

"What do you mean Jews?" I said. "Am I going to put big schnozzles on them and earlocks, or what?"

"You'll know best what to do," he said, in moist-eyed confidence. "Maybe you can put black stripes on the bottoms of their dresses, so they'll be like prayer shawls. Maybe you can make their beards so they shouldn't look like strings, maybe . . . maybe . . . Who knows what an artist can do? Who am I to tell you about your own work?"

"But you *are* telling me," I said. "And I'm telling you, nuts! Nuts to you and to Max and to Kimmel, and to the rest of the nitwits who advised you. I've got one more strip to do and I'll finish it the way I started."

I got back up on my ladder and tried to go on with my painting. But I trembled so much I made a real botch of it. Still, I worked until suppertime, when Julian and Adeline arrived. They knew all about my troubles, of course, and now I told them the latest installment.

They were wonderful. They knew the jam we were in but never for a moment suggested a violation of my artistic integrity.

"I've got to get some clothes for the kid," I said. "I'm worried stiff. I don't think we'll be able to eat here any more either."

"I get my next pay check a week from today," said Adeline. "We can manage to stall everything off until then." She was paid every two weeks, so she was going to receive seventy dollars, which was a lot of money for those days. Still, I had to get around to hustle some cash on my own the first thing in the morning.

But the first thing in the morning was my visit to Nettie in the hospital. Here, too, I had bad news. It seems that Nettie had been so worried about our circumstances, the night before, that she had hardly slept at all. Dr. Van Lengen had left word for me to drop in on him before I left the hospital. So after I'd stayed with Nettie for a while and dutifully inspected the baby, I went around to the doctor's office.

He was a shade less cheerful than usual. "Your wife should not be worried at this time," he said. "She wants to feed the baby herself and if she is upset it will affect the child too."

"Thanks, doctor," I said. "I think I can help to cheer Nettie up right away. Is there a phone in her room?"

"No, but there is one out in the hall that has a very large extension cord. It will reach right to her bed."

"I'd like to put in a long-distance call to her mother," I said. "Nettie is very devoted to her mother and she doesn't want to tell me how much she misses her."

Van Lengen beamed. "A wonderful idea!" he said. "It will pull her right out of it."

It did. After the doctor had explained to me that there was such a thing as a person-to-person call, I even got around having to talk to the menfolk in Nettie's family. Her poor worried mother was so stricken with joy at the sound of my voice that I had to give her half a minute to control her feelings. After she had pulled herself together, she instantly came through with a noble sentiment. She said, "Please tell the operator to reverse the charges."

Then I put Nettie on the wire. They laughed and wept their way through a whole symphony of emotions, and in the end Nettie was radiant. She was completely purged of misgivings. As I stood on the sidelines I realized how desperately I was lacking in some of the commonest human consolations. But I was happy for Nettie's sake.

After I left the hospital I took a long walk down South Salina Street, which was the fashionable street of Syracuse in those days. Dawdling along without any special purpose in mind, I stopped in front of a really chic department store, which belonged to somebody called Addis. Maybe it still exists, maybe it has gone the way of cotton, and wool, and silk, and real wooden furniture; at any rate, it was a fine store. Only one thing was corny about it—the permanent backgrounds in the show windows were cluttered with meaningless ornate carvings. They were eyesores.

So I had myself another idea. I would talk to the owners, whoever they were, and suggest to them that they ought to change these dreary backgrounds for some more-up-to-date settings.

I went into the store and asked to see Mr. Addis. You will be pleased to learn that such a man really existed; the name Addis was not just a commercial fiction that merely represented the initials of five absentee owners. Mr. Addis was there, and, what's more, I was admitted to his presence within less than ten minutes.

In looks he was an upper-class trade version of Dr. Crimmins. He was just a little shorter, and he wore a well-tailored blue serge suit.

I told him I was passing through the hinterlands to find customers for my New York studio; that I designed and redesigned windows for smart stores; also, that I had a staff available that could come on in short order, and that we were prepared to perform minor jobs right on the spot.

Mr. Addis was definitely interested. He agreed that his windows, in which the merchandise was tastefully displayed, were basically a little old-fashioned.

He asked for my card. I fumbled around in my pockets and told him I'd left them in my other coat at the hotel.

He was neither suspicious nor disturbed. And then I did the one thing that clinched the deal.

"If you'll let me have some paper," I said, "I'll sketch you out a few suggestions that occurred to me while I was looking at your windows a few minutes ago."

I had nothing to worry about. I was an unusually dexterous draftsman, and my subject was at the tip of my pencil. With a few deft strokes I sketched a landscape with two stylized figures. They were Chinese under weeping willows.

Mr. Addis was delighted. "Let's draw up a contract," he said.


And now a really hectic period began in our lives. First of all we moved back to the hotel, so that Mr. Addis would be able to get in touch with me. We rented an enormous room with three beds and plenty of floor space. This room had once been a small banquet hall, and I planned to live there with Nettie and the baby after they came home from the hospital. Meanwhile it became my studio. I went up to the college art-supply store and laid in a stock of oversized illustration boards, and I also bought six quarts of different-colored India inks and a couple of dozen water-color brushes.

But there really was no hurry. We even had time to stall around, because I had to allow time for my staff to arrive from New York. My staff was, of course, Julian and Irving. I made preliminary sketches for all the sixteen windows, since I didn't intend to paint one stroke without Mr. Addis' approval. He was going to pay me twelve hundred dollars, of which I had already receive half in advance.

God was good. The world was good. And I was good. We threw no parties, we did no splurging, and I even went back to silently finish my murals at the restaurant. The atmosphere at the Schlesingers' had suddenly undergone a great change. I suppose Irving had blabbed to them about my job with Addis. Harry, like all front-office-executive types, had a permanently wet finger in the breeze of public relations, and at that moment the currents were definitely pro-Chinese. When my murals were finally finished and I was removing my debris from the restaurant, I couldn't resist blowing a farewell blast at the Schlesingers'.

"I'm doing a job for Addis' store," I said. "I'm going to paint Chinese settings in their twelve front windows on South Salina Street. When you boys next see Adolf Kimmel, you must remember to tell him that Mr. Addis just likes the way I paint Chinese, and he doesn't have the slightest intention of turning his place into a chop-suey joint, or into a kosher delicatessen, either. I'll be seeing you boys around!"

Irving had abandoned his job at the Schlesingers', since I was going to pay him twenty-five dollars a week. Julian had stopped peddling his books, too, and finally we went to work full blast. But somewhere along the line I had miscalculated my schedule, and I had only three of my panels finished when it was time for Nettie and the baby to come home.

Now, then, with all my foresight and my multifarious activities, I had not yet made any proper preparations for this one unavoidable event. I had bought a few diapers and some clothing for the child and had, of course, taken them out to Nettie at the hospital. I had reckoned that if these supplies proved scant the nurses would manage, for a few days, to eke out from their own stock of baby garments. But, on the very eve of Nettie's return, I suddenly realized that we needed a whole raft of stuff for the kid, at least. It was already late in the afternoon when the shocking immediacy of this theme first struck me.

"In heaven's name," I said to Julian, "I've got to get three or four dozen diapers and some shirts and sweaters for the baby. I've got to run down and get them this minute, Nettie is expecting me to pick her up at the hospital at nine o'clock in the morning."

Then Irving piped up. "I think diapers have to be hemmed by a seamstress," he said. "I don't think they're sold hemmed, ready for use."

"That's fine," I said. "Well, the kid will just have to pee unfashionably into seamless diapers. I doubt if Benjamin

58

Franklin had any better, and it never stopped him from saving a buck."

"The stores close at five-thirty," said Julian softly, "and it's now ten after six."

All three of us sat down, like the last surviving members of a beleaguered garrison after their last bullet turns out to be a dud, and now we were so smeared with dirt and color that we would have caused astonishment even in Greenwich Village.

Then the phone rang. It was Harry Schlesinger.

"What is it?" I said.

"I'm sorry to bother you," he said, "but it's getting on suppertime."

"Yes, yes," I said. "If you want Irving to help you out tonight, I don't think he can make it. We're all bushed."

"I don't want Irving," he said. "I just want to know if you can get somebody to move this crate out of here. It's blocking the way to the cash register."

"What are you talking about?" I said. "We didn't leave any crate in your place."

"No, you didn't leave it. The express company left it," he said. "They left it this morning already."

"Just a minute," I said. "Whose crate is it? Where is it from?"

"It's from New York," he said. "It was insured and I signed for it. Whoever sent it got the address from you probably when you were working here."

"I'll be right down," I said.

We washed up a little and tumbled downstairs to look at the crate.

It was from New York, all right. It was large and enigmatic, but it was definitely addressed to me. We hauled it back into the kitchen and pried it open with a cleaver.

It contained a small department store of baby clothes. Diapers, layettes, nightgowns, sweaters, stockings, booties and all sorts of rubberized disaster preventives emerged out of that box. Then came jams, jellies, preserves, tonics and a whole array of patented food supplements, for the mother. For her, also, there were lacy bed jackets, frivolous sleeping garments, and an all-silk quilted bathrobe.

Nettie's mother had sent it all.

How about that? We danced around that kitchen like demented Isadora Duncan acolytes and nobody minded a bit. The bounty that had poured out of that crate, the generosity hovering about those benefactions, affected the whole kitchen staff.

We had dinner at the Schlesingers' that night. When Irving also sat down at our table, Harry Schlesinger raised his eyebrows so high he looked as if he were wearing bangs; but they served us with smiles and with curtseys, because good will was shining over the world and everyone enjoys warming up his tepid soul in the radiance of real kindness.

Next morning, mother and child arrived at our bed-sitting-room-nursery-studio and were installed with due ceremony. We had decorated the place with paper lanterns and colored streamers, we had pasted silhouettes of nursery themes on the windows, and we even had put colored bulbs into the electric sockets. It was a real, happy homecoming.

Of course, in the next few days the studio-household management became a little complicated. First of all, Nettie's natural milk supply gave out, so we had to prepare formulas for the baby. The diaper problem became staggering at once. I learned right then and there that the human infant is nothing but a gluttonous funnel. You pour stuff into it on top and it runs out in a less attractive form, almost instantly, at the bottom. A drag! It is fortunate for the race that somebody in the family cares a lot for the little swine right at the start, or I think most of them would probably land in the garbage can.

I must admit that I myself was slowly getting used to the looks of the monster. I even began to discern minute human attributes in it. The hands and the feet were unquestionably masterpieces. The face was still a disaster, but, even there, the nose and the lips showed a certain skill in execution. I had a few sculptor friends who would have been willing to underwrite that nose and those lips.

In the midst of our household complexities we had to go on painting. Color got into everything. There were streaks of green in the milk, touches of magenta in the diapers and even the baby's hair once had some strands of bright blue in it. I thought it improved the kid, but nobody agreed with me.

Nevertheless, the work proceeded. Everybody performed heroically. Irving certainly proved his value to us in more than one direction. Since he originally came from a family of eleven children, our baby situation was like old home week to him. He knew every conniving trick for making one diaper do the service of three.

But the whole messy layout wasn't too easy on my poor wife. Despite my youth, I had already met some dopey gals in the Village who would have grooved this combination of paint shop, cookery, and baby crap. They would have found it "interesting" and antibourgeois. But Nettie happened to be painstakingly fastidious. Once, twenty-five years later, she reminded me how, despite her resolution to be brave and understanding, she had flipped her lid one evening. It seems that one of us had left some egg yolk splashed all over the sink, while another of us had thrown some soiled diapers on the hot steam pipes. It broke the dam. The little woman bawled the bejeezus out of us.

And through it all, and despite it all, flocks of carefully painted Chinese ladies and gentlemen continued to emerge from under the fine camel's-hair brushes and to live their own quiet, poised existence under the stylized willow trees.

A strange thing occurs to me now. None of us ever talked about our plans for the future. And yet I'm certain that by common consent we took it for granted that, once our job was finished, we had not the slightest intention to remain in Syracuse. Even Irving.

Well, finally, one day, the job was done. We delivered the last batch of work after hours at the store and stayed up almost a whole night to help the window dresser install it. It was three-thirty in the morning before the last panels were in place.

We raised the window curtains and went out on the street to look at them. It was a wonderful sight. Mr. Addis, who had suddenly appeared out of the night, was delighted. I went across the street with him and we got a full load of it. I felt damned good. If I had let myself go, I could have bawled. Instead I said a prayer of thanks. I've said many such prayers since, it is always the same prayer, and its substance is one thing I'm not going to tell you about.

Before we parted for the night, the window dresser asked me about my next job. Because he was a nice guy, and because my heart was full of gratitude, I leveled with him. I told him I had no job and no plans. He didn't mind.

"You ought to go to Chicago," he said. "Marshall Field spends a mint of money each year on their windows and they ain't anywheres near as good as these. I've got a brother who dresses for them and I'll write him a letter about you, if you like."

"Thanks," I said. "I'll stop by and see you tomorrow."

I went there the next day to get his letter and to pick up my check. Mr. Addis beamed on me when I stepped into his office. All morning he had been showered with congratulations, newspaper reporters and photographers had already called, and his two chief competitors had invited him to lunch.

"I expect you'll be around again next spring," he said. "We'll try to do as well again, won't we?"

"We'll do better," I said. "We'll always do better."

"This whole thing has given me a great deal of pleasure," said Mr. Addis. "I've taken the liberty of changing some terms in our contract. I'm sure you won't mind."

He handed me my check. He had given me a three-hundred-dollar bonus. If I had dared, I would have embraced him.

And that, dear children, was the end of the hegira to Syracuse. It all happened forty years ago, and, in all the time since then, I never once went back.

## CHAPTER EIGHT

THREE TIMES a day I eat boiled rice with stewed vegetables or bananas. I can't have any milk, butter, eggs, meat or fish. I can't put any seasoning on my food whatever. Because the Jews, who were probably suffering from high blood pressure even then, left Egypt with unsalted bread, I can also eat matzos. The world is still my oyster but I can't eat it. I'm on a salt-free diet.

I have been in constant pain all down my left side for the last three years, ever since I had my stroke. At least I'm not paralyzed. Also, for the last three years I have been off drugs.

I often recall those long sleepless nights in Lexington, and how much I was sustained, this side of madness, by my retentive memory. I speak and read five languages—Hungarian, Yiddish, German, French, and English. While my roommate, Manny, down at the narcotics farm, would be enmeshed in his own private nightmares, I, wide-awake, would conjure the great poets out of their graves and out of their books. In five different tongues they brought their wit, their wonder, and their ecstasy for my consolation. Petöfi, Schiller, Hölderlin, Raizin, Heine, Goethe, Rimbaud, Verlaine, Shakespeare, Donne, Rilke, Eliot, and Cummings were all ghostly visitors at my bedside. I particularly cherished Villon, who had often been in prison, always an outcast, and frequently in bad jams, like myself. Also, in 1928 I had illustrated a special new edition of Villon which Pascal Covici had published in Chicago.

Like so many significant rapes on reality, my success as a book illustrator was achieved through no purposeful strategy on my part. I fell into it as one falls into a gold mine or a mud puddle.

In the latter part of 1924 I had accumulated about twenty black-and-white drawings, which I submitted not too hopefully to various magazines. They weren't the sort of drawings the magazines generally printed, and I wasn't too hung up when everybody rejected them.

And what sort of drawings did they use?

I can tell you about that very specifically. Some years before, a close friend had written me a letter of introduction to the art editor of *The American Magazine*. That publication, like most magazines at the time, was a constantly warmed-over compilation of maudlin trash. I needed money very badly and my friend thought that this art editor might possibly find something for me to do. He assured me that this functionary was in every way superior to the stultifying requirements of his position, that he was a man of intelligence and taste. Let me hasten to tell you that all this proved to be quite true.

The art editor received me kindly, and he seemed quite impressed with my work. In fact, he offered to buy one of my drawings for himself.

"I should like to do some work for the magazine," I said.

"That, I'm afraid, will not be possible," he said. He didn't hem or haw about it. He just told me quite plainly I couldn't make it.

"But why?" I asked. "You seem to like my stuff. You're the art editor, aren't you?"

"That's right," he said, "but your work is absolutely unsuitable for us. You see, my dear boy, you haven't the vaguest idea of our formula."

"What is the formula?" I said. "Whatever it is, I'll learn it."

"No," he said. "It's really quite hopeless."

"Come on, now," I said, "give me a break. Tell me the formula and I'll accommodate myself to it, whatever the hell it is."

He looked sadly at me for a moment. "Well," he said, "the formula is this: We want the sort of pictures the readers would make if they knew how!"

He was, of course, dead right about me. I couldn't even imagine their readers, much less what they would try to draw. So I never really expected to score with my new batch of drawings. But you just go on making pictures whether anybody wants them or not, if that happens to be your particular affliction.

One day when those twenty drawings had bounced back on me again I showed them to an old friend, Minna Bodenheim, who happened to be visiting. She looked at them speculatively for a while and then suggested that I send them up to Horace Liveright, the book publisher.

"Liveright is a weird character," she said. "He sometimes goes for the most unlikely people." She had a good reason for thinking so, because he published her husband Max Bodenheim's poetry. The poetry was excellent but Max was certainly unlikely people.

I had nothing to lose, so I sent my batch of drawings up to

Liveright's. A week later I got a note from them telling me to call at their offices. The note was signed Donald Friede.

And that's how I happened to meet a person of supreme consequence in my life. He turned out to be the junior partner of the business, quite new in his role and eagerly on the lookout for new talent of all sorts.

The firm occupied a remodeled four-story building up on West Forty-eighth Street, and most of the people who worked there were a lot of noisy extroverts. Not Mr. Friede. He seemed like an interloper. Dark-eyed, long-jawed, elegant and prematurely balding, he had a bland, foreign-office air about him. He acted like someone from the embassy of a powerful country who had been instructed to muffle the national dynamics for the sake of a benign public policy.

I had Donald all wrong. On our first meeting he seemed to me like a toothy, well-bred, constipated Englishman. As so often happens with real British types, he was of Russian Jewish descent. He spoke beautiful French and had a warm, sympathetic heart despite his good manners.

If you think I'm exaggerating about British types, I want to point out to you that the late Leslie Howard was sired by a full-blooded Hungarian, and was even a Jew. And if he wasn't the very essence of the old Empire, I don't know who is.

Anyway, Donald Friede liked my work. He didn't quite see how they could make use of it in the near future, but he was personally so beguiled by my samples that he asked me to submit some more.

The following day I toted up a whole new load. Come to think of it, my work was pretty strange, when you consider the time and the place. For instance, I remember one painting of a couple of elderly people, nude and repulsive, sitting opposite each other inside a tightly sealed bottle. The woman's feet were splotched with purple and lavender varicosities, and the man had some sort of magenta-colored skin rash. It was obvious by their looks that these two ancients simply loathed one another.

The title of this little opus was "The Old Folks at Home."

I say my work was strange, when you consider the time and the place, because in 1920-24 American artists just didn't graze in such pastures. I discovered some four years later that in Central Europe men like Thomas Theodor Heine, Alfred Kubin, Pascin, and George Grosz had gone over that terrain pretty thoroughly. But in the good old sentimental U.S.A. my stuff was definitely freakish. Book illustration never seemed to have attracted particularly talented people in this country; the few good artists who had worked at it were already dead, or dying, by the time I emerged. In my time, pictures for books were made by refined spinsters with three names, like Mildred Huntington Quagmire, or Eleanor Sweetfish Wanderfogel.

The only people who ever really encouraged my work were H. L. Mencken and George Jean Nathan. By encouraged, I mean they had bought covers from me for the old *Smart Set*. That was a magazine in whose pages many of the best writers in the country had cut their eyeteeth. Mencken gave me carte blanche for seven covers once, and what's more, he paid me on acceptance. *Smart Set* was the only magazine that didn't make a poor writer or artist wait for his fee until his stuff was printed six months later.

I remember very well the old *Smart Set* office at 25 West Forty-fifth Street. The magazine was published by the Warner brothers (no relation to the movie people), and they got out a whole flock of pulpy adventure tales, too. I think Mencken had stock in the corporation, because once he asked me to try my hand at writing some gruesome stories for *Black Mask*, which was another Warner-brothers production. I did write a couple, mostly because I liked to illustrate them, and one summer when I went fishing I wrote up my experiences for still another of their magazines, called *Field and Stream*.

Well, anyway, at Liveright's I was now involved with a book publisher at last, but nobody was as yet asking me to illustrate anything. Not for another year and a half. Friede, who was a rich man, or the son of a rich man, had happily decided to stake me for a little while. He suggested that I go away to the country for a few months and prepare some new work for a possible exhibition in the fall. He thought we might hold the show in the Liveright waiting room.

Now this waiting room was something special. First of all it was a good size, was comfortably furnished, and even had a little shaded veranda out over the back yard. In this waiting room you were liable to meet Sherwood Anderson, Ben Hecht, S. J. Perelman, Theodore Dreiser, Eugene O'Neill, E. E. Cummings, William Faulkner, Ernest Hemingway, Hendrik Van Loon, and a lot of other people you have since heard about. Liveright published them all, and for a good many he was their first publisher. He had quite a flair.

So I took my wife and my kids up to Lake Mohegan and started working for my show. I was on top of the world. I could draw and paint to my heart's content, and I was even promised an exhibition at a famous publishing center. Plenty cool!

I didn't know then about exhibitions. I didn't know that unless you already have a famous name an exhibition, for an artist, is like a ghastly public denudement before an audience of blind flagellants. In short, I didn't know the art racket. I've become better acquainted with it since.

I did one more thing before I left for the country. I competed for an art prize that the Liveright people had set up quite a while before I got to know them. I suppose the competition had been announced all over, but I never got wind of it until I read about it in their waiting room. I think I submitted my entry just two days before the whole thing closed.

The point of the competition was for artists to submit drawings for a book by Heywood Broun, called *Gandle Follows His Nose.* Unless you're as old as I am, the chances are you've never heard of this opus. The book had been published a few months before and had obviously already laid an egg. Some of the critics, in reviewing it, had maintained that Gandle, the hero, had been described by the author in five or six contradictory ways; and so, to stir up some possible interest in this dying swan, the publishers had offered a prize to the artist who could best realize the physical aspects of the elusive Gandle.

Although I loved Heywood Broun, I had to confess that he had pretty extensively fluffed the characterization of poor Gandle. But I was willing to try. After all, I couldn't miss it any worse than all the other artists.

I'm telling you all about this because we had a surprising experience while crossing an empty lot up in Lake Mohegan that summer. My older boy, who was going on six, picked up a water-stained newspaper and ran up to his mother with it. She was just going to bawl him out for his retrieverlike tendencies, when her eyes suddenly lit on a reproduction of the very picture of Gandle that I had submitted in the competition. It was a week-old copy of a New York *Herald Tribune* book-review section, and it announced that I was the winning artist.

I took it as a very good omen. I also took the check that accompanied it. It spurred me on to still greater labors, and by the time we were ready to come back to New York I had completed forty drawings and eighteen paintings. The paintings were in oil, gouache, and water color. In other words, I was ready to be launched.

And now the time has come for me to tell you something about Horace Liveright himself.

He was quite an astonishing-looking hombre.

In those dim, backward years when Waldo Frank used to write all the *New Yorker* profiles, I remember he devoted one of them to Horace Liveright, who was his publisher. Later, when a compilation of these articles was printed in book form, I illustrated the piece about Horace, and I recall making a drawing of him looking out from behind a shower

66

curtain. This was no flight of fancy on my part; Horace actually had a complete shower in his office.

He was not a man one easily forgets. He was of medium height, dark-complexioned, with markedly Semitic features and a mass of thick, curly, almost snow-white hair; but what had an immediately shocking impact on me were his wildly protruding hyperthyroid eyes. He was certainly the most volatile and restless man I have ever known. I think Horace was originally a stock-market gambler, and he remained a plunger until the day he died. When I first met him he was gambling on manuscripts, on people, and on ideas. Although he owned perhaps the most enviable publishing list in America, he was still untamed and he proceeded to expose his nervous system to other more dangerous urgencies. He produced plays, for instance, some damned good plays, too, but he also lost fortunes in the theater the way another man loses buttons off his coat sleeve. He was a dangerous enemy and a still more dangerous friend, and he was frenziedly searching for something that he certainly never found while he was still alive.

He spoke very fluently, but too loudly, on every subject under the sun, including some that by common consent are only whispered about. I think he deeply envied, and yet loved, all people of real talent, and I suspect that somewhere in his personal effects there were a few yellowed pages of a manuscript that he had himself composed and written. I know that he gave enormous advances even to writers who had never produced any justifiable piece of work and who, in return, often befouled him with denigration and ingratitude. I think he was capable of stupendous generosity because he had no particular liking for money. Also, Horace had overwhelming charm and he could turn this mystical fluid on and off at will, like a faucet.

If I knew enough about his personal life, I would gladly write his biography, as an act of commemoration not only to his person but to a period of which he was one of the most colorful and potent symbols.

You will ask, how did such a man pick Donald Friede to be his partner? Surely it would have been impossible to find two more ill-matched people for any imaginable kind of collaboration. The answer is very simple. Horace needed a hundred thousand dollars in a hurry, so he took a partner who was in a position to put that amount of cash on the line.

You may not know that Liveright originated and owned the Modern Library, probably the most profitable reprint publishing idea of his day. Well, he sold the Modern Library when he needed another hundred thousand dollars. Sold it to

Bennett Cerf, who is making a mint of money on it to this very hour.

The Liveright publishing business of the twenties earned enormous sums, but the expenditures of the publisher were always several digits beyond the firm's wildest income. He was the central, dynamic force of a vortex of willful waste at whose bottom yawned only disaster. Particularly, personal disaster. But Horace's troubles came much later on, and the mad rigadoon was actually at its height when I first came to know him. (The business still continues under the same name, under less dramatic auspices, to this day.)

At any rate, all this will give you an idea in whose waiting room I was going to have my first exhibition. I must say, Horace was always very nice to me. Or almost always. Sometimes it wasn't easy for him. You see, he had already squandered the hundred-thousand-dollar dowry that Donald had brought him, and so his never too certain affections for his now obsolete partner had begun to grow altogether pallid; and because the moneymoon was over, he was naturally not so keen about Donald's special friends and protégés, of whom I was definitely the most outstanding.

Let me say in all fairness to Horace, though, that he submitted me to the ice treatment for only a very little while. A couple of weeks, perhaps. Eventually he gave me books to illustrate, even long after Donald had left the firm.

But I'm anticipating again. Nobody had the vaguest intention of giving me any jobs as yet, and even the possibility of my exhibition still hinged on the good will of the big boss, who was a notorious and unpredictable mind-changer.

And he was the boyo who came from Arroyo, who owned the stick that might strike the dog that might bite the cat that could chase the mouse that might nibble the bread that was fed to the brood that sat down at my daily table.

Donald remained his usual calm self all through the time before my exhibition. He had my pictures framed, and he also had a most elaborate catalogue printed. I think it contained ten large black-and-white illustrations, and it finally turned out to be a pretty fancy art folder. We mailed these to the various critics, and to some influential journalists as well, and I must say the advance notices on those prints were remarkably favorable.

I remember sending one to Ezra Pound in Rapallo; three months later (in Paris) I got an answer full of hectic spelling, hysterical punctuation, and cryptic marginal notes. The gist of the letter was get the hell out of America, which is quickly turning into Neo-Palestine.

Well, the evening of my exhibition arrived at last. I went

up to Liveright's quite early, but when I arrived the place was already jammed.

You know, I find art mobs more depressing than the mobs in subways, because they are even more joyless than the other lemmings. In the subways, at least nobody pretends to be having a ball. In the art galleries, the brittle pretense of amusement, the cynical smirks of alcoholic superiority, the constant collisions of shopworn laughter fill me with a sense of heart-breaking depression.

I'm talking only about opening days, of course; the rest of the time the average art gallery successfully simulates the atmosphere of an underground chapel, where bank deposits are expected.

Well, I, at least, had my first show in a room where on ordinary days some damned intelligent people used to forgather. But about two thirds of the mob that came to my opening—and goes to every opening—were either androgynous monsters, nymphomanic divorcées, part-time pimps, or all-time drunks.

Of course, there were some nice people, too. These and a few dear old friends approached me commiseratively in the course of the evening, pressed my hand, murmured a few gentle words of sympathy, and then stepped back to disappear once more among the smilers with the knives. These friends and well-wishers acted as if somewhere in the room, behind the curtain of cigarette smoke, I had laid out an embalmed stiff for final display, and they had come by only to offer their last condolences.

Man! It got me!

Horace came up from time to time, convoying some of his literary lights, and they would shed a momentary baptismal gleam on me. I'm glad to say that most of them were charming and felt decently ill at ease in this congregation of cackling phonies.

I sold a few pictures, too. Quite a few, as a matter of fact. Donald felt the evening was turning out a howling success. But a couple of my customers talked to me at some length, and I got the feeling that they were buying my stuff mostly because they were sorry for me, or, because they wanted to please Donald. What they really wanted to buy were Gauguins and Modiglianis. (Both of those characters starved to death.) Some of them told me that they could have bought their canvases quite cheaply, too, just a few years ago, but that they had missed their chances. They could have corralled a whole mess of French impressionists for a few thousand dollars, they said, and look where they all were now. 'Way up there! My own pictures cost really very little and I had an idea that if I sold them all I could afford a good second-hand car. So, naturally, as I listened to my clients, I felt like a mendicant who at Christmas, in front of Bloomingdale's, gets the small change that people are too lazy to put into their pockets.

But I did get introduced to Otto Kahn, and I did have my first meeting with Elinor Wylie. She was angelic to me, too.

"You musn't be afraid of all these people," she said. "They're only thistle balls. Squeeze them, and they'll disappear."

While she said this, she looked more frightened of that mob than I was.

Quite a few people got drunk, and one or two even had their elbows on my pictures and were leaning up against them. I started to wonder whether I ought to beat it before I got sore and busted one of these relaxed aesthetes in the nose, when Nettie, who had all evening been impersonating the demure, understanding wife of genius, fortunately happened to look at me. She swam quickly over toward my side, took my arm, and the two of us trod muddy water together until we hit shore. Out on the street, we were both deeply and wordlessly depressed, and I, at least, felt unaccountably humiliated besides.

You can see I was just an ungrateful swine. Can I explain it better now, what it was that got me down so? I think I can.

I had spent months doing my work, bringing to it as much ingenuity, skill and passion as I was able to muster. I drew it all, as the anonymous Hindu said, "from that unimaginable source of certitude."

It was great! To do the work, I mean. It was the greatest!

The pictures hardly ever turned out as well as I had conceived them in my mind, but even so, invariably, the last one—the one that I was just working on—had more merit than the others.

And then they were done. Each had been a peculiar problem, whose solution had caused me quite a bit of anxiety and pain. On rare occasions I had had certain brief but poignant spasms of satisfaction. I had surely left some significant aspect of my identity in each of those pictures, and part of me was palpably present in all of them for anyone who had eyes to see.

And what, in God's name, had the people at my exhibition to do with all this? Who were they, anyway? Most of them were professional booze lice who crawled from one *vernissage* to the other, who were already making multiple appointments to meet again at the next art shindig. When they talked to you they would speak permanently past your face, because at any moment somebody more important than you might possibly smile at them. And if this somebody, perhaps fifty feet across the room, *failed* to smile at them, or ignored the smile which they had grimaced or catapulted through space, then their afternoon fell into shattered fragments. They would frantically mop their faces, roll their eyes, and waggle their heads like half-decapitated herrings. I'm reporting to you now on one actual case I witnessed myself, in which a woman who fancied herself so snubbed finally broke into uncontrollable convulsions of hysterical belching and had to have medical attention before she could be taken home. And who in the world had brought on this shattering collapse? Who had snubbed her? I'll tell you who. A stammering paranoid gasbag who occasionally commented on musical publications for *The Saturday Review of Literature*. But, enough. Let me get back to my story.

After my second and third meetings with Otto Kahn, the substance of which I have already told you, I had a big heart-to-heart talk with Donald Friede. Donald warned me not to be too optimistic about my coming financial situation in France. The French had again manipulated their currency to the disadvantage of foreigners living in their country, and he felt I might not be able to manage as well as I had anticipated or as Mr. Kahn had expected.

"I don't want you to get into difficulties and have to ask Otto Kahn for additional help," he said. "He is too valuable a person to irritate with what might seem to him bad management on your part. Suppose I send you a small allowance each month, then I'm sure you'll be able to stay at least a year."

That's what Donald said to me before I started out for Europe with my family. And now I'm about to unveil for you the true nature of Donald's stupendous generosity.

He was really not a rich man on his own account. His father had left a large fortune to the family, but Donald had to manage with a definitely restricted allowance, which was administered under cast-iron trust conditions. Any monies he gave to me, and to others I shall name later, he had to take out of his own allowance.

I'm not pretending that he had to take oleomargarine for breakfast, instead of butter, because he was staking a couple of artists to a small living. But I am telling you something nobler and more surprising. When Donald eventually landed in a really tough money jam and had to strip himself of all his negotiable possessions, and even had to sell his wonderful collection of books, we, that is to say us protégés, were the last ones to hear about his debacle. He had gone right on sending his voluntary, generous, allowances, until he no longer could, because, finally, he didn't have either a pot or a window left, himself.

In short, he was, beyond his means, an infinitely greater patron of artists than Otto Kahn. I gladly roll back these thirty years to make him a profound bow. "A Russian bow with the forehead to the floor."

## CHAPTER NINE

BUT WHAT the hell kind of a biography is this, anyway? What is the meaning of all these vaguely related anecdotes? An autobiography ought to begin somewhere in childhood and proceed in some decent order toward its conclusion in old age, shouldn't it?

Well, perhaps my life was only a series of just such anecdotes and was, properly speaking, no biography at all. One of the finest autobiographies I ever read was *Paul Gauguin's Intimate Journals.* I don't mean *Noa Noa,* which is just a peppery piece of journalese tripe, I mean the journals that were translated years ago by Van Wyck Brooks and published by Horace Liveright, of course.

That book hops and skips around quite a bit, but every paragraph is a nourishing bouillon cube. Unfortunately, popular taste tends to run to hogwash, to thin, sentimental drippings, like Lust for Lust. Artistic or literary bouillon cubes are too much bother. You have to furnish your own heat and cook them in the sweat of your own enthusiasm and perception. It's a drag on people, I understand.

I don't think Gauguin talks much about his childhood in the *Intimate Journals,* and I fancy his reason for keeping away from it might easily have been the same as my own. I find it difficult and painful to write about my childhood because I don't like to confess that I ever lived in a world of such uncritical exaltation. Yes, even the sorrows of my childhood were unique and noble.

In 1910 I was ten years old. You see, like Cellini, I came in with a new century. I helped inaugurate the new era. Maybe that accounts for the new era. It certainly accounts for me.

At the age of ten I was staying with an elderly spinster aunt, Aunt Catherine of the warts, in a summer resort, a little town on the shore of the Danube called Deutsch Altenburg. In 1910 the Danube still ran to the Black Sea in three-quarter time, and Austria's chief exports were chocolate wafers and Strauss operettas.

This town of Deutsch Altenburg had in ancient times been an important Roman settlement, and the neighborhood was still rich in Roman ruins and artifacts. Sometimes, when I walked across the fields after a summer rainstorm, I would find antique bits of cameo and old toga pins nestling in the churned-up furrows. There was even, on the edge of the town, a Roman amphitheater in a good state of preservation, where on Saturday evenings visiting orchestral groups would serve light seasonal tidbits to the insatiable Austrian appetite for music.

What can I tell you about my summer days among those wine-heavy hills? Well, most significantly, that I fell in love. Don't laugh! Don't even smile. The love affairs of children are inevitably tragic, since they can never have a happy ending. Except in India, maybe. In the old days.

But my juvenile involvement has become particularly memorable to me because, for a while, it had almost magical overtones.

My aunt and I lived in two tiny rooms at a place called the Kurhaus, a crazy architectural concoction that looked like a birthday cake. Kurhaus means literally Cure House, and it was so named because Deutsch Altenburg was famous (even in Roman times) for its thermal baths. That's the reason my aunt had come to stay there in the first place—to cure herself of something, I don't know what. Homeliness and spinsterhood I suppose; if so, nothing ever came of it. Aunt Catherine was around fifty-three at the time, and even in the most flattering old photographs she looked like a female version of Punch. To my childish perception she was a sort of animated wart plantation. She had only three of these mysterious excrescences, but they were so effectively placed I always noticed them, even before I saw *her*. The biggest one, the one I called Attila because he sprouted a hair out of the top of his helmet, was situated on her right nostril. The second one, without a pennant, was smash in the middle of her left eyebrow, and the smallest one, about the size of a ripe pea, led an agitated life on her right cheekbone. Every winter I used to overhear family confabs about an impending operation on these warts, but when the poor soul finally died, in 1912, I noted with satisfaction that they were buried with her. I also remember that while lying in her coffin she was still wearing her eyeglasses.

Aunt Catherine was really nobody's sister, at least nobody I knew. Like many elderly spinsters in those days, she had come by her appellation through common usage. I think she lived in mortal terror of me, and yet she hardly ever trusted me out of her sight, because she considered her guardianship over me as a sacred responsibility to my parents. I was an only child, and hence an irreplaceable jewel.

So Aunt Catherine and I were involved in a summer-long

cops-and-robbers game that invariably left her with frazzled nerves and made her swear, at the end of each season, never to go to the country with me again.

At Deutsch Altenburg she subscribed to a series of curative baths at the Kurhaus, and, because I was under age and there was no extra charge, she made me share them with her. These sulphur inundations, which smelled like rotten eggs, took place in sunken stone tubs of enormous size, and there certainly was room in each of them for a whole committee of active cripples. I simply loathed those daily dunkings, and I'm sure that those curative baths drained whatever little strength I had right out of me. The only reason Aunt Catherine dragged me along to them was that while they lasted she was able to keep an eye on me. She was absolutely adamant about those rigorously clocked stink immersions, and I couldn't stand the smell of cooked eggs for twenty years afterward.

Luckily, the doctors had prescribed for her a long siesta after each bath. Enfeebled by the therapeutic experience, and further exhausted by my irritating bathroom manners, she would crawl upstairs to her cool, shaded bedroom among the chestnut leaves and pass out for a couple of hours. And then at last would come my daily chance to take off and have a life of my own.

I generally roamed all over the Koppelberg or crawled around the stone seats of the amphitheater or spied on other children who were collecting plant specimens for their herbariums. It was an old Austrian custom to combine profitable nature studies with summer vacations. I rarely spoke to these kids, not because I was leery of them, but their jokes and their games seemed as pointless and silly to me as the goings on among the grownups.

I did have one friend in the neighborhood, a boy called Walter Schwaller. His father was one of the Emperor's foresters, and the walls of their home were beautifully stocked with the antlers of deer and chamois. The Schwallers lived in the country the year round and Walter, who was only nine, had read almost as many books as I had. Indeed we had both just finished *The Memoirs of a Physician,* those wonderful novels by Alexandre Dumas. Walter and I had another bond in common; we both had a tender regard for the girl at the cigarette counter in the Kurhaus. Her name was, inevitably, Mitzi, and she was engaged to the head barber, Heinrich. (There, ready-made, you already have a couple of characters for the subplot of an operetta.)

Walter and I used to lie on our backs in the tall grass on the hills and talk about Mitzi. Nothing dirty, you can be sure. We were just interested in her words, in her gestures and even in her clothes. Walter too was an only child; perhaps because we had no sisters, a new blouse on Mitzi or a new colored ribbon would send us off on pleasant conjectures and speculations. Neither one of us ever referred to her betrothed in any other terms except the Hedgehog. We weren't envious of him, he was just an anomaly in her life that we never cared to analyze or explain. It was one of those mysteries that grownups got involved in. They were capable of the most astonishing attachments, to houses, to people, and even to animals, that defied all taste and common sense. The Hedgehog was certainly a flaw in Mitzi's character, but we suspected deep and secret reasons for her grotesque choice and by common consent we never tampered with this enigma. Mitzi was generally very nice to all the children in the Kurhaus but she had a special little manner of almost amorous teasing for the both of us. We brought her little presents—flowers, and Roman coins that we happened to find—and she in turn would slip us chocolates and peppermints that she abstracted from the loose assortment of candies under her jurisdiction.

This, however, was not the love affair I was going to tell you about. Mitzi probably represented our first delicate, precocious experience in gender awareness, a fragile and unpossessive liaison in which there was no room for jealousy. I was glad that Walter also cared for Mitzi, it made my friendship with him complete.

My serious love affair happened toward the end of summer, when the late afternoons turned surprisingly cool under the wild chestnut trees, and Aunt Catherine would suddenly descend upon me with a flock of hairy mufflers and sweaters.

I saw my great passion for the first time while she was taking a matutinal walk with her mother in the Kurhaus garden. Now, this mother was something worth seeing on her own account. She looked like Cleo de Merode. And if you're too green to know who that was, let me inform you that during my childhood Cleo was the official mistress of the old King of the Belgians, and that her unique coiffure changed the hair styles of a whole generation of European women.

Tall, dark-haired, white-skinned, sleepy-eyed, the mother of my beloved trailed the train of her lace peignoir regally across the Kurhaus lawn. I dubbed her Semiramis on sight, although I already knew that her real name was Bianca de Tolnay and that she was a Hungarian countess. I had gathered this information the day before, when my aunt had spoken to another pseudo invalid about a new arrival, a Hungarian countess. I hadn't listened carefully at first until my aunt started whispering, and then I naturally perked up.

"She's a divorcée," my aunt said, with a reptilian hiss, "and

I don't understand why they allow such a woman here. I thought this was a respectable hotel."

Please remember, the year was 1910 and Austria was a Roman Catholic country, and although my aunt was not a Catholic she was a typical idiot of her time.

Of course, I hadn't the vaguest idea what a divorcée could possibly be, but Aunt Catherine's manner convinced me that it must be something both harmless and interesting. So when I finally saw the lady in person, I was instantly convinced that to be a divorcée was surely the most desirable state for a woman to be in.

Now let me tell you about her daughter.

She was eight years old when she became my fate. She had auburn hair, green eyes, and the most delicate complexion, and she was of a slenderness that one generally associates with fragile, aristocratic animals. Because of her fair skin she wore large Italian straw hats, and her costumes, her gestures, her posture, and her walk made all the other little girls in the Kurhaus look like awkward female impersonators. Her name was Ilonka.

After all I have been through since then, I am still not rid of the spell of enchantment that she cast over me almost half a century ago. What ever could have happened to her? What was her mysterious destiny?

What has become of you, Ilonka? Were you married to an Austrian officer? An officer like the one who came every evening to call on your beautiful mother and who used to walk around the Kurhaus park with her? I remember him very well. He was like an elaborate mechanical toy, complete to the last details, monocle, spurs, medals, and long cavalry sword trailing on the white gravel walk beside him. Mme. de Tolnay, dressed mostly in white, would just barely rest her hand, like an exotic flower, on the chevrons that corrugated his sleeve.

Did you marry such a man, Ilonka? And was he killed in the First World War? Did he die on the Isonzo or in the Masurian swamps? And when the red film blinded his eyes and the taste of death rose bitter on his tongue, did he muster his last breath to say your name, Ilonka? And whom did you marry after that? And after that? And after that? Are you dead? Or are you perhaps still alive and flickering out your final days as a dim candle of faith in some ancient Austrian cloister?

A few hours after I had first seen her I offered her a Roman coin, one of my real treasures. She took it from me without embarrassment or the slightest sign of obligation. She had the self-possession and authority of a beauty that is so great it has never had occasion to question itself. She was aware of her power over me, as if we had had the same fixed relationship through fifty previous incarnations. Her mother, from the very beginning, seemed to favor my devotion to her child, but my Aunt Catherine nearly swallowed her upper plate when she caught me talking to them. She didn't actually yank me away from them in public, but she threatened that we would leave at once unless I solemnly vowed to abjure such sinister company.

I vowed, of course. It made life more difficult but also more interesting, and I happily contrived and executed the most elaborate stratagems to be near my diminutive enchantress.

I remember that once I reproached Ilonka for going off on an excursion down the Danube after she had promised to go with me to some Roman ruins. She stared at me for quite a while in genuine surprise.

"If you are really my friend," she said, "you should be happy I had a chance to have a pleasant time on a boat." (She actually said, *"Das ich mich freudig erholen konnte."*) "It was a wonderful trip," she said, "very cool and refreshing under the awning on the top deck. I can go to the Roman ruins any time. Can't I?"

For nearly fifty years I have recalled this conversation every few months. It comes unbidden into my mind from the depths of memory, and sometimes I used to feel that its emergence signified a key, a clue, or a parable applicable to some current emergency in my life. I finally grew content not to search for any mysterious cipher in that little dialogue but to ascribe its psychic regurgitation to an unaccountable whim of my willful subconscious.

I remember that I didn't accept Ilonka's stupendous selfishness without qualms and, sometimes, even anger. She doesn't care a rap about me, I told myself. I'm going to ignore her from now on.

I tried it, but I couldn't keep it up. Not even for a day. I was parched and aching for the mere sight of her a couple of hours after my bravest resolution.

And then one day the earth opened up, the sky fell down, and I nearly lost the rest of my mind, such as it was.

One afternoon I was up in my room, spying, when Mme. de Tolnay stepped out into the garden with Ilonka. Suddenly on the other side of the mother there appeared a second redheaded little girl, who was the absolute mirror image of my green-eyed tormentor.

I was standing at the window one flight above them, and I found myself desperately clutching the window frame to keep myself from falling out. A frightening pulse had started to pound in my throat and I nearly gave way and screamed for help. Only the thought of Aunt Catherine brought me back to my senses. But even so, I was willing to risk all to go down into the garden and get to the bottom of this crazy devilish riddle.

I daresay you have guessed that Ilonka had an identical twin sister. Her name was Mariska, and she had arrived only that morning at Deutsch Altenburg.

And how did my poor childish heart cope with this additional dilemma? It accepted the precious mirror image with the same passionate frenzy as it had the original. They could be told apart only by a tiny mole which Mariska had behind her left ear. She showed me that mole, once, by way of identification. I never looked for it again. I didn't need to know which one was exercising her fascination over me, or who was sending me panting across the hills on urgent, pointless errands. I was in thrall to both the little bitches and they well knew it.

Although Walter was my best friend, I never told him about my infatuation! It seems that under the circumstances I might have spared him one of the vixens. But I had nothing to spare. I had fallen under an enigmatic spell and I accepted my strange condition with all its unsolvable complexities. I had only one real fear, that it would end.

And it ended, one rainy September day at ten o'clock in the morning. When my aunt and I came down for breakfast, about twenty suitcases and three large trunks were lined up between two pillars in the lobby. My prescient heart knew the worst even before I had read the name on one of the luggage tags. My aunt had a tight grip on my arm as she piloted me into the dining room. I can still remember the stiff white damask napkins, the fresh field flowers in the tiny cut-glass vase, and my aunt peering nearsightedly at the old familiar bill of fare. I kept looking at the luggage on the other side of the glass door. There were wonderful, romantic labels pasted all over their belongings: Nice, Milan, Tunis, Athens, Paris. They were the great world, and I was just a squirming little worm, staring at those beautiful gummed pieces of magic and feeling myself dead, dead, dead, and utterly discarded. Dead, never to wake up again. What would I do? What was there to look forward to, after they were gone?

And then I saw them coming down the central staircase. The mother covered with undulating furs and the children wearing identical dark-blue coats, each carrying a tiny red umbrella.

I got up from the table. My aunt spoke to me but I didn't even turn my head. I went out into the lobby and walked toward the little family group because an irresistible force was propelling me.

Mme. de Tolnay smiled and gave me her hand. "How sweet of you to see us off," she said. "We're going to Rome for six weeks, but maybe we'll see you again in Vienna this winter. You must give the children your address."

"I won't be in Vienna this winter," I said. "I'm going to Bagdad."

"Oh, really," she said. "We've never been there. We've been to Beirut. Are you going with you aunt?"

"No," I said. "I have an older brother who is physician to the king, and I'm going to live with him."

"How nice," she said. "Well, goodbye, till we meet again. Say goodbye, children!"

I would become a great physician. Like Gilbert in the *Memoirs of a Physician,* I would come back years later, rich and proud, and treat these poor girls for tuberculosis. My uncle Joseph Balsamo, the great Cagliostro, had perfected a secret cure for tuberculosis, and I would look in their eyes and say, "Don't be afraid, I have come to save you."

Later when my aunt picked me up out of the wet grass behind the hotel, she displayed for the first and last time in her life a great deal of imagination and human compassion.

"Come," she said, "let's go upstairs and get packed. We'll catch the night boat for Vienna. I think we've had about as much pleasure as we can stand for one summer."

If you think that a child of ten could not possibly have experienced all that I have related, let me remind you that this same child five years later took Nettie for an outing to Nepera Park and only eight years after Deutsch Altenburg had become the father of a son. Remember, great is the magic of the white man.

## CHAPTER TEN

As I SIT HERE under the old trees, contemplating the grandeur and the superb indifference of nature, it comes home to me what a bundle of petty idiosyncrasies and prejudices I have become. I believe, for instance, that most professional aviators are politically very conservative. And where do I get such an idea? Well, partially from the life and confessions of people like Lindbergh, St. Exupéry, Rickenbacker and Ernst Udet. I'm quite aware that Udet, whom I met a few times in New York, was not an orthodox Nazi and was probably liquidated for it, but that still doesn't make him an outstanding liberal. I think the loneliness of flying, the sense of absolute power and the constant imminence of disaster are not particularly conducive to all-embracing, democratic feelings. It tends to breed the *Herrenvolk* type. The aristocracy of death.

I also have the feeling that most table-rappers and occultists are almost instinctively anti-Semitic. I met a lot of those cuckoos when I was doing religion for a while, on *Life* magazine, and I found the majority of them to be violently anti-Jewish. I can figure that one out, too, I think. You see, the Old Testament doesn't really talk very much about heaven or paradise with any great insistence or conviction. The stress of the Old Book seems to be on decent behavior down here below, and not too much promise of pie in the sky later on. Well, that must make the professional psychics, mystics and pseudo metaphysicians pretty leery of Jews, who are certainly indoctrinated from infancy to keep their heads out of the fog and their feet on the ground. Of course, there may be a much simpler explanation. It may be that all those swamis that I ran up against had once been married to some revolting Jews and had naturally developed a deep loathing for all of them.

Now, another one of my cherished beliefs is that you can sell the American public anything, if it is properly publicized and sponsored. I firmly believe, for instance, that if somebody put a couple of million dollars into an advertising campaign, you could make the chewing of king-sized goat droppings into a national hobby that would put Wrigley out of business. I can already see the "scientists," in white pajama tops, looking earnestly and scientifically at millions of television viewers. "The Greeks worshiped the goat as a god," they are saying. "The goat is the most ancient symbol of natural virility. Let this powerful symbol carry the burden of your worries and anxieties. Let it be your Scrape Goat. The purest natural product on the market. It reaches you directly from its original source without adulteration of any kind. The pure goat pearls are packaged scientifically three seconds after they were hatched. Remember, Scrape Goat in the gold-foil wrapper. Scrape Goat for livelier liveliness!"

Offhand you'd say I had a natural aptitude for the advertising business. Well, you'd be wrong, because I tried my damnedest to make a corrupt easy dollar in that line, but I never made it. Or hardly ever.

My first big chance came shortly after I had illustrated *The Magic Island*, by Bill Seabrook. That's a book about voodoo doings in Haiti, and my illustrations show some pretty tough colored folk in various stages of somnambulism, catalepsy, and catatonia. The book was a world-wide best seller and everybody reprinted my illustrations.

So it came as no great surprise to me one day to receive a telegram from an advertising agency which said:

# Tom Ryan

It was from the Pedlar and Ryan Advertising Agency, on lower Park Avenue, and they certainly seemed to be in a big hurry. Of course, they could have called me on the phone, since I was listed in the book, but it wouldn't have been good agency practice. Shake people up! Get them on their toes! Ring a fire alarm! That's the way they operate.

So an ancient Western Union lady, with a pencil haplessly snared in her hair net, had to drag her asthma up four flights of stairs just to give me a heart condition.

Well, kid, I said to myself, you've finally made it. The agencies are after you, they're already sending you wires. I didn't know then that they also sent wires to find out the weather prognosis for the following day.

At any rate, I let a decent time interval elapse, half an hour at least, before I got into a cab and dawdled up to their offices. This was quite a few years ago, but it is still as fresh with me as my first memorable contact with poison sumac.

Let me tell you at once that if their reception room had been contrived to intimidate people they succeeded magnificently with me. On the wall they had an original drawing of a cat that was the well-known identification symbol for a toilet preparation called Liu. This cat had me completely bulldozed. I couldn't stop gaping at it. I finally decided that it had been sprayed onto the paper with an ink-filled cooky-shooter. Well, I thought, if that's the way it's done, that's the way I'll do it. I'm nobody's El Greco.

Don't get the wrong impression. I didn't antechamber Mr. Ryan for more than fifteen minutes. Then an underdeacon materialized beside me and, guiding me safely past a few wayside shrines, whispered me discreetly into the Presence.

I entered and bowed to a tall advertising man who was wearing a beautifully tailored pearl-gray suit. I noticed at once that this suit was more than a garment, it was the extension of a personality, and I could feel that it was oozing energy at every seam.

After giving me a sincere, manly handshake, Mr. Ryan without a word proceeded to walk very briskly toward a door at the end of the longish room.

But believe me, no matter how fast *he* walked, I was trampling with both my feet right on his shadow; because I too was demonstrating something. I was demonstrating youth, eagerness, and love of money. I tell you, when we got to that door there weren't two inches between us.

And then an unbelievable piece of craziness happened. Mr. Ryan, without calling any warning signals, suddenly wheeled completely around and nearly knocked me down in a heap. I made a remarkable recovery and quickly skipped behind him as he dashed off in the opposite direction. This time I kept about ten inches between us, and when he wheeled about again I executed a brilliantly successful veronica, without cape or sword, of course.

I tried once more. This time we walked in somewhat less close formation up to one of the filing cabinets, but when I caught him staring disapprovingly at me over his shoulder, I finally got the hang of it. He wasn't going to go anywhere. He was just letting off some excess vitality. He was simply churning with unspoken ideas. I might as well sit down. He didn't need me.

After he had taken a few more vigorous turns about the room, he finally stopped in front of his desk and picked up a book. It was *The Magic Island*.

"I've looked at your illustrations on the train coming down from the country," he said. "I think you might be able to do something quite important for us."

"Something to do with Negroes?" I asked.

"Oh, no! It isn't at all settled yet, and I'm not free to discuss it in any detail, but it's a big campaign for a hair tonic."

Something inside me gave a strange tremor, and an unaccountable whiff of wilted cauliflower came to my nose.

"A hair tonic?" I said. "For white people?"

"Certainly! We're planning a nationwide newspaper campaign. I'm sure you'll do an excellent job. Here, for instance!" He held up one of my illustrations which showed a fierce Negro wearing an admiral's hat. Not a hair was visible anywhere.

"You see," he said, "this is the way I visualize the art work in this campaign. Just in this sledge-hammer style! With all this ruthless force! It's going to bowl everybody over!"

He kept staring at my illustration, so he didn't notice that I was passing from mere despondency to the first stages of imbecility.

"This campaign needs power," he said, "and you've got it!"

I was touched by his simple faith in me. I was going to do my best for him.

"Tell me," I said, "what sort of man do you imagine would be the hero of this hair tonic?"

I could see Mr. Ryan didn't care for my sloppy terminology.

"The art work," he said, "should visualize the message through a well-set-up man between the ages of twenty-five and thirty-five, wearing a clean-cut athletic undershirt."

"Just a minute," I said. "What should this man look like? Like me?"

"Of *course* not!" Mr. Ryan didn't even try to disguise his disgust.

"Well, who then? Should he look like *you?*"

"No! No! No! No! No!" He stalked over to a rotary bookshelf, took a magazine off the top of it, and purposefully started to riffle the pages, like a man who knows exactly what he is looking for.

Well, I thought, here's my break. Whatever the hell he shows me, I'm going to copy it. Better still, I'm going to trace it and make myself a little easy money for a change.

Finally he stopped searching and flattened the magazine out on his desk. "Here" he said, "look at this!"

I walked briskly up to him and took the magazine out of his hands. It was a double-page ad for Buick cars. You can't imagine how I stared at that goddamned ad. There was a lot of text all over the left-hand page and the open door of a car in the extreme right. The biggest lump of illustration was a dimpled tootsie with a picture hat who was just getting out of the car, and the layout was so cunningly arranged that her fat, sloppy leg seemed to be stepping straight into my lap. This doll was pink all over, like a freshly spanked suckling pig. A discreet hunk of lace, from her drawers, very likely, was fluttering over the artist's signature.

I must have stared at this invention for quite a while, because Mr. Ryan finally took it out of my hand.

"Well," he said, "there you have it!"

"There I have it?" I said. "I thought I was supposed to draw a man?"

"Of course you are," he said impatiently. "It's a liquid hairdressing for men."

"Well," I persisted, "where's the man in the Buick ad?"

"Come," he said, "you see this woman, don't you?"

"Yeah, what about her?"

"Don't you understand?" said Mr. Ryan, and as he spoke he raised his eyes heavenward; he grew fifteen feet tall, and his voice suddenly had overtones of vast interstellar spaces and of eternally reverberating echoes, because his voice was the voice of Pure Creation.

"Take a good look at that woman," he said, "because what we want in this campaign, and what you are going to give us, is—*this woman's husband!*"

He was wrong, of course. As at my previous attempt with the magazine editor, when I couldn't even imagine his reader, let alone what the reader would draw, I was now completely stumped by the pink fetish in the Buick ad. I couldn't imagine her, either. And what's more, I didn't want ever to find out what in hell her husband could possibly look like. No. Not for all the cash in Coney Island. There is a limit to my curiosity; and even to my greed.

A little while later I did get a job from an advertising agency, but luckily it didn't require quite so much creative imagination. It was an interesting and even lucrative experience and it happened some time early in 1929.

One morning I got a letter from an agency up in Hartford that sounded like unadulterated good news. It seems that the Linweave Paper Company, a powerful and far-flung enterprise, was proposing to publish some notable literary tidbits once a month for a whole year; and it was further planned to have each of these morsels of good will illuminated by a well-known illustrator. Since I had already done *Gulliver's Travels, The Emperor Jones* and *The Magic Island,* I seemed to have qualified for one of the jobs.

Now, remember that you can get type-cast in the illustrating business just as readily as on the stage or in the movies. Two out of my three books had been about Negroes, so I was slowly but inevitably getting to do all the loose Negroes that happened to be around. Not quite all of them. My dear friend Miguel Covarrubias used to split the black belt with me for a while, and a little later on a still closer friend, Al Hirschfeld, began to cut in on both of us. So, when I first got the letter, I wondered what sort of Negroes the Linweave people would probably want me to do. At any rate, I notified my correspondent in Hartford that I was available, and a couple of days later he showed up in my studio.

He turned out to be quite a nice guy who really seemed to know something about my work. His name was Stevens, I think. Naturally, in America you don't go on calling a man Stevens very long; you call him Hank or Butch or Mitch, or something, ten minutes after he has crossed your fate line. From then on you are buddies until an hour afterward, when you get to loathe him for the rest of your life. That didn't happen with Stevens; we really grooved it from the start, and it stayed that way until the end. Now, although this new buddy of mine came from out of town, he too had the standard agency look: tall, clean-cut, anonymous, and, of course, with the usual smile of healthful dentition. I don't know what the hell I expected; Carl Sandburg or Bertrand Russell, I suppose. Well, anyway, he was a sweet guy, and he came straight to the point.

"We're thinking of doing a fine poem or a famous piece of prose, once a month," he said, "and we'll print these on some of our best paper stock. We plan to send them to all our dealers, distributors and customers free of charge and alert them to the fact that these beautiful color jobs may in time become valuable collector's items."

"Fine," I said, "and do you have anything specific in mind for me?"

"Yes," he said. "The piece that was unanimously selected for you was 'The Congo,' by Vachel Lindsay."

(So, they wanted Congo Negroes.)

"I know the poem," I said, "and I'll do my best with it."

"I'm sure you will," he said. "I've brought you some samples of our finest papers, and perhaps you will find yourself inspired by using some of our colored stock for your first sketches."

"Very good," I said. "I'm glad you brought them. By the way, how much are you planning to pay each artist for his work?"

"Well," he said, "that will naturally vary with the individual artist. We are prepared to go up to fifteen hundred dollars in your case, and we'll pay the same to John Held, Jr., if we use him, but we'll try to shop around a little on the other subjects."

"Will you be in town for a while?" I asked.

"I'm planning to stay a week," he said, "because I'm hoping you might have an idea for us by then."

"I will," I said, "don't worry."

I had a complete idea ten minutes after he left me, and two hours later I had completed the final drawing. But I kept my peace for the next seven days. Such, I had been told, were the well-established ways of commerce, and I had no intention of inaugurating a new traffic system. During that time I made all my "preliminary" sketches and when the week was over I called Stevens at his hotel.

He was up at my place within half an hour, and I must say my sketches simply gassed him. Of course he had to submit them to his sponsors first, but he was sure that these sketches surpassed their wildest expectations.

And so it turned out. A couple of days after he got back to Hartford, he wired me to go ahead. I let another two weeks elapse before I wired him that I was finished. He came down on the next train, and when I handed him my drawing he was more pleased with it than I was.

So everything had gone off hunky-dory.

I poured him a drink and we bared our amiable fangs at each other.

"And now," said Stevens, "I have a real problem ahead."

"What's that?" I asked.

"Our next poem," he said, "is a translation from the Chinese."

"So, what?" I said. "That oughtn't to be too hard."

"Well," he said, "we'd planned to have Cyrus Baldridge do

it for us. He's done a number of books on Chinese subjects, but it seems he's off to China at the moment."

"That is a drawback," I said. "I wonder what the hell he's doing in China."

"His wife writes stories for children which have a Chinese background," he said. "I guess they like to keep in touch with their sources."

"Naturally!" I said. "So what are you going to do?"

"Frankly, I'd hoped you'd be able to advise me. I thought you might know somebody who specialized in drawing Orientals, and that you might be good enough to tip me off."

"I'm glad you asked me," I said. "I know a real old-timer, a Frenchman, who used to do such illustrations years ago. I doted on his work when I was a child. His name is Victor Helleu and he lives out in Jersey somewhere."

Stevens was so delighted he put down his drink. "Gee," he said, "would you get in touch with him for me? I'd stay a couple of days longer if you think it's worth my waiting."

He sure was anxious to get the right guy to do those Chinese for him. Little did he know that he was talking to the man who, in sheer frenzy for the picturesque East, had put pagodas and weeping willows, as well as Chinamen, on the walls of a kosher Jewish restaurant.

"You go home," I said. "I'll find the guy in the next couple of days, and if I do, you'd better let me handle him. He must be ninety and he's probably a pretty crotchety party by now. I'll tackle him with kid gloves and if he can still hold a brush he'll come through for you."

Stevens was delighted. "Do that," he said, "and if you have to pay the top tariff it'll be all right. We'll manage to save on the other subjects."

"Very good," I said. "I think the old codger lives with his daughter, out in the wilds of Jersey somewhere. I understand she's a widow and pretty well heeled. But, don't worry, if *man* can do it, it shall be done."

Well, it *was* done.

It stands to reason that there was no such person as Victor Helleu; and his illustrious past, and his well-heeled daughter, the Jersey widow, and all the rest of it were just picturesque improvisations to give what Pooh-Bah calls "artistic verisimilitude to an otherwise bald and unconvincing narrative."

Do you know, it was a great deal of fun for me to get back to the Orient after all those Negroes, and, honestly, I think I did a better job over Victor Helleu's signature than over my own. Better still, the sponsor and the agency were absolutely delighted with the work of the old Jersey recluse. He surpassed himself. He illustrated a poem called "The Lute Girl," by one of my old favorites, Po Chü-i. I had to work very hard to disguise the real hand that had perpetrated the work, and in the end, I think, I succeeded quite well.

Al Hirschfeld saw the illustration a few years later and, completely ignoring the signature, asked me if I had done it with my left hand, and if so, why?

But hardly anyone else ever caught wise. Certainly not the agency. They got so much credit for those first two jobs, they openly decided to engage me as a consultant on the rest of their campaign. They had six or seven more knotty problems on hand, and they rightly felt that I might prove invaluable to them.

I did my best. Let me say in extenuation that my best was really not too bad.

I don't quite recall whether I was eight or nine of that select group of artists that did the Linweave series that year. All I remember is that it was quite a bit of money and that among the bunch of us we copped quite a lot of graphic prizes and honorable mentions in the trade publications. I had to open bank accounts under all those names, too, and of course I had to invent suitable biographies that were printed alongside their drawings.

But finally it was all over, the money collected, new outfits for the whole family, happiness all around, and even a new trip to Europe planned for the fall. And then one morning I got a telegram from Hartford:

LINWEAVE SALESMEN AND DISTRIBUTORS WILL MEET AT COCKTAIL PARTY TWENTY-FIFTH PLEASE INVITE ALL ARTISTS TO HOTEL ROOSEVELT FIVE THIRTY
GREETINGS
STEVENS

There it was, the one unexpected gambit in the whole screwy game. What was I going to do? How in hell was I going to get out of this one? It was the damnedest corner I'd ever gotten myself into; I was really rattled. I couldn't possibly present any substitutes, because anybody I could produce was either a lush, or a professional joker, or both. Anybody I framed it with would be sure to offer mad toasts and wild praises to every other fictitious character on my roster. That was a cast-iron certainty.

No, that was out. I could easily do without Victor Helleu, he was an old crock and his daughter might reasonably object to his risking his life for a mere cocktail party. But I had one Rockwell Kentish, outdoorsy character who had lewd nudes tattooed on his biceps; what could I do about him? I might say he was off on a yacht race to Bermuda, but that still left me with quite a mob of people to account for. It was a real drag!

I nearly went wild trying to find a solution, but I didn't come up with a thing by the time that ghastly afternoon came around. Well, I finally decided to trust to some last-minute inspiration and started out for the hotel around six o'clock. I must have dawdled quite a bit on my way up there, because I didn't get to the Roosevelt till nearly eight.

Obviously the Linweave people had rented a whole floor, and when the elevator spit me out on it I could hardly find a place to stand. The joint was thick with smoke and amiability, and I suddenly had a glass in my hand, without even seeing who the hell had dished it to me. A few seconds later I was part of a chain of chanters who were going around in a circle singing "Mademoiselle from Armentières." Despite the imminent pressures of a demanding camaraderie, I kept an alert eye open for my nemesis, Stevens.

At last I spied him, cut myself loose with some difficulty, and wallowed over to him. He was delighted to see me. He'd had a few, of course, but he was all the better for it.

"Where are your friends?" he asked. "I want them to meet the boys."

"They're doing great," I said. "They're singin' it up in the other corner."

"Fine!" he said. "We want them all to have a good time."

While he was saying these few words to me, five or six affectionate arms were placed around him, moist-eyed comradely glances rested on his face, and glittering bifocals concentrated their gleams on him.

"I'll see your friends in a little while," he said. "I just have to take care of these boys first."

"Don't hurry," I said, "everybody's doing fine."

Because I don't drink (kidneys, remember?) I went down into the lobby and got myself a magazine. I stayed for an hour down there and then decided to risk another visit.

Well, things were really humming now. People had taken off their coats, and barrages of fountain pens, screw pencils, collapsible rulers and every sort of office hardware had come into evidence. The gaiety and good will had become a flood tide that washed all conversation into a multiple-voiced incoherent roar. I had a drink in each hand when I spied Stevens again. He'd had a few more. In fact, so many more that I decided to take an uncalculated risk.

"See my friends anywhere?" I asked.

"Friends?" he said, looking vaguely about.

"Yes," I said. "Charlie and Gus and the tall blond girl I left you with."

He tried hard to become master of his really hard-pressed faculties. "Tell you the truth," he said finally, "I haven't seen them in quite a while."

"Don't worry about it," I said. "I'm sure they're all having a good time."

"Sure," he said. "Everybody is having a good time. Everybody and his uncle is having a good time. Drink up!" he said. "There's plenty more where that came from!"

"Right!" I said. "See you later."

I did see him, too. And because he had an agency man's memory for names, he told me he'd waved to Charlie and to Gus but hadn't been able to get near them.

After that I thought it was safe for me to beat it.

## CHAPTER ELEVEN

THIS LITTLE New England town has seen better days. As who has not? It once had a paper mill, a shoe factory and a cannery, but some competing Southern states offered lower local taxes and a free, nonunionized, labor market, and so the glory has departed.

But five years ago the American Savoyards company took up seasonal residence here, and a small prosperity of summer resortfulness has come back to the community since then. Gilbert and Sullivan are also responsible for my presence here, because my wife sings second leads with the troupe and we live in a small house within walking distance of the theater. I generally attend these productions at Wednesday matinees, and at the same time I make my weekly visits to the local library. This is also the one day of the week when they have cookies for sale at the library and I always like to stock up on some fresh baked goods. Of course, I'm not allowed to eat any of these delicacies myself, but I get them for my wife and for occasional callers who drop in to see us.

I sometimes think how pleasant it would be if I could someday stop by the Forty-second Street library and pick up some hot blueberry pies in the main reading room. I think it would humanize the grotesque old monster and add a badly needed dimension of grace to its soiled austerity. I suppose I'm really terribly ungrateful, since I've spent so many profitable months of my life in it, but I was young then and I didn't notice its uncomfortable chairs, its backless benches, its unyielding tables and its oppressive atmosphere. Come to think of it, there aren't any really comfortable libraries. Not yet.

What distinguishes this particular one is its remarkable, colorful clientele. A city as vast as New York is bound to yoik up some pretty strange bibliophiles, and I think the Forty-second Street library attracts the most unusual specimens. Perverts, too, I have no doubt. I was once told by one of the employees that they were cautioned to watch out for certain customers who have pocket mirrors fastened to the bottoms of their walking canes; it seems that with these simple devices such browsers manage to catch titivating reflections from under the skirts of unsuspecting women readers.

You sure can spot some weirdies there. I once saw a proud, brittle woman, with a wonderfully dated coiffure, munching crumbly refreshments out of a mildewed muff. She kept carefully scanning some ancient playbills through a lorgnette that had been fastened to her bodice with a chain obviously derived from an old-fashioned toilet tank. It was also perfectly plain that her elaborate eyepiece didn't have lenses in it.

Well, she wasn't hard to figure. She'd trod the boards, fifty years ago, and now came up here to warm her poor, tepid blood with the kindling of old press clippings. And maybe not. Maybe she had just *yearned* to go on the stage in the days when she was wearing bloomers and middy blouses; and maybe, after life had mislaid her in some dingy back pocket, her imagination had taken over and become her stage manager and now she was just reveling in a picturesque, theatrical past she had never known at all. There are many such benign cases of self-deception and lunacy abroad in the land. I see no urgent reason for curing them.

There was one character, who for a few weeks used to sit across the table from me in one of the main reading rooms, who really had me bulldozed. I couldn't keep my eyes off him. He seemed to have no shirt on whatever, but each morning he wore a fresh editorial page from the *New York Times*, which he'd stretched over some kind of a cardboard dicky. It looked neat, too, and it is surprising how few people noticed his unusual haberdashery. If you weren't too observant, that ponderous editorial page could pass for a pale-gray pull-over. I also noted that the books this guy consulted were technical works on engineering and physics, mostly, and I figured him to be some kind of inventor. I'd had some experience with inventors and they were a strange lot, even when they were comparatively normal.

I proved to be right about him. We got to know each other one day when his fountain pen had run out of ink and he seemed reluctant to use a pencil. I leaned across and offered him the use of my pen, and, after a moment's hesitation, he took it. Later on, around lunchtime, we went downstairs together and he introduced himself. His name was Oliver Rykoff, and he lived 'way over near the East River, on Grand Street, a real Italian neighborhood.

He told me he was sixty-eight, and I thought he looked every single hour of it, despite the fact that he was a food faddist who kept crunching raw carrots and turnips all the time. I guessed he must have been over six feet tall once, too, but now he was so stooped he was hardly taller than I, except when he took a few breathing exercises out in Bryant Park, when he would suddenly gain about seven inches. Then he would collapse again. He had no hair, but I don't think he'd ever had any. He was one of those hairless wonders without eyebrows or eyelashes. To keep the chill off his dome, he wore a tight, homemade skullcap which the library people let him wear even in the reading rooms. He told me he had only six teeth left, had lost all the others through eating cooked food, so he warned me to look after mine. He still had perfect vision, though, and his quick dark eyes were not altogether suspicious or frenzied; sometimes I saw compassion in them, and occasionally even a certain childish humor.

After a while, we got to be real friends and he confided in me about his work. He'd had a lot of stuff patented over the years, but people had robbed him or swiped his ideas; the usual inventor's megillah. But the critical smashup in his life had happened long ago, when he'd patented his one really big idea, the six-handled chamber pot. It *was* quite a notion. Just think of it! Before his invention, people used to fish around for this piece of comfort under their beds, and, just when they were under the greatest pressure, they were rarely able to locate that goddamned handle. Oliver's six-handler eliminated all such hazards. It was revolutionary.

"So what happened?" I asked.

"Oh, well," he said, "the toilet trust was going to buy my patent. They stalled me along for a couple of years. I was very foolish. I kept dickering with them—for a fair royalty arrangement, you know—but they were just keeping me on ice."

"What did they do?" I said. "Did they swipe the idea from you?"

"No," he said. "They were gambling on a lot of different angles of the game. They were secretly backing half a dozen different people, and then one of their boys came up with cheap concealed plumbing, and I was left holding the pot."

He smiled at his little joke, but I could see the scar from this wound had never healed.

I must anticipate and tell you now that some years later I held an auction for charity at the Waldorf, and that the main items that I put up for sale came out of Oliver's collection of models. I got three hundred dollars for the original six-handler (it was covered with gold leaf), but poor Oliver got nothing out of it; he had died six weeks before. The bids were all quite high, too, because it was for charity and the customers were all well-heeled editors and executives of *Time, Life* and *Fortune*. Clare Boothe Luce sponsored the sale, and everybody thought I'd invented the items myself; they didn't realize that a whole lifetime of agonized hopes and aspirations was wrapped up in those strange novelties.

I also sold the original Oliver model of an early vacuum cleaner. In fact, I suspect it was the real granddaddy of them all. It was a shiny metal pipe with a suction cup at the bottom and a long wooden stick that fitted snugly into the pipe. Not too snugly; it could be moved, of course. Well, then, if you hovered with the suction cup over a dust pile and drew the wooden stick quickly upward, the dust would automatically rise up into the pipe. Fine. The trouble came when you plunged the stick back into the tube again; then, unfortunately, all the crap would fall right back on the floor. The apparatus really looked very slick and efficient, you just had to resist the temptation to use it.

Oliver had once had quite a lot of correspondence with Thomas Edison. He showed me some of his letters and I gathered from them that the old wizard didn't think too much of Oliver's inventions. But they did have a real bond in common, they were both devout atheists. Ollie used to write pieces for one of the atheist papers that Edison was financing, and when I read some of these articles I noticed that my poor inventor friend had so cabalized and circumscribed his disbelief, it had become just another form of religion. One without consolations.

Oliver was one of those truly rare people, a real New Yorker. He'd been born over on East Thirty-second Street, of pretty well-to-do people, I suspect, because he still used to get a little dribble each month from the old family loot. My mother would have said, too much to die on and too little to live on. But he managed.

I used to visit him quite often, down on Grand Street near Baruch Place, where he lived in a wonderfully cluttered flat over an Italian grocery store. Although he was certainly very weird-looking, nobody in the neighborhood ever poked fun at him. Not even the kids. I suppose their elders had told them to leave him alone, that he was a learned man, and that learning often manifested itself in strange ways. Most simple people like to believe that too much brain work leads to madness. It make them considerate of madness and reconciles them to their own simplicity.

Then I lost track of Oliver for a couple of years, but one day when I happened to stray into his neighborhood I knocked at his door. After a while a crack opened but it was forbiddingly crossed by a hunk of chain. A wire-haired gnome proceeded to screen me through enormous shell-rimmed glasses.

"Is Oliver in?" I asked.

"Who wants to know?" The creature had a giant's hollow voice and a strong Irish accent; also Irish blue eyes and fair, baby skin.

I told him my name, and Oliver's voice came at once from the next room.

"Let him in!" he said. "Let him in, and let him see me stretched out in my mortal misery!"

So the doorkeep undid the chain and grudgingly let me pass. Oliver was lying in bed and looked like a corpse that some apprentice embalmers have finally abandoned. For some reason the little Irishman planted himself truculently between us.

"What's this?" I said to Oliver. "Don't tell me you're taking a siesta at six o'clock in the afternoon."

Oliver smiled and I could see he'd lost the rest of his teeth.

"I'm making ready for my eternal siesta," he said.

"Aye," said the gnome, " aye, with the pope's trimmings and the stink of the Jesuits all over him." I could see the little man was trembling with anger.

"Hush!" said Oliver. "I want you to meet my friend, Hugh Latour, who is all bark and no bite, like a cork tree."

"Pleased to know you, Mr. Latour," I said. "Offhand I'd have judged you to come up with an Irish name."

"So you would," he said. "But I'm the great-great-grandson of a Frenchman who ran from the bloodshed of France to the bloody penury of Ireland. Devil a choice he made."

"Sit down," Oliver said to me, "and tell me how the librarians are treating you these days."

I told him I was working on *Life* magazine and didn't have so much time to spend with books.

"The more's the pity," he said. "I daresay they pay you good wages, but you're part of the big swindle now; corrupting and flattering the silly masses. Well, I won't be around long enough to see much more of it."

"What's wrong with you, anyway?" I asked.

"Raw vegetables!" boomed Latour. "Raw vegetables and priests, that's what's wrong with him, goddammit!"

"Come, Hugh," said Oliver, "Mr. King will get a wrong impression of you."

"And what sort of impression will he have of *you?*" demanded Latour. "Just listen to this man," he said. "The priests have been at him morning, noon and night; and this scientific

93

thinker, this friend of Edison's, is going to take holy orders, if I'm not mistaken."

"Please!" said Oliver. "Please, don't get us all upset with your insinuations, Hugh!"

"Insinuations is it?" Latour turned to me again. "Just ask him if the priest hasn't been here twice, this very day; and if he's not about coming again tomorrow morning, right after holy mass. Just ask him!"

I did ask him, and a strange and troubling story came in bits and splinters out of poor Oliver's toothless mouth. In the end, when I pieced it all together, it was just the sort of story I'm particularly partial to.

It seems that when Oliver had become bedridden, a few months before, Mrs. Maracotti, his landlady, had begun to look after him. She was an elderly widow who, in the manner of her people, had worn the black shawls of her mourning for twenty-five years; years during which she had also become a local landmark of kindness and Christian charity to all the Italians in the neighborhood.

Now, in the course of her ministrations to Oliver, she had suddenly discovered his appalling state of godlessness. You can imagine the effect on her. She at once began to overwhelm him with her concern for his immortal soul, and to plead with him to repent before it was too late; and, since she could not really imagine a human being entirely destitute of religious faith, she begged him, daily, to send for a minister of his own denomination. When Oliver confessed himself out of touch with any Christian creed whatever, she had fallen to weeping and bewailing his condition so bitterly that he had finally softened and allowed her to bring a priest to his rooms. But his was not just the banal tale of a sick-bed conversion. Not a bit of it. You see, poor Oliver still clung, more tenaciously than ever, to his old atheistic principles, even while he was receiving daily instructions in the Catholic faith.

"I don't want to hurt the poor woman," said Oliver, "She has been kindness itself to me, not only since I've been ill, but for years she has looked after me, better than my own flesh and blood ever did. If it makes her happy to see me buried with all those hideous, nonsensical trimmings, well, I'll just do it to please her. I've done damned few things for people in these last years of my life, and I might as well make my exit in a state of graciousness, if I don't believe in Grace."

And that's just what he did. He died a couple of months later and left half his collection of models to me. His funeral was attended by only two people from uptown, Hugh Latour and myself. The rest of the large crowd was made up of neighborhood Italians, who looked reverently at Mrs. Maracotti, who, before their very eyes, had saved a human soul from eternal perdition. Maybe she had, at that. Surely, the roads to salvation are frequently devious, and always incalculable.

## CHAPTER TWELVE

I SPEND MOST of my time indoors, writing these reminiscences, but nature leans in at every window and the shadows of passing clouds move in gentle procession across my paper. I have nothing against nature, but in large doses it tends to oppress and diminish me. It is like hearing the Ninth Symphony, conducted by Toscanini, on a record player that can't be stopped. I do go out once in a while, of course. Yesterday, for instance, I went for a visit to the town cemetery, which is located on a sweetly sloping hillside, and I found some of the finest-looking old trees up there.

I lay down against an ancient graveside and let the sun make jigsaw patterns all over me while I lost myself in harmless reveries for a while. Across the path from me there was a large stone pillar on which somebody was still going on with his all too earthly boasting. At the bottom of this phallus they had caused to be engraved "PERPETUAL CARE."

Well, Perpetual is a long time, and I'm just ready to make book they'll get fooled. In the stillness and otherwise quiet nobility of this scene (there were no television antennae on these graves), it came to me what a presumptuous ass I really was, to patronize this little backwood community. After all, what difference does it make where you are? You're bound to take *yourself* along wherever the hell you go.

Emily Dickinson, who lived in just such a town, not too far from here either, didn't have to go to Damascus or Samarkand to know what the magic of the Orient was. As a matter of fact, she's a great gal to read in such surroundings. It makes the wonder of her genius even more sublime. I had gotten a book of her poetry from the local library and I had it in my pocket when I was lying there in the graveyard, under the weeping-willow trees. I don't seem to be able to escape them long, do I?

You know, they have some remarkably good books here in this library. Naturally they have all the latest crap, too, that's what the cooky sales are for, but a few scholarly people with pretty wide literary interests seem to have endowed it with their own fine collections. They have Gogol, and George Moore, and Charles Doughty, and I even found Baron Corvo,

95

appropriately bound in pansy pink. All these books are standing silently and modestly on their shelves, waiting for the eager searching eyes of that young curiosity which will not be appeased by *McCall's* magazine, no, nor by *Reader's Digest,* either.

By the way, if you think I was being unduly facetious about the absence of television antennae in the cemetery, I must tell you that some time ago when I was in the South, around Charleston somewhere, I happened to pick up the business card of a local undertaker, which said "Bember Brothers, Morticians and Embalmers." In the lower right-hand corner, in smaller type, they had printed "Underground Novelties"! I carried that damned little card around with me for many years, for I never got over puzzling about those Underground Novelties. What could they possibly have furnished you? Ice water? Intergrave telephone service? Or what? Great country, ain't it?

Since I've started scouting the territory around here, I've also gotten myself a local haircut. The barber takes care of you in a back room of the house that he lives in with his family, and, in many ways, I found my visit with him very rewarding. First of all he's a New Englander, so he didn't have a single sound to say to me all through the shearing process. Nothing enlivening or conjectural came up about the weather, the state of his arthritis, or his corns. What's more, the shop had not been planned to impress anybody as being flagrantly sanitary. It was clean and even had a refreshing, improvised quality. There was only one mirror and it had obviously once been the top of an old-fashioned oak dresser. All the tools and implements in the place were honorably aged with service and there was no pretense of male beauty parlor about these works. A haircut was a bitter necessity and you got through it with a minimum of motion and a maximum of silent concentration. There were no foam-rubber divans for the waiting clientele, either. An old trolley-car bench had been nailed to the floor, and a fresh Sears, Roebuck catalogue and a recent *Farmer's Almanac* seemed to be the only reading matter that had been provided. Refreshing!

This town has two groceries, no drugstore, and no five-and-dime. But it does have an antique shop and a beauty parlor. It figures. At the antique shop they sell some fly-specked children's dolls that are about thirty-five years old, about as old as my youngest son, and they unblushingly ask forty dollars for these antiques, while they point out to you that they have just been provided with brand-new wardrobes. The beauty parlor has only a homemade cardboard sign in the window but it scintillates with all the curlers, dryers and torture implements that are required equipment for such an emporium.

I'm also getting some driblets of information about our more colorful neighbors. An old lady who has fallen into the uncharacteristic habit of talking to me in front of the post office has kindly briefed me about a large and slovenly-looking family that lives down the street from us.

"They're very poor," she said. "Her husband went hunting in the fall, a while ago, and he was shot dead. She had to get help then, with all them children and all. And she isn't too well, neither. She got vericorse veins in her legs, that she's been suffering with all her life. Well, those children all got married before they finished school, any of them, and had themselves some children of their own, too. And now they're all living together in that big shambly house."

"And are they still poor?" I asked.

"Ayeah, they're poor, all right. As poor as they come, I guess."

"Well," I said, "seems like I've seen a pretty good-looking car in their back yard!"

"Ayeah, they got that, all right. They got three or four cars out back there, I'd say. 'Course the eldest boy married the first car. Station wagon it was. And the others just came after that one."

I liked her explanation. It proves again how right my friend Richard Lindner is when he says that America is the only true surrealist country in the world. In vain do the Germans and the French try to dip their schnozzles into the authentic well-spring of surrealism. They haven't got a chance. Only here in the U.S.A. is it possible for out-and-out mendicants to become so elegantly mobile, and only here can it happen that this should be calmly accepted as quite a natural phenomenon. In Italy or France those people wouldn't even own a three-legged donkey, let alone a brand-new Chevrolet station wagon. Well, I must say I'm all for it. It is all dear, dear, dear to my heart. I just love those neighbors of ours. I've always been enchanted with the craziness of everyday life, which I've often found so much more startling and unpredictable than the clinical craziness in insane asylums. Most official madmen are comparatively conventional in their aberrations, and their manias are rarely distinguished by any sort of originality. You'd imagine when a man has taken the trouble to go out of his mind and is free, at last, from the bonds of all logical, responsible compulsions, he'd really let himself go. Not a bit of it. Lunatics are generally as hidebound and consistent in their frenzies as the most ultrarespectable people who are confined in their sanities. That is, that within the framework of their established lunacies they are only too boringly predictable and bourgeois. Of course, you can find some real novelties among madmen too, but a genuine original is as rare in an asylum as he is on a campus. I must say, though, that I did meet a few lulus once at a Dr. Moreno's sanitarium up on the Hudson one summer.

I landed at Moreno's a few weeks after my second agonizing visit to Lexington. I had, of course, relapsed into my addiction, but I had earned a couple of thousand dollars ghost-writing a book for a plastic surgeon, so I decided to try my next cure in a private clinic, for a change. Somebody told me of a famous junkie cleanery called Towne's, on Central Park West, and I went up there to look them over. The doctor I talked to told me they'd knock me off the stuff in two weeks, and I don't doubt they could have done it. I asked the doctor if I could bring my own radio and he seemed quite agreeable about it. That's when he lost me for a customer. After all, I could have filled that goddamned machine with enough narcotics to poison the whole Upper West Side. Maybe they would have frisked the little apparatus, but I happened to own a complicated German radio, with all sorts of extra tubes and secret interior grottoes, that I could easily have loaded up without anybody but an expert mechanic catching wise to me.

So I decided against Towne's, because it was certainly senseless for me to lay out a lot of dough on my own self-imposed honor system, since I had a pretty good notion what that was worth once the pains came on and the vomiting started. While I was shopping around for a more suitable retreat to park my disaster, a friend of mine told me about the Moreno Clinic out in the country. This place wasn't a drug-cleaning joint at all. It handled only genuine cuckoos, and it treated them with an entirely new method called psychodrama, a system of psychotherapy I'd never even heard about. My friend told me that the patients at this boobyhatch acted out all their difficulties on a real stage, under the guidance of special clinical directors, and that some remarkable results had been achieved there. I liked the idea, so I phoned Dr. Moreno, and he told me to call at his New York office the next day, since he was coming into town anyway.

Let me tell you, I was much impressed with Moreno during that first interview. He proved to be an unusually intelligent person with wide human and cultural interests, and for any man who presumes to function in the capacity of a psychiatrist or psychoanalyst that is surely a basic requirement. Of course, that is still no guarantee of his having any special gifts for this highly exigent calling, but it is certainly an absolute must as a starter, isn't it?

Now, Dr. Moreno, who was also Viennese, which did him no harm with me, told me right off the bat that he didn't generally tackle dopeys. But I liked his manner and his looks, which were a cross between Rembrandt and Diego Rivera—

that is to say, plump, bright-eyed, curly-haired and alive—so I decided to persuade him. Not that I believed for a moment that any, or all, of his attributes were necessarily going to cure me of my addiction, since that, in the final analysis, was entirely up to me; all he could really provide for me were certain routine, clinical facilities and his own sympathetic medical and human perception. My liking for him had hardly any connection with my own malady at all; he just sounded like a gifted person who, in an emergency, could tie a package better, or more originally, than the next man. I asked him earnestly to take me on, and he finally agreed.

The following day I landed at his aviary, which was located in beautifully landscaped grounds on the left bank of the Hudson, opposite Newburgh, I think. They gave me a fine corner room but confiscated my radio and all my eleven tubes of tooth paste, which showed that despite their inexperience with junkies they had a pretty cool idea of what such varmints were capable of. Otherwise I had the run of the place, and I was particularly invited to attend my first psychodrama session that afternoon.

Since I'd had my lunch on the train coming up, I had over an hour to kill until showtime, so I meandered into the doctor's library. He had a marvelous collection of books in many languages, and, to my delight, I found a few volumes of poetry that Moreno himself had written many years ago in Austria. Now, listen to this, this stuff of his was quite self-respecting. It was not the amateur ranting of some rhyme-crippled medic and I was delighted that he had lived up to my hunch, that he was a cool stud and really had something on the ball.

You may have surmised by now that I have deep prejudices against psychoanalysts and psychiatrists, and, believe me, I have. The majority of the practitioners I have personally known, and I have known about twenty-five during the last three decades, were a bunch of presumptuous pfooshers who shouldn't have been allowed to treat an introverted turtle. Of course, I *have* seen people who had been helped by psychotherapy, but I wouldn't go so far as to say I've seen them cured. The patients generally have to go back to their refueling stations for the rest of their lives. These psychotherapeutic udders become as indispensable to them as opium is to a drug addict; and I say, pfui! You might point out that it is still preferable to real drug addiction, and I will grant you that it is, but only because it isn't illegal. But that's about all I'll give it. I'm fully aware that there are dedicated, scholarly, and earnest workers abroad in the field, but I tell you that, at this moment, too much of the actual therapy is just a hit-or-miss proposition and has about as much relation to real science as alchemy has to modern chemistry. I'll tell you, further, that at the present stage of its growth too many of the operators who function in its ranks are dangerous ignoramuses, or out-and-out scoundrels who just like to make themselves a fast and easy buck. You might reasonably object that there are more fakers in the art world than in psychotherapy, and you would be quite right. I'd just like to point out that when a wretched artist makes a bum picture it just means a waste of paint and a ruined canvas, but when a blundering ass of a psychotherapist sticks his dirty fingers into an already infected mind it is liable to cause some unfortunate creature the permanent loss of his sanity. That, I think, is pretty obvious, and there you have the reason for my truculent and censorious attitude.

So you can imagine that it wasn't exactly a dreamy little boy who attended that psychodrama séance up at the sanitarium that afternoon. The session I witnessed took place in a tidy little theater which had been especially constructed for these meetings, and when I arrived about twenty-five persons were already scattered about the auditorium. These people faced a slightly raised circular platform, which eventually proved the main stage of action. I can see now that this theater was the forerunner of the playhouses that some well-heeled off-Broadway producers have since constructed and utilized to present their much less interesting dramas.

Dr. Moreno opened the session by announcing that a visitor, a Mrs. Mehlmann, was expected to arrive the next day. Before he stepped down from the stage he asked whether Mr. Mehlmann cared to express himself, one way or another, about the impending reunion with his wife.

Mr. Mehlmann slowly rose from his seat in the audience and said, "I'm glad she's coming."

"You're glad?" said Dr. Moreno. "That's good. Not like a month ago when you refused to see her, eh?"

Mr. Mehlmann scratched his large nose and looked at the floor.

"What happened to change your mind about her? Would you care to tell us, Mr. Mehlmann? Suppose you step up here and tell us why you didn't want to see her on her last visit."

Dr. Moreno stepped down and Mr. Mehlmann dragged himself reluctantly onto the platform.

He was a short, pale, flabby man, almost bald, with colorless eyes and a long, untidy Slovak mustache, like mine. He was around fifty and I judged him to be a hardware dealer. He had that unhealthy hardware-dealer's skin. When he got on stage he looked around for a moment, blinked in the direction of Dr. Moreno, pulled at a pretty substantial ear lobe, and smiled foolishly.

100

"It was your wife's birthday," said the doctor, "and she brought you a piece of cake, didn't she?"

"Yeah, she did," said Mehlmann. "I watched her from upstairs, when she got out of the car with the packages."

"Where did you watch from?" asked the doctor.

"From Joe's room," said Mehlmann.

"Suppose," said the doctor, "you arrange the furniture on the stage as it looked up in Joe's room."

Mr. Mehlmann turned around and began to lug at some characterless furniture that had been waiting in the shadows behind him. Still farther to the back, I noticed, was a child's blackboard on some wooden rollers.

It was plain to see that Mr. Mehlmann was an old trouper in psychodrama, and he was gaining authority and poise with every passing moment; as a matter of fact, he proceeded to crouch down, without self-consciousness, behind one of the chairs, to simulate his actions of the month before.

"Did your wife come up from the right side of the house?" asked Dr. Moreno.

"No, she came from the left," said Mehlmann. "She couldn't open the door with her hand account of the packages."

"Just a minute," said the doctor. "Would Miss Mathew please be good enough to take the part of Mrs. Mehlmann?"

A young woman, who, I later learned, was a trained practitioner in psychodrama, rose from the audience and approached the stage from the left side. She made believe that she was carrying some bulky packages in her arms, and, as she stepped onto the platform, she pretended to kick open an imaginary door.

"No!" said Mehlmann. "No! no! She kicked the door with her right foot! She don't use her left foot much, she has arthritis in the knee."

I discovered later that the woman assistant was instructed to make carefully calculated and prescribed mistakes, for the very purpose of rousing the patients' critical and corrective faculties.

I've bothered to tell you about this Mehlmann person not because he was particularly interesting; he was, as a matter of fact, just a mediocre paranoid performer, with the usual persecutionary overtones. But something happened during his turn that was really wonderfully exciting. While describing a breakfast he'd once had with his wife, he happened to mention the word *beigel*.

No sooner was this word out of his mouth than a pretty, dark-haired woman, called Millicent, jumped out of her seat and shouted, "Wrong!"

Mehlmann stopped and peered nearsightedly out into the audience. He finally spotted Millicent, who raised her arm and

101

once more shouted, "Wrong!" Her arm slowly came down, but she still trembled with excitement. I noticed that a nurse had suddenly materialized in back of her.

"You don't say *'beigel,'* " said Millicent. "You're supposed to say 'bagel.' " She passed the back of her hand across her forehead and chuckled to herself. "You talk like a Galician," she said, as she sat down again.

Although I was quite a distance from her, I felt waves of excitement surging around Millicent, and I couldn't understand why Dr. Moreno had suddenly crossed the room and placed himself just a few feet from where she was sitting.

"Come, Millicent," said the doctor, "go up on the stage and show Mr. Mehlmann the correct way of pronouncing 'bagel.' Why don't you write it out for him on the blackboard?"

After a moment, Millicent got up again and slowly, in complete stillness, like a trance-walker, proceeded down the aisle toward the stage. She walked as one who, after a long illness, is relearning how to properly balance her body's equilibrium. In passing Mr. Mehlmann on her way to the blackboard she stopped and smiled at him, and he good-naturedly smiled back at her and even patted her on the shoulder. It was a perfectly commonplace tableau, in which a woman of Russian Jewish descent had corrected the pronunciation of a Polish Jew, and the correction had seemingly been accepted with kindly tolerance. So what?

Just this: Millicent had, for almost a year, been a totally uncommunicative un-co-operative patient and had, during all that time, failed to respond to any form of physical or psychological stimulus. It seems that a few days after childbirth she had encircled herself within a complete wall of silence, which had been breached for the first time only that afternoon, when she heard Mr. Mehlmann give his parochial twist to the word "bagel."

I know that such small miracles happen every day in sessions of group therapy, but I'm maintaining that group therapy was only a twinkle in somebody's eye in those days, when nobody had as yet bothered to kibitz this valuable aspect of the Moreno technique. Incidentally, Dr. Moreno was not at all doctrinaire about psychodrama in the treatment of his patients. He freely utilized all established methods of psychotherapy at his clinic, but I've heard psychodrama scorned and belittled by practitioners who have shamelessly plagiarized his most significant discoveries.

I spent only a few weeks at this sanitarium but, when I finally left, my dosages had decreased to a minimum. Of course I wasn't cured, because I wasn't ready to be cured, because mine enemy within had still a few desperate resources left in his destructive campaign against my health and my sanity. But those weeks up at Moreno's brought me the knowledge of some strange and wonderful people who have pleasantly troubled my memory for many, many years.

For instance there was Gabrielle, who was only nineteen, the prettiest, most winsome schizophrenic I have ever met. Dark-haired, dark-eyed, tall and slender, she looked like Arthur Rackham's illustration of Titania, out of *A Midsummer Night's Dream*. She was a refugee and spoke nine languages, including Latin and Greek. On her way over to America she and her family had been detained for some months in Portugal, and Gabrielle had whiled away her time by learning Portuguese, so that she might later translate Camoëns into English.

And what was wrong with this paragon She stanchly maintained that her stepfather had sexually violated her. It seems that her mother, a rich and still youngish woman, had, some time previously, married a man several years her junior—a gifted and handsome man, to boot; and now Gabrielle insisted that this person had been making a play for her affections from the start and had, finally, cold-bloodedly seduced her. Of course, it could all have happened just the way she told it, except that there was no question in Dr. Moreno's mind that the girl was lying. She had, in fact, first made her wild claim after she had publicly disrobed in front of her whole class at college and had, for this piece of originality, been taken to Bellevue Hospital. By the way, for whatever it is worth, I'd like to tell you that she had perpetrated her shocking public exhibition during a class in civics.

When I came to know her, I was told that Gabrielle was already much improved, and I often played cards with her without ever thinking there was anything wrong with her. Indeed, I was so much impressed with her altogether-balanced behavior that, the night before I left the sanitarium, I couldn't resist the asinine impulse to talk some straight sense to her. No psychological crap, you understand, just plain, honest, intelligent-man-to-intelligent-woman business. I was suffering from that common failing that makes presumptively sane people talk horse sense to clinically certified psychopaths. It is hard to resist when you see how rational they are. You can't stop yourself from telling them to straighten themselves out, to pull themselves together, and to put their shoulders to the wheel. You know what I mean.

Well, I was sitting with Gabrielle out on a darkened porch, a little after supper, when I suddenly heard myself pronouncing noble sentiments on the subject of rational deportment. "You are too gifted a person, Gabrielle," I said, "to go on sitting in this nut haven and waste your time among all these sick characters. You are too valuable to the world to be lost in this way. Get out of here; you've been here a long time; you have work to do out there. This bughouse has just become your ivory tower; you've got to make an effort and decide to rejoin the human race." That's what I said, among other things.

I couldn't see her face very clearly, but I could hear plainly enough that her breathing seemed much troubled by my straightforward, common-sense approach. I thought I had been very wholesome and manly, and I had never once hinted that with a little encouragement I might get very stuck on her. I waited for her to say something, but she just sat there in the darkness, all clammed up, until, by slow degrees, I began to get a little uneasy. After about five minutes of silence, I even had certain misgivings whether my appeal to reason had been in altogether good taste.

Finally, she reached across and put her hand on my arm. "I'm sorry I was mistaken in you, after all," she said. "When you came here, a few weeks ago, I thought at first that you were a glib wisecracker, a superficial *bon vivant*, with just a surprisingly good memory. But later on, when you read me Peter Altenberg and told me about your life as a young immigrant, I decided that you had a heart, that you were really intelligent, and that, most important of all, you had a lively imagination."

"Yes?" I said. "And how, exactly, have I let you down?"

She removed her hand from my arm. "I'll tell you," she said. "You see, you don't believe at all that my stepfather really violated me. You think I'm just hopelessly in love with him and that's what's really wrong with me. Well, let's suppose that that is the real truth about me. Suppose I'm just sitting here and slowly wasting away only because once he actually did kiss me, under the poplars on the road to Antibes. Is that so utterly incomprehensible? Remember, Petrarch saw his Laura only once, in a laurel grove, and she was another man's wife, and yet Petrarch begot, on that one vision, all his miraculous sonnets. Where has it been stipulated, and by whom, that we would all have been better off if, instead of his hopeless longing, he had somehow managed to marry Laura and had enriched the world with half a dozen snotty children instead of with sonnets? I mean, specifically, that if you heard or read somewhere that somebody, three hundred years ago, had perished of unrequited love, you would be deeply moved. So, what has suddenly gone wrong with your lively imagination? Tell me, how did you decide at what point in history it had become improper or unfashionable for anyone to die merely of a broken heart?"

Luckily it was dark out there on that porch, and Gabrielle couldn't see me too clearly, either. I was sure, when she stopped talking, that I should have been wearing some kind of face that would have been appropriate to the occasion, but, whatever the hell kind of face it was, I didn't have it.

You can see my dilemma, can't you? You can see, as I did, that her madness had so much more reason and style than my so-called sanity. I was deeply ashamed that I had blunderingly and arrogantly presumed to bring order into the fixed, cold beauty of her poetic aberration.

I met a couple of other fascinating characters at Moreno's, such as the ex-auditor whom I had never seen without three old cigar boxes under his arm. He was introduced to me by Gabrielle one morning when I was sitting in front of the house with her and he happened to greet her from the porch. She asked him to come down to us, and he did.

"This is Mr. Parroni," she said. "He writes letters to the world that never wrote to him. Don't you, Mr. Parroni?"

He seemed flattered by this introduction and smirked at us like a young bride who has just been complimented on her root-beer muffins.

"Pull over a chair," I said, "and sit with us a spell."

"I think I will," he said, "but I prefer a rocker. I'll get myself one from the porch."

I thought he was going to have trouble lugging that rocker while he was also trying to hold on to his cigar boxes, so I suggested that he park his baggage beside us until he got back.

He gave me a suspicious, almost vindictive look. "No, thank you," he said. "I'll manage my own affairs without anybody's help, mister." Then he took off.

Gabrielle laughed softly. "He's funny," she said. "He's written a hundred-and-twenty-six-page letter of peace to the chief rabbi of the Jews, offering to have himself circumcised, provided the rabbi will submit himself to baptism."

"There is no chief rabbi of the Jews," I said.

"I don't think there is a Mr. Parroni either," said Gabrielle.

But there apparently was, for he was just emerging from the porch and, what's more, he was having a hell of a time clutching his boxes and dragging that rocker down the steps toward us. He was a skinny little runt, about fifty-five, with straight sandy-gray hair whose color had all run out, long ago, in the wash. I had already noticed that when he talked, the tip of his nose moved up and down as if he had some kind of extra mobile joint in it. During all my stay I never once saw him without a coat or a tie, and he also wore high, leather-laced brogans on all occasions.

Well, he finally rassled his way successfully across the lawn and sat down beside us.

"I've just told Mr. King that you've written a hundred-and-twenty-six-page letter to the chief rabbi of the Jews," said Gabrielle.

"In rhyme!" said Mr. Parroni. "In hexameters! I have it with me." He took a bulky envelope out of his coat pocket and handed it to me. It weighed about half a pound and I could see it was no machine-made envelope; he had built it himself out of a brown paper bag. He'd made the stamp himself, too; it was just a small photograph that had obviously been cut out of a magazine, and he had painstakingly pinked the edges in exact imitation of a real stamp. When I looked closer at the picture, it turned out to be a miniature of Sally Rand, fans and all.

"Looks great!" I said. "How come you never mailed it? I'm sure the rabbi would be delighted, particularly by that stamp."

"Dr. Moreno won't let me mail it," said Parroni. "I've got over seventeen hundred letters upstairs, all sealed and stamped. He never let me send any of them. I hope you'll be good enough to take this one out with you when you leave here. I'd be much obliged to you. It's a letter for interreligious brotherhood."

"Yes," I said. "Gabrielle has told me."

"She hasn't told you about my boxes, though, has she?"

"No," I said. "What about them?"

He'd kept them in his lap all this time, and now he opened the top one and disclosed some neatly stacked but quite unrelated objects, such as some short pieces of colored ribbon, the top of an ice-cream container, a piece of used sandpaper, and some stained cigarette holders. At least, that's what I was able to spy at first glance.

"Interesting," I said. "Quite a collection."

"Yes," said Parroni, judiciously, "it is a rather interesting collection. It has important connections with certain stages of my life, with my whole career, you might say. Now, this chicken bone, for instance!" He took the winning half of an old wishbone out of his box and held it up in front of us. "This," he said, "is a memento of a dinner, a Sunday dinner, I once had in a small town called Memlick, a little north of Buffalo. Perhaps you've heard of it?"

"No," I said, "can't say that I have."

"It's been in the news lately," he said. "Birds Eye people are putting a new freezing plant up there. I once worked for the Birds Eye people, and I like to keep track of things. Well, anyway, I was up in Memlick before the plant was started; went up there with a lady friend, a librarian from Buffalo, a widow, who went to visit her eleven-year-old son, who was in school there. I'd driven her up in my Chevrolet convertible, and all three of us had dinner together, chicken dinner, at a place called Billson's. Well, I only eat the white meat, so I got hold of the wishbone; and the little boy, his name was Herbert, and I, we decided to try our luck on it. As you can see, I won. I thought it was a good omen. You're not supposed to tell about your wishes, but that was nine years ago, and it doesn't really make any difference now. To tell you the truth, I wished for that lady, her name was Thelma, I wished for her to marry me. Well, she didn't. Married somebody called Hastings, a nickel-plater, who took them all out to Utah. And this is the lucky bone that I got left from that event that I'm telling you about. Things sure happen funny, don't they?"

He gave a deep sigh as he replaced his fraudulent relic and picked up the top of the cardboard ice-cream container. "This is one I think about often," he said. "Happened seven years ago. I was visiting some friends in Portsmouth, it was a hot day, and on the way to the house I stopped off and bought a quart of vanilla ice cream. Tell you the truth, I was interested in their daughter, a girl called Clarice. A lovely girl, but very restless. Artistic too, and reading the theater pages of the papers all the time, and subscribing to the Book-of-the-Month Club, and all that intellectual stuff. A little above me, maybe, but I was very devoted to her and I had a very good job with General Electric at the time. Semisupervisory job, with nice pay. Well, anyway, I got to the house and the mother and the father made a big fuss about my bringing all that ice cream that I bought. Clarice didn't say much. She was in one of her moods. She didn't want any ice cream. Later, when the old folks left to visit their married son, who lived the other side of town, I asked Clarice what was wrong. 'Everything is wrong,' she said. 'My job, my parents, and you, too,' she said. 'My God! I wish I could leap right out of all this. I want to get away from here and get some real joy out of life.' I told her that I cared for her, that I could do a lot for her, that I had a good job, with nice pay, and that we could have all kinds of holidays and lots of parties together; and then she started to laugh. You never heard anybody laugh like that. It was awful. She just laughed and laughed, and couldn't stop herself. I was almost scared, the way she carried on. Then, after a while, she quieted down, but, even so, every once in a while she gave a wild laugh, more like a bark, you might say. I told her I was sorry, I hadn't meant to upset her, and so on. And Clarice said, 'You're a nice guy, Joe. It was only, when you started to talk about our holidays and wild parties, I just saw you coming home, one night, with a real big surprise—a quart of *chocolate ice cream!*' and off she was again. Laughing

107

like she was having a fit or something. When I left, I picked up the top of the ice-cream carton that had been laying there all the time. And here it is. I never went back to that house again, and I never seen hide nor hair of any of them, ever since. Not ever."

So the poor bastard was just lugging around a whole kitchen midden of commemorative debris from each of his disastrous romances. He was prepared to go on indefinitely with the rest of his calamitous dossier, if Gabrielle, who had heard it all before, hadn't managed, very tactfully, to shut him off.

I guess we must have laughed a couple of times after Parroni left us, because suddenly, Professor Lunting appeared before us and waggled a reproachful finger over our heads.

"Shame!" he said. "Shame on both of you, and a demerit for bad manners."

"We weren't laughing at anybody," I said. "We were just laughing at life in general."

"I suspect you have just been laughing at poor Parroni," said Professor Lunting, "and that is a breach of the house rules."

Before I go any further, I'd better tell you about Lunting. He was an honest-to-God professor, a professor of ancient history, and was even something of a celebrity in his field. He was a refugee, too, who had been teaching at a Midwestern university and would have been teaching there still if the local D.A.R. hadn't gotten after him about not eating all his farina, or something. As a matter of fact, nothing subversive was ever proven or even specifically charged against him, but the poor dislocated old scholar flipped his lid, and through the help of some friends he had finally landed at Moreno's. He was tall, gaunt, and clean-shaven, with somber brown eyes and a wild mop of upstanding gray hair. He looked, altogether, like a Hollywood ideal of a European history professor. He had a fine speaking voice and I loved to hear him tell about his childhood in Sweden and his young manhood in Paris. He belonged to a dying species and I treasured him accordingly. The murky tides had washed him ashore here for my delectation, and I realized that his kind was vanishing forever from the academic scene. This was no joiner, no easy laugher, no handball player in Bermuda shorts; he was as completely steeped in learning as some people are in opportunism, in cunning, and in moneygrubbing. He judged human endeavors and achievements by hallowed classical standards, but not too severely, since he had a lively sense of humor and saw that the earthly dilemma only too frequently lapsed into redundant travesty.

"You should not laugh too much at Parroni," said the professor, drawing up a chair, "because it will some day dawn on you young people that every man carries around with him just such a sinister bundle of horrors. Parroni, at least, can take a look at his package. He can even put it down. It is, at least physically, separate from himself. But what about the bundle that each person carries around with him that nobody can see, not even himself? Are they any less real? No, you do wrong to patronize Parroni. He has, at least to some extent, externalized his inner turmoil, he has totemized his fears, and let us hope some day he will burn them all up, in a grand auto-da-fé of liberation."

The professor was a cool cat, and I used to have long talks with him on everything under the sun, excepting his retirement from academic life. But one day we came close to it. We had been talking of the difficulties that confronted the elderly immigrant in making his adjustment to American ways, and the professor said that most people didn't realize that, indeed, the immigrants themselves were quite unaware of the severe psychic damage that must be the inevitable result of such a late transplantation.

"Of course they are aware that they suffer," he said. "But they think it is homesickness for a little forest, or a church steeple, or a lake, or sometimes even just a dirty street in a dirty city. Nostalgia can make an Eskimo yearn for his frozen igloo. It has no logic and no morality. But the trouble with the older immigrant to the United States is more serious than that. You see, *near* that lake, and *by* that church steeple, or *in* that dirty street, in the old country, people work, and play, and eat, and dance, and sing, and talk and use words that are worn round with use, like pebbles on a shore. You know, I attended quite a few baseball games when I was teaching out West, and I understand the principles of the game well enough to keep an accurate score card and to follow the complexities and the tensions that develop, with reasonable alertness. I used to get up and stretch in the seventh inning, and have my frankfurters and soda pop along with the rest of the crowd. But I don't have to tell you that that whole elaborate rigmarole of anxious mimicry never actually succeeded in making me into a baseball fan. There is the slang, for instance, so rich and terse and sometimes so fiendishly accurate, since it springs directly from the very needs of a constantly growing vocabulary. And then, you have many popular, established misconceptions which are altogether harmless and go unchallenged because they aren't really important. What do you think a citizen of Hamburg, Germany, for instance, would say if you served him one of our hamburgers? You know what he would say?"

"Yes," I said, "he'd say that it lost a lot in translation."

The professor laughed. "You're quite right. And there is the essence of the whole matter, everything loses a lot in translation."

He suddenly looked very disturbed and said in a stricken voice, "You see, *there*, I'm afraid, is the basis of *my* whole calamity. It seems that somewhere along the line I, too, got totally lost in translation."

I will tell you about one more patient at the sanitarium, a girl called Monica Schuyler. Monica had the good looks of Helen Wills, the tennis champion, complete with permanent sun tan, but, happily, she lacked Helen's humorless, astringent personality. I suppose I should tell you, my grandchildren, that at one time this Helen Wills girl had been an All-American ideal, a female fetish of enormous potency to all the busy-biddies of the women's clubs and the women's magazines. But, as happens so often with All-American girls, some incalculable factor came to taint her central essence to such an extent that, in the end, she wound up being devoted to dogs and horses. Such characters don't cotton much to people. Not *really*.

Well, this Monica Schuyler was not only good-looking, but she had some sort of a social worker rampant inside her that made her do fifty things a day for people she couldn't possibly have cared very much about. That isn't always admirable either, but she carried it off so casually that there was never any sauce of do-goodism slopping over her kindnesses. She had me completely fooled for a while; I thought she was employed at the sanitarium, until one of the nurses wised me up and told me that she'd been terribly sick just a year before, and that when her condition improved she had seemed so anxious to be of use around the place that Dr. Moreno had finally allowed her to assist him even in the laboratory.

This Monica doll played tennis, too, and I must say she seemed just about the nicest kind of girl for anyone to come home to. I'd heard that she was married and that her husband, a personable young man, came to see her from time to time. I was also told that he didn't come as often as he wished, because, for some reason not known to anyone, Dr. Moreno had spaced these visits rather sparsely.

And then one day I was sitting in the library and looking over some Austrian literary magazines, when I heard Monica talking in the next room to a Mrs. Albertson. I didn't catch the beginning of their conversation, but it was easy to guess that Mrs. Albertson had probably asked Monica something about her marriage.

This Mrs. Albertson had been with us only a few days,

and she seemed like a quiet, untroubled, Midwestern matron of about fifty, and the only thing queer about her was that she wore her hat and her fur piece all day long, as if she expected to quit the place at a moment's notice. Also, I never saw her without her knitting, at which she was expert; but I sometimes wondered whether she too, like Penelope, always unraveled her daily production just before she went to bed, because, despite her ceaseless work, her sock, or her scarf, or whatever the hell she was knitting never reached completion.

So, as I said, these two girls were talking together in the little sitting room next to the library, and I first started to pay attention to their chatter when I heard Mrs. Albertson saying, "And how long were you married before your husband had his breakdown?"

"Two years," said Monica. "I guess it really began that morning at breakfast. We were supposed to go and visit some friends of ours that evening, the Mitchells. Tony Mitchell had been my husband's roommate at Princeton, and Victor, that's my husband, had known Stella Mitchell, too, when she went to Vassar. So I suppose they were probably our closest friends."

"Did you like them?" said Mrs. Albertson.

"Yes, I liked them as well as anybody," said Monica. "Of course, I had no special, old bonds with them, like Victor, but we sometimes had nice parties with them that were sort of fun."

"And did you go to visit with them that night?" said Mrs. Albertson.

"We were just talking about it, at breakfast," said Monica. "I didn't really want to go, that day, and Victor seemed quite upset about it. 'I can't understand you,' he said. 'We've had this appointment for three weeks now, and it seems we hardly ever go out and meet anybody any more, at least, not anybody our age,' he said. You see, I had a couple of old friends that used to come to the house, friends of my grandfather's —ever since he died, they like to come over and talk to me about the old days."

"Your grandfather been dead a long while?" asked Mrs. Albertson.

"He died two and a half months after I was married. I lived with him ever since I was a little girl. I lost my parents in the flu epidemic, and my grandfather brought me up. He was a wonderful man, my grandfather. We lived in this house that he had built a long time ago, and I had the upstairs all to myself and it was fixed up like a real boudoir, with fluffy curtains and lace bedspreads and fine carpets that he had gotten himself in Persia and Afghanistan, and in Kerman and Marrakech and such far-off places."

"He traveled a lot, I take it," said Mrs. Albertson.

"Oh yes. He'd been all over the world. In his rooms, downstairs, the walls were full of African masks, and knives, and spears, and he had many presents that African chiefs had given him—carved stools, and headrests—and he always wore a ring that a big Somali chief called Ngakoura had given him. It was made of ivory, but it was so old it had turned deep brown. If you want me to, I'll show it to you sometime. I have it here with me."

"I'd love to see it," said Mrs. Albertson. "But didn't you have any friends, your own friends, I mean, when you were a young girl?"

"Oh yes, I used to have a tutor, a man called Crabshaw. He was a little lame, but spry and lively like a youngster, and we used to have wonderful times together, the three of us."

"Seems to me," said Mrs. Albertson, "that your grandfather ought to have sent you off to a school somewhere, to some nice girls' school where you could have met some people your own age."

"That's what Victor said. He thinks Grandfather spoiled me. He did, too. Sometimes, when I'd had my breakfast upstairs, I'd come down to his study, and he'd just be eating, and I'd sit on his knee and he'd put some of his honey on a piece of buttered roll and put it into my mouth; and that piece of roll tasted better than anything I'd eaten at my own breakfast. He had some special honey from Greece, from Mount Hymettus, the kind that the gods had eaten in the ancient days."

"And how did you meet your husband?" said Mrs. Albertson.

"Oh, Victor lived right near us. I've known him all my life, you might say, but not really close, you understand. I didn't know anybody too close."

"Well, you must have gotten to know him a lot better, to marry him," said Mrs. Albertson.

"Oh, that. I guess Victor had been fond of me for a long time. He used to come around, and Grandfather was always very nice to him. And then, when he got out of Princeton, I think, he came over with his father one day, to talk about Victor getting married to me. They were locked in with Grandfather for almost an hour that day, and later Grandfather talked very seriously to me about the future. He told me that he was an old man and didn't have very much money to leave me, that he'd been reckless and foolish with his money before I came into his life, and that Victor was a fine boy and would be able to take good care of me after he was gone."

"You mean you weren't in love with him when you married him?" said Mrs. Albertson. And it was obvious that one of her absolutely sacred conventions was about to be outraged.

"I guess I liked him a lot, all right," said Monica. "The way Grandfather put it, I saw no reason for not marrying him. Victor is a good husband, and he's very fond of me, really."

"So what was wrong, then?" said Mrs. Albertson. "What made him fly off the handle that way?"

"Oh, like I told you, that morning at breakfast, when I'd balked about going to the Mitchells', he was arguing with me about it, and I said, 'What's the use of going there again? I know the majolica umbrella stand in their hallway, and the etching of the two Scotties with their heads cocked to one side, in their bedroom, and the dried babies'-breath in their Mexican vase, that stands on the Spanish shawl on their piano. I've seen them all, time and time again.' And Victor just got pale as a candle and stared at me with great big eyes, and then he said, 'You know what you've just described? Do you know what you've just finished describing, Monica?' 'What?' I said. 'You've just described our apartment here,' he said. 'And, what's more, I'm good and sick of watching you drink four, five cups of coffee every morning.' And he took the cup right out of my hand, and, wrought up as he was, he put that cup right to his own lips, and he nearly passed out."

"He nearly passed out?" said Mrs. Albertson. "Why would he do that?"

"Because," said Monica, "there was straight gin in that cup, that's why. I'd gotten into the habit, lately, of taking quite a bit of gin, every day, and I drank it out of cups so nobody would notice it. But then, suddenly, he knew. I guess it was quite a shock to him. Anyway, Victor drank the rest of that cup, all of it, at one, crazy gulp. And then for the next three weeks neither one of us drew a sober breath, till his father found out about it, and they took us both away. And that's how they brought me here, about a year ago, and I've been here ever since. I like it a lot here."

## CHAPTER THIRTEEN

BEFORE I CAME up to New England I picked out some books at home to take along with me, and, in an old volume of prose poems by Peter Altenberg, I came across a dozen lapsed pawn tickets, which were all dated the latter part of 1945, the earliest days of my addiction, when obviously I still had some things left to pawn.

It was certainly fitting that I should have chosen that particular volume as the repository for my passports to perdition, since Peter Altenberg, the author of the book, had been chronically insolvent the better part of his existence. Perhaps you've never even heard of this guy, and yet he has had the most enormous influence on my ways of thinking and feeling about the whole baffling earthly conundrum. I am deeply in his debt, not only for the wonderful essences he distilled in his writings, but for being a potent spiritual mentor who guided my vision to those beauties that he himself so often found in the most common manifestation of life. That's what Eddie Guest did, too, for some people, I suppose, but Peter Altenberg was not just a rhyming house painter, he happened to be a divinely gifted poet. For years and years now, he has helped me to see, accurately and humbly, the heart-filling miracles that happen every day in God's lovely, self-tortured world.

In a short biographical piece about himself, he once wrote: "I never dreamed of being Shakespeare or Goethe, and I never expected to hold the great mirror of truth up before the world; I dreamed only of being a little pocket mirror, the sort that a woman can carry in her purse; one that reflects small blemishes, and some great beauties, when held close enough to the heart."

And who was this wise man, this poet, this seer? He was an Austrian writer who, in the early part of this century, floated like a swamp blossom through the cynical sewers of Viennese coffee-house life; among people to whom only their own petty interests were sacred, he lived like a Columbus of the soul, whose chief aim was to widen the horizon of human sympathy and understanding.

From time to time, when the pressures and anxieties of existence became too acute for his sensibilities, he used to take flight and find sanctuary at a place called Steinhof, a famous lunatic asylum outside Vienna; and, since my own memorable visit at Dr. Moreno's, I have felt even closer to poor Peter than ever before.

Luckily, he had some exceptional friends who understood, valued and loved him, and one of these, the architect Adolf Loos, delivering the funeral oration at Altenberg's grave, said, among other things, "You all know that our dear, good Peter, in his quaint, quixotic way, looked up to children, to women, to servants, and you also know that he spent quite a number of his years among us in actual poverty. And now that this beggar has gone from us, how poor *we* all have remained."

True, noble words. Unfortunately, you will have to learn German to know his real worth, because he, also, gets quite lost in translation. I'll risk giving you, at random, a tiny vignette by Peter Altenberg, which is not fair to him, but, as the French say, what would you?

> *He and she are sitting side*
> *by side on a bench, at night,*
> *in the ducal garden. In the*
> *stillness she says, "Would you*
> *like to kiss me?"*
> *He: "Yes."*
> *She: "My hand?"*
> *He: "No."*
> *She: "My mouth?"*
> *He: "No."*
> *She: "I think you are revolting!"*
> *He: "I wanted to kiss the hem of your gown."*

I know it loses almost everything, but a little something is still there, because you cannot altogether becloud the Altenberg magic. I have made my translation very freely, since the volume I own doesn't contain this particular item, and I hoped to catch his real flavor more successfully by not having the original right in front of me.

Speaking of translations, I mentioned to you, some pages ago, that I'd once had a very strange experience with the love books of Ovid, and I think the time has now come for me to warm up this crumbly, mildewed tidbit.

It was back in those lush days of easy grazing, when I was not only well established as an illustrator, but when almost any book I chose to do was sure of a definite sale among collectors, that this benign little cancer ripened upon my professional life. I had quite a lot of work on hand at the time, and I used to do most of it up in the country, at Kent Cliffs, New York, where we had bought ourselves a modest little summer home. That is to say, it had started out to be modest, but, like a qualifying sentence in brackets that finally eats up the whole story, this modest, bucolic retreat eventually nearly ruined me. But such an experience has become so common that I have no intention of going into details about it; I'll just confine myself to telling you that there came a time in my life as a landowner when my family ate home-grown cucumbers that cost us seventy cents apiece, and, what's more, a couple of thousand of them all came up in one night, and I already saw myself smothered alive in an avalanche of popping, dropsical cucumbers. I'm probably the only man in the country (not sponsored by government) who for weeks on end buried bushels and bushels of decaying broccoli. Other people were digging up *their* vegetables; I spent a whole summer burying mine. But enough!

It was in those ink-happy times, then, when my work was hardly ever absent from the book-review pages, that one day a man came to my New York apartment who told me that his name was Calhoun and that he wanted me to illustrate the love books of Ovid for him. I couldn't have been more surprised. I had never seen anyone who looked less like a book publisher. I know there is no standard type for the breed—who knows that better than I?—but I had always found that certain ineradicable smears of literacy tended to accrue to the most ambiguous of these creatures. That is, until the day Mr. Calhoun showed up. At first glance there was nothing particularly disturbing about him, excepting perhaps a certain steely compactness of person, and an unusually concentrated display of quiet resolution in his shadowed face that indicated, to me, that Mr. Calhoun might prove an extremely arduous father-in-law. By the way, his face was shadowed because not once throughout our curious communion did he ever find it necessary to remove his hat.

There was nothing demonstrably illiterate or even awkward in his speech, quite the contrary. In good New Yorkese, he expressed himself fluently and to the point, and I think he even showed me a couple of books that his firm had already placed on the market. And yet it was the *manner* of his speech that baffled me, because Mr. Calhoun spoke so softly that he could hardly be heard, and the only other person who had ever whispered to me in that singular way had somehow managed to project, by that very suppression of voice, a certain unmistakable quality of menace. My previous whisperer had been a notorious Brooklyn hoodlum who had persuaded me to copy his dead brother's portrait from a hideously tinted photograph. Now Mr. Calhoun, afflicted with a similar personal mannerism, which conveyed no actual threats, nevertheless managed to get me quite rattled.

Also, I was aware that, at the time, a lot of very strange people looking for an easy buck had suddenly launched themselves into the shmootzig waters of the limited-editions business, since in a limited edition you could print a lot of unprintable stuff that the suckers were paying heavy money for.

Frankly, I didn't particularly want this job, but I was somehow reluctant to refuse. So I agreed to work for Mr. Calhoun. I told him that I was familiar with Publius Ovidius Naso's handiwork, and that I would at once set about illuminating the book to the best of my ability. Mr. Calhoun

116

didn't blink when I mentioned my rather stiff price; as a matter of fact, he produced a filled-out check from his pocket and paid me half my fee in advance. I promised to make delivery within the next two months, and I began, the very next day, to design my frontispiece.

I phoned him about five weeks later to apprise him that the job was done and he told me, in his confidential way, that he would come by to pick it up at my apartment the following afternoon. And so he did. I had inserted twenty explanatory slips of paper in my copy of Ovid, to indicate the appropriate pages for the various illustrations. When I explained this piece of business to him, I noticed that Mr. Calhoun was looking at me with an expression that I chose to interpret as quizzical. It was just the tiniest fraction of a muted smile, if you like, but the man seemed definitely beguiled by some secret comic fancy. I wondered what it was that amused him so. I didn't have to wonder long.

"Do you really think," he finally whispered, "that any publisher in his right mind would invest his money in putting out an expensive book that was written in poetry?"

"What do you mean?" I said. "Didn't you want me to do this Ovid?"

"Sure I did. But I had no idea that the book had been written in poetry."

"You mean to say you've never seen this book before?" I said.

"Never. Why should I? Somebody suggested it. There was no copyright on it, the title sounds saleable, and that's all I cared about. But the condition this thing is in now, you couldn't give it away. That poetry's got to go."

"Well," I said, "there must be lots of prose versions of it around. Let's just use one of them, if that's the way you feel about it."

"It isn't the way *I* feel about it," he said, "it's the way the public feels about it. The public just don't seem to go for poetry. Now, why don't you go to the library and see if you can dig up a prose version of this thing, and call me later in my office."

And that's the way we left it. Not very pleasant, but still, nobody was really hurt, except maybe Ovid.

At the library I found out the real disaster. There were two English prose versions extant, which were, unfortunately, copyrighted, and I didn't have to be told that Mr. Calhoun didn't intend to pay royalties on a book that had been in the public domain for over a thousand years. I realized that I was stuck with my pictures, or Mr. Calhoun, or both.

Mr. Calhoun, you will be surprised to learn, had not yet troubled to pay me the second half of my fee. Get it?

Well, here was another goddamned mess, and I had a grim notion that somebody was going to have to make a new prose translation of Ovid, and that that somebody was going to be *me*. I've never quite decided whether that soft-spoken son-of-a-bitch had known from the start that only poetic versions of Ovid were freely available, and whether he had not deliberately and in cold blood whispered me into that little classical quagmire. Maybe somebody had tipped him off that I was the sort of platypus that would start swimming when the water got up to my schnozzle, and that, in a pinch, I would somehow emerge with a new translation.

Whatever the hell it was, I had to make a fast decision. I called up Calhoun and told him we were stuck.

"That's too bad," he said, "because I got a contract with a printer to deliver all the copy at his shop this coming Monday afternoon."

"Next Monday!" I said. "You must be out of your mind! Do you realize that today is already Thursday? How in hell can you get it all done by then, even if you did find a sucker who was willing to do it?"

"Well," he said, "I don't see how I can get out of my contract if I want to stay in business, do you?"

To make the agony brief, I told him I'd take a shot at it but I'd have to have help.

"What kind of help?" he asked.

"Somebody who knows Latin and who can type like a demon, and who's willing to go up to the country with me for three days."

He was willing, he said, to pay three hundred and fifty dollars for the hire of such an all-round guy, but Monday, he insisted, was his absolute deadline for delivery.

I knew only one person who could possibly qualify for the job, a scholarly friend of mine, Jack Borut, who happened to be out of work at the time. So I called him up, and without entering into specific details I persuaded him to go up to the country with me the following day.

My friend Jack was a long, lean, crisp-haired myopic who never really quite approved of me or my doings. He was nevertheless quite devoted to my interests because we had met years ago in Paris, when both of us had still been rather tender packages, full of wistful hopes and youthful misgivings.

So, when we arrived in Kent Cliffs, around noon, we got out the typewriter, I outlined the general proposition to Jack, and we started to translate.

It was a drag. A terrible drag. I had brought along four versions of Ovid—the original Latin, one in German, another

118

in French, and finally the English, poetic version by Christopher Marlowe. It took us about five hours to do five pages, and those pages just stank. It had the flavor of powdered eggs cooked in stale clam juice, and at one point I got so disgusted and frantic, I threw all the goddamned books smack up against the wall. So Jack decided to go out for a walk, and when he was gone I picked up the books, sat down again, and started to read the different translators' prefaces. They were something awful, too.

However, by the time Jack returned, about two hours later, I had finally decided that there was only one way in which I could possibly do this thing at all; I was going to write it as if Ovid had perpetrated his little opus in a funny kind of Italian just a couple of weeks ago; I was going to cut through all the classical crap, and I was going to dish up a version that really moved its can.

There was just one trouble: My friend had perfectly understandable objections to massacring an ancient masterpiece just to make a King and Calhoun holiday. I reasoned with him for a long time, but in his own rational spinsterish way he had worked himself into a state of scholastic self-righteousness that seemed impervious to common sense. Finally, in despair, I copped out to him completely. I told him I had no option in the matter, that I had to produce the gravy by Monday or the consequences were likely to be deplorable.

As an old and loyal friend he was of course horrified by my jam, and so he finally sat down at the typewriter and proceeded to take my dictation. By midnight we had finished sixty-four pages, and then both of us simply fell away, slaughtered by exhaustion.

The next morning at nine we were at it again, and we kept up this unremitting pace until Sunday evening, when we put the last page, numbered and clearly typed, into a binder. As a glib Latinist might have said, *"Vires acquirit eundo."*

When I offered Jack his money, he pursed his lips and with two fingers lifted just one fifty-dollar bill out of my hand.

"I shouldn't take *anything*," he said, "because I don't like to profit by the results of crime. However, I've performed a certain amount of manual labor, and I need the money, so I'll settle for this. Let the blood of Ovid be on *your* head."

I delivered the manuscript to Calhoun the following morning, and that fine man never even bothered to raise the cover. He just took another check, already made out, from his pocket, and handed me my final payment.

And that, I thought, was the end of it. But not quite.

After the book was published, Jack Borut called me up to ask if I'd seen a review of it in the *Sun*.

"No," I said, "I didn't see any mention of it in the papers so far."

"Well," he said, "let me read you one paragraph, because the piece is too long to quote in its entirety in a telephone booth. The man who reviews it is a professor of classical literature up at Columbia University, and he says as follows:

> " 'Here at last is a translation that warms the cockles of a scholar's heart. It revives more than a classic, it breathes new vibrant life into an old masterpiece that has in the past been treated with so much starched reverence that the previous translators seem to have, inadvertently, embalmed poor Ovid, instead of presenting him to us in vital, contemporary language.' "

Jack kept quiet for a moment. Then he said, "Well, I suppose you think I was an ass, not to have taken the rest of that money, but I'll tell you something: You know, I'm sort of embarrassed that I even took that fifty-dollar bill."

And that still wasn't the end of it. You see, I had made the translation under the name of Charles D. Young; and when Calhoun asked me to write him a translator's preface I offered to do it for nothing, on condition that he include in the same volume, intact, the poetic translation of Christopher Marlowe, for such readers as fancied something a little more traditional. To this Calhoun had agreed, and the book had gone to press that way.

Now get this: There was in those days a reprint series of famous books, called the Black and Gold Library, and the publishers of these books naturally made the usual racket about their painstaking selection of editors and translators for the relaunching of these classics.

Fancy my astonishment when I read in a Sunday paper that they were bringing out a new, popular-priced edition of Ovid with a preface by the celebrated Latin scholar and translator, Charles D. Young. They went into a small gavotte of ecstasy over the judicious care with which this little jewel had been polished, and, what's more, they quoted reams of favorable reviews from savants all over the country to prove it.

Obviously, the old whisperer had unloaded this noodle pudding on them, reviews and all, and I have no doubt it will go on fermenting through the centuries as a typical scholarly contribution of our time. Serves our time right!

This edition, of course, has no pictures in it. If you want to see that copy, you'll have to go to the Forty-second Street library, and, after proper identification and the signing of a few documents, you may take a gander at it in the rare-book department.

Incidentally, the Black and Gold Library was also published by Liveright, so they gained an Ovid, but by that time they had already lost their Horace.

## CHAPTER FOURTEEN

I HAVE KNOWN Al Hirschfeld for more than a quarter of a century, and during all that time he didn't know how to swim. The few times I saw him dunking himself in water he was about as buoyant as an anvil. And then last summer, under the aegis of his young daughter, Nina, he suddenly became glibly amphibious. Consider that during all his previous years he had shown no interest whatever in any body of water which could not be encompassed by a cocktail glass, or, at the most, by a very shallow bathtub, and then you will begin to grasp the true nature of the miracle I have described.

Yesterday we had a note from Dolly Hirschfeld; they are in Italy at the moment. Since they are our closest friends, I'm delighted they're having a fine holiday abroad; at the same time, in my parlous state of health I'm a little uneasy to have them all so far away from home.

I also had a letter from my dear friend, Joanie Castle, today, telling me that the Billy Roses are spending their summer in Europe and that Billy, too, was taking swimming lessons. This piece of news simply gassed me, because I love to imagine all those middle-aged, gray-haired Jews disporting themselves aquatically in Venice, while all the dolphins in the Grand Canal are gaping at them. As Sid Perelman said on another occasion, "It shouldn't happen to a Doge!"

Of course, Al and Billy have finally taken to water because their little daughters playfully goosed them into it, and I'm just jealous because I never had a daughter. Nor a grand-daughter, either, for that matter. This lack, which I have always felt pretty badly about, accounts for a good many emotional ramifications in my life and explains to a certain extent my paternal attitude toward most women. It was also probably one of the decisive reasons why I married, a couple of times, girls so much younger than myself.

I might as well confess that all through my life women have somehow seemed a little pathetic to me. I don't mean

121

pitiable, you understand, but needing and deserving a lot of extra consideration; and not just the male-etiquette type of consideration, but rather an all-encompassing awareness of their eternal, basic frailty.

I've always found their physical defenselessness, for instance, terribly moving, and what makes it even more poignant for me is the elaborate pretense, on all sides, that this is no longer true.

Just look at a naked woman and see the sad, pear-shaped droop of her buttocks, the anomalous pubic goatee, the breasts so overtly accessible to injury, and you will be looking at the most vulnerable creature that walks this earth. I'm fully conscious that there are also lots of rugged, muscular dames around who are as tough and rowdy as any man, but that has nothing to do with what I'm saying, because if that's the sort of woman you're mixed up with you're in the wrong book, anyway.

Look at a woman when she's dressed. In the machine age she tends to discard her natural habiliments and to assume mannish, sporting outfits; slacks or modified jock straps, for instance. These ghastly transvestitisms merely emphasize her fruity buttocks, and the poor creature becomes an ambulant exhibit of all her dangling sexual giblets.

You may not think this is sad, but I do, because I rate women pretty high. They have helped me greatly and taught me much. And I'm afraid I shall never be able to square my many obligations to them. Simone de Beauvoir, in her book *The Second Sex,* makes out a fine case for them, but I'm sure her final conclusions are dead wrong. What women need is not absolute equality with men, they need wider sympathy and appreciation for their special qualities, their unique endowments, which only the poets of the world have ever recognized and evaluated justly.

I don't mean that cooking fifteen meals a week for some adenoidal ape requires any unique endowment. Nothing of the sort. I know that all repetitive domestic chores are absolutely soul-destroying and will, I hope, in the foreseeable future be largely dispensed with. I too like to do a little cooking once in a while, as long as nobody expects it of me, and I don't see why women should feel any different about it.

What women *do* contribute to the richness of life is their astonishing capacity for making poetry and drama out of the most unpromising substances. Believe me, I have seen them wring elements of beauty out of pretty gruesome involvements. I have known women who have spun shimmering cocoons of wonder around the most boringly commonplace love affairs that have ever desecrated this planet.

You will say this sort of magic works both ways, and you'll

only show that you've hardly given the matter any serious thought. Certainly, men will glorify their sex symbols and endow them with nonexistent virtues during the mating season. This is the divine blindness which nature bestows on all its creatures to assure the continuation of the species. But a woman goes infinitely further, and stays a hell of a lot longer, than this camouflage job requires or justifies.

She doesn't only think that the uncouth truck driver of her dreams is "cute," she manages, for her own mysterious needs, to bring his crudenesses into relationship with the mythological oafs whose winsome simplicities inspired Shakespeare. She ennobles her dolt because it is her great gift to do so; because it is her great gift to ennoble the boring prose of life with a cadence of splendor.

My Marxist friends may object, at this point, that the real reason for a woman's making so much of her man is simply that she wants to apply a little extra glue to her legally contracted meal ticket. Let me point out to these immaterialist logicians that some of the most considerate and devoted wives I have ever known were ladies who either *had,* or *earned,* a great deal of money, and who seemed delighted to support their husbands in conspicuous style.

Now, I'm not pretending that all women or even most of them are up to the high standards I have outlined, I'm just telling you that *my* women were.

I'm aware that there is a rising quota of unfeminine horrors abroad in the land who seem, at this moment, to jeopardize the psychic equilibrium of the country. I also know that even during the best of times women have too frequently carried a dark side to their virtues, a side where dull timidity and foolish caution were flagrantly rampant.

Just remember this, that *men,* real *men,* were never deflected from their serious aims by the obtrusion of these minor gender deficiencies. Consider that when the racket in the house got too damned loud, old man Socrates took it on the lam and aired his views in the market place.

Many good men have been helped by dames, and don't you exercise your pretty wit by saying that just as many have been *stopped* by them. That's only the easy excuse that comes to the lips of those who shrink from attributing their failures to their own deficiencies.

When the waters first began to recede from the land, and some daffy fish who'd been experimenting with air bubbles suddenly suggested that it might be a good idea to grow a couple of lungs and maybe even get onto some solid ground, I know damned well what his wife did about it. She screamed bloody murder. And you know what she said? She said, "Everybody else is satisfied, everyone is perfectly happy with

123

the temperature, and the algae; and the snails have never been running fatter or more plentiful; all the neighbors are delighted. But not him! No, he's going to go out and find us a new place to live. Oh, yes, the minute I've put up the new seaweed curtains, he wants to move. But my poor sainted mother told me, she even told me after we had our first twenty thousand children, she said, 'Don't flounder around with him, you're still young, get yourself somebody steady who'll look after your eggs instead of wasting his time staring at bubbles all day long.' That's what my mother said, and I should have listened to her. All our family has lived in this puddle ever since puddles first started, and nobody ever wanted to go any other place. But not him. No, he's going to go and die on dry land even if it's going to make widows and orphans out of the three hundred million of us. Oh, heaven give me strength to bear my miserable lot!"

That's what that little fish wife said. And how do I know? I know because her husband was the lineal ancestor of a friend of mine, and the male line has carried the story through all the millennia, straight down to him; and he tipped me off.

There are still quite a few fish wives around who are carrying on in the old tradition, and their husbands have also confided in me, and sometimes, in the damp twilight of hushed saloons, I have commiserated with them. But that original fish genius, 'way back in the swamp age, who spouted off about growing lungs and living on dry land, he *did* make it, didn't he? And damned lucky for all of us that no wide-mouthed, carping wife was able to stop *him*. But when a guy really has something on the ball, they never can.

Now, I expect somebody is ready to bring up Sappho, Emily Brontë and Mme. Curie. Please, don't bother. I am surely the last person who would deny women any amount of intellectual and creative capacities. These mysterious qualities are probably potential in all genders, in an equal degree of unlikelihood.

I only think that women are inclined to scatter their greatest gifts on filigrees of graciousness which are destined to perish unnoticed in the glutted appetites of dull men. Too many lovely women expend their poetry trying to live it, and they pass their years full of high expectations in a world which rarely ever lives up to its promises. Because some women, almost at birth, know all they want to know, they learn very little from sad experience, and, far too often for my comfort, I have seen these ladies weaving heroic laurels for the brows of torpid, preoccupied troglodytes.

Goethe, who was a good kid when he *had* it, said:

*Ehret die Frauen sie flechten und weben*
*Himmlische Rosen ins irdische Leben.*

124

Honor all women, they weave and they plait
Heavenly roses in man's earthly fate.

I hope you have gathered from this chivalrous exordium that all my four marriages were happy ones. That three of them quietly dissolved only proves my point that it is indecent to go on living with a woman in whom one is no longer passionately interested.

I've told you before that I don't believe this life of mine is only a curtain raiser for a much finer production, one that is scheduled for an infinite run later on. So, you see, with my limited little existence I couldn't, just for old time's sake, continue in any marriage which had ceased to be meaningful and vital. Because two people have been lugging the same cart for years together and are now afflicted with similar harness sores doesn't seem a sufficiently compelling reason for them to go on pulling their burden indefinitely, particularly if they've had intimations that their load was slowly turning into garbage. That sort of arrangement is hardly compatible with a rich and significant life. Remember my picture, "The Old Folks at Home"? Well, I was twenty-three when I painted it, and my reaction to such embalmed sentimentality hasn't changed one bit.

I believe quite sincerely that it is possible for a man and a woman to grow old together in grace and affection, and I certainly think monogamy ought to be given a fair chance by everybody. It is surely the ideal arrangement for an artist, since he never has leisure enough to play the *flâneur*. To keep chasing after women all the time, to be constantly romantic on that adolescent level, is a career in itself. No, to be artistic with such pathological overtones is the prerogative of people with secure incomes who live in studio apartments and who, above all else, have no important, absorbing work to do.

I was never married less than five years to anybody, which proves that there was nothing trivial or temporary about my love affairs. Indeed, my first marriage lasted almost twenty years, and during those two decades I had only two brief extramarital involvements; and on my next three wives I never cheated at all, and I didn't find it a bit difficult to stay straight, because I always lived only with such women as I happened to prefer to all others at the time.

By the way, I might as well bring out that one of those extramarital excursions was not such a complete breach of virtue, after all; it was more like a down payment on a lay-away plan, since I legally married this doll after Nettie and I had parted.

And now it suddenly comes to me that I did pull a fast one on my second wife, Annis, too, and since it is not my inten-

125

tion to whitewash myself in these pages, I freely confess to this additional peccadillo. It happened after eight years of contented married life, and I am pleased to report that the charming young woman who beguiled me into this parenthetical experiment in adultery became, shortly afterward, my next cherished connubial partner.

So, you see, there is a very consistent pattern of almost conventional decorum to these seeming trespasses, and you can understand that in sexual matters, at least, I consider myself an eminently respectable and moral man.

## CHAPTER FIFTEEN

HAVE YOU EVER read anything by Grace Livingston Hill? I've just heard about her for the first time, although her career is one of the great American phenomena, largely contemporary with my own life.

She was, as you probably know, a lady novelist who wrote, altogether, 117 books, besides heaven only knows how many articles and short stories, and her major works alone have sold well over three million copies.

Now, then, where in hell was I while all those things were going on? I thought I'd read some pretty esoteric fiction in my day. I've been through Leonard Merrick, Gilbert Cannan, Karl May, Eugene Sue, Caradoc Evans, and even Mrs. E.D.E.N. Southworth, but this Niagara of ink never once splattered in my direction until three weeks ago.

I happened to come across her biography, very competently written by a man called Jean Carr, who not only admires her literary output but quite rightfully extols her as a daughter, a wife, a mother, a lecturer, a church worker, a niece, and a little friend of all the world. Get this thing straight, she wrote 117 books in one life span, which averages three a year, and, by the record, she must have written most of them in her spare time.

But let me tell you about her. It will not surprise you to learn that she was born the daughter of a clergyman, since that seems to be a favorite opening gambit with a lot of prospective authors. When I started reading this biography the Brontës instantly came to my mind, and they have been hovering on the edge of my awareness ever since, because, I suppose, they were so completely and elaborately unlike her.

Anyway, Grace Livingston Hill grew up to be a healthy

126

normal novelist and published her first book at the age of twenty-two. I just got through reading that one, also, and it tells the story of a bachelor's-button who regales a bunch of delighted and astonished field flowers with his past adventures on a Chautauqua circuit.

At this point I couldn't help wondering what effect it would have had on her if she too, like the Brontës, had had an acute alcoholic for a brother, and how it would have influenced her work if every once in a while she had stumbled across him in the upstairs hallways with his head nestling in the family spittoon. But at the time when I pursued this idle daydream, I was a mere fanciful child. I have since read eight of her major works, and I am certain that her creative efforts would have remained quite unaltered if her father and her mother had run nightly marihuana sessions in the parsonage; and I am convinced that the pure stream of her art could not have been polluted or diverted from bringing its message of hope and cheer to the panting little flowers, even if all the fecundating bumblebees in the whole damned world had turned into drunkards and dope addicts.

A great woman! From time to time her staggering output even baffles her biographer, but I must say that at one point I find him a little smug and even obtuse. It is when he comes to remark on the uniqueness of Mrs. Hill's gifts and tells us that several unscrupulous authors who attempted to imitate her invariably failed. The discerning public instantly spotted the imposture and would have no part of it, he says.

Why? asks Mr. Carr. What was her secret? He thinks we shall never know.

But Mr. Carr is wrong. He is wrong, because *you* and *I* know, don't we? Because you and I know the *formula*! Yes, we *do*! And the formula is: Mrs. Grace Livingston Hill wrote the sort of story the *reader* would have written, if the reader had known *how*!

But that's not the whole of her secret. No, not altogether.

In another of her novels, a young girl steps up to the altar as a substitute bride because the original marriage candidate has, at the last minute, taken a powder in company with another man. So, you see, Mrs. Hill didn't only write books about garrulous bachelor's-buttons, or squander all her gifts on a lot of anthropomorphized weeds; if it came to a showdown she was prepared to tackle the complexites of real life in their most confused aspects.

Now, you just listen to what her biographer has to say about this yarn of the pinch-hitting bride.

"The story of her romance, beginning at the altar," he says, "was woven around the events of the decade of the 1830s. It has all the quaintness of the old stagecoach days, of a chivalrous society, and of a growing country in the making, highlighting at the climax the invention of the steam railroad."

*There* you have it! The charm of the *stagecoach,* with the force of the *steam engine.*

And there you also have the final fraction of Grace Livingston Hill's wonderful secret. Such a combination couldn't possibly fail at anything, and by these standards the poor Brontës were just a lot of hopeless pfooshers and I think they're damned lucky to have made the Modern Library.

Just think of Emily writing *Wuthering Heights* and dying off before even the reviews were in. One book, one single book, and basta! What an awkward, inefficient performance. Neither stagecoach nor steam engine, she failed to give her novel either charm or locomotive momentum. And what did she do with her whole brood of unwholesome characters? She marooned them all on such hopeless outposts of disaster that they finally had to be abandoned beyond any possible chance of rescue by a happy ending. Her only book, too.

Depressing!

You know, I have also decided it definitely helps an author if she's a mother and a housewife, because it makes her instinctively aware of usable leftovers. A woman who has to look after a family knows how to cleverly eke out several sustaining meals from the residue of one single pot roast. She knows better than to throw in the whole works at one delivery. You can see that the Brontës were an improvident and shiftless lot, and the great wonder is that with all their depressing tendencies anybody ever bothered to read them at all.

It goes without saying that Mrs. Hill's output was serialized in all the mass-circulation magazines, at least those that were lucky enough to secure her services, which leads me to think that right at this moment some other charming locomotive is probably doing a very similar job, and I just happen not to be aware of it. Excepting, of course, that mass-circulation magazines have lately undergone a decided change of policy; nowadays, they feature a lot less fiction and print more of the do-it-yourself type of crap.

Which reminds me of a weird thing that happened to me down in Lexington in the summer of 1951. A doctor, in the course of an interview, asked me what had been my most sustained period of suffering during my stay at the hospital.

I thought about it for a moment, and then I told him that the longest duration of acute, unrelieved agony had been a whole weekend, when, for clinical reasons, I had had to remain in a room by myself and the only reading matter available to me had been *The Saturday Evening Post.* Now, don't get this thing wrong! This was no psychological test of any sort, the magazine had been left on the bed by a kindly nurse

128

who just tried to help me pass the time; and that's how it happened that, after God knows how many years, I again had occasion to look at a *Post*. I think the last one I'd seen had a cover design by F. X. Leyendecker. That'll give you an idea.

When I told this doctor how sick I'd gotten from reading that one blasted issue, he only gave me a superior, psychiatrist's smile, because that's just about the sort of exaggerated, wiseacre remark he'd expected from a professional sophisticate like me. But he was wrong. I was in dead earnest.

To tell you the truth, it was not the contents that got me down so completely, it was the ads. Since I'm a very rapid reader, I soon brushed through the piece that told you about a woman who had been much improved by cancer; and the ghost-written article about the man who makes rhinestone-covered G strings for strip teasers; and another piece about a Texan who was elected mayor of a town after he ate twelve full-sized blueberry pies; and so by Saturday noon I had already gotten around to looking at the advertisements. Maybe it wouldn't have been such a soul-shattering ordeal for me if I had looked at them only once, but in the next day and a half I must have scanned those gruesome pages at least ten or twelve times.

It was a waking nightmare of the most sinister dimension and variety. My whole past life was insidiously evoked, ruefully demonstrated, and mercilessly indicted. It suddenly came to me that the reason my three marriages had smashed up was, simply, that they had been frivolously ratified on the wrong kind of mattresses; I realized with unshakable conviction that my social and financial calamities had been caused by my improperly sanitized apertures; and, as I went on reading, it became brutally clear that all through my life I had washed only with soap substitutes, had worn unmasculine underwear, and had never decently neutralized my offensive bodily effluvia.

For seventy-two hours I wallowed in accusations and self-reproaches, and when the nurse finally let me out of my isolation cubicle I was a psychic tatterdemalion.

I remember saying to the doctor who interviewed me that rather than have another such weekend, I would prefer to spend three days on an army cot, lashed to a belching, gonorrheal Eskimo prostitute, who had just finished eating walrus blintzes.

*He* didn't believe me, but I hope *you* do.

And yet I know, and I've had it demonstrated innumerable times, that most American magazine readers skim through the editorial contents of their periodicals with haste and impatience, but settle down in slavering relish to the slow mastication of the advertising pages.

So I can't imagine that any great numbers of these people could now possibly ' object to the imbecilities of television commercials, unless they find themselves disappointed that these deadly bludgeonings are spaced too sparsely and pass far too briefly for their thorough enjoyment.

✳

# CHAPTER SIXTEEN

TWO DAYS AFTER I finished the last chapter I was dragged off to the hospital with, of all things, a bleeding ulcer. During the last week I've had six blood transfusions and my doctor seemed quite surprised by my final recovery. I suppose when a man gets to be my age and starts helter-skelter downhill, there really isn't much brake lining left to stop him.

Just like me, though, isn't it, to bloody up the whole neighborhood with my ulcer while everbody else is quietly dying of cancer and heart disease. In my daffy way I seen to be unorganizable even on the very brink of the grave. When news of my disaster got out, my darling Margie was besieged with offers of blood on all sides, and, finally, seven good men did march off to the hospital to offer their precious life juices in my behalf. Among them was Don Freeman, the artist, and I couldn't have been more surprised than when I heard about it. I've known Don and Lydia for about twenty-five years and I've had a harmless unexceptional friendship with them during all that time. Nevertheless, if anyone had asked me offhand if Don would stand good for me for a fountain-pen refill, I honestly wouldn't have been too sure about it. And now he has utterly shamed me by giving almost a quart of blood merely because Margie stopped him in the street and told him I needed it. My profound bow to him, and I sincerely hope that he may never require the like service from me, although, God knows, I'm certainly ready to give it.

The hospital was, of course, the usual nightmare of ghastly incompetence and inhuman cruelty that is par for all such places. I find that all hospitals have certain well-established routines that are not going to be disturbed by the mere needs of its ailing patients. I've been to many such places and all of them seemed organized exclusively to bring profits to the management and comfort to its working staff. Crazy, isn't it? But I've never yet been in a hospital where the beds were not too high, the service was anywhere near functional, and the employees anything but greedy, sadistic savages. That anyone ever recovers under such circumstances is ultimate testimony that the human body is surely the most miraculous apparatus extant in the entire world.

During my sixteen days in this hellhole, the doctor came once a day to tell me that I was a very lucky guy indeed. Whether my good fortune consisted in the fact that I had a strong constitution, or that he happened to be my doctor, or that I had a beautiful and loving wife who hovered near me most of the time, the good medic never managed to make quite clear to me. It doesn't matter. I know I was close to death because I fainted a couple of times from sheer weakness, and that sort of behavior isn't my style at all. At least it never has been in the past.

I also noticed a special technique of service that happened to obtain in this hospital, and I can't make up my mind whether it was altogether accidental or not. They had an almost exclusively white staff on duty during the daytime. Males and females both. But after sundown, strange amorphous Negresses would make their appearance and pull up near one's bedside like mortally wounded sea monsters. I would also observe that these ominous creatures administered my necessary hypodermic shots through half-broken lead pencils and, by way of refreshment, would spill water liberally all over my bedclothes. I finally concluded that these dark angels of nightly disaster either cost the management less money or did a lot of dirtier work, or something, for I can't believe that these creatures of darkness were hired for symbolic reasons alone. Capitalism just isn't that sophisticated yet.

I suppose this is about as opportune a time as any for me to make clear my attitude on race prejudice. I'm sure I'm completely free from it. I want Negroes and others to get all possible rights of equality because only then will I be able to esteem them, or to loathe them, *individually,* as I do white people. But at this time I'm still compelled to stand a lot of rudeness, boredom, and nonsense from some of my darker brothers, simply because some of these specifically offensive individuals happen to belong to an abused and injured minority toward whom I have an unavoidable sense of guilt. I must personally lick up the memory of all the insults, all the humiliations and all the lynchings that their race has suffered, and so I shall never be able to treat them as true equals until all this color iniquity stops, once and for all. You understand?

It goes without saying that I hardly slept during my sixteen days' stay at the hospital and so, God knows, I had plenty of time to think about my past and to tremble about my future, if any.

And now, here I am home again, limp and damp with recuperation, prepared to set down my memories of my years on *Life* magazine. As they say, it was quite a while ago, but I recall it all as if it had happened just yesterday.

Of course I had heard about the new publishing venture about a year before the first issue of *Life* appeared. From time to time carefully placed newscrackers would explode in various columns about it, and I was particularly interested because I had once published a sort of picture magazine of my own, in 1931. It was called *Americana*.

I had never been a particularly avid reader of the other Luce publications, like *Time* for instance, because I had found its general attitude toward the world and its affairs to the last degree conservative, that is to say, uncreative. Nothing whatever has happened in the intervening years to change my mind about this. *Time* is just as wrongheaded, misinforming, and stuffy now as it was twenty-five years ago. It is still snobbish, antiprogressive, chauvinistic, arrogant and frightened to death. I'm fully aware that some very clever people have worked for *Time* and some of them have even pretended to be dancing in their chains. I also know that from time to time some members of the staff are allowed to get very sassy and to spill some prune juice on their betters. But don't let anybody fool you. These Dionysion capers are as carefully controlled as a free election in Virginia, and the people who perpetrate such iconoclasms are never allowed to pick on a really sacred cow of any rank or standing in the Republican Party, for instance. They generally pick on a foreigner, a Jew, a Negro, or somebody who is politically unimportant or on the skids anyway. Their national- and international-affairs editors have been, and are, notorious sail-trimmers and crow-eaters, and the chief appeal the magazine actually has for the readership is based on its columns of medical and news curiosities in the back of the book.

Now, then, it happened some years ago that somebody on the staff of *Time* invented a new method of captioning photographs. These captions were clever, allusive and tantalizing rather than just informative, and in due time this became one of the distinguishing features of the magazine.

So far so good. They got a lot of favorable comment on the way they handled their photo material, and so they naturally got to thinking about publishing a sheet in which pictures alone were to be the important part of the works.

It turned out to be a hell of a tough job for them. When the first dummies of the new *Life* magazine arrived at my home, I happened to be living out in Greenwood Lake somewhere with my second wife, Annis, and it goes without saying that I found my copies hideously stupid and unimaginative, and just about the sort of picture magazine the editors of *Time* and *Fortune* would manage to eke out from the giblets of their more serious ventures. It was obvious to the meanest intelligence that the editors hadn't the vaguest notion of picture values, and I was thoroughly convinced that they had a definite contempt for photography altogether. I could just see these antipictorial copy boys completely adrift in a world of nothing but photographs, and I could understand only too well that they did their damnedest to make a lot of text points that had nothing whatever to do with the picture impact.

And yet I was quite sure that a good deal of expensive help had been hired for this new venture, and in certain nooks and crannies of the magazine it was possible to discern small traces of such outside influences. But, at the basic center, one could clearly feel the dead hand of an editorial authority that took little joy in the marvelous multiform aspects of life with a lower-case *l*.

So why did these bozos bother to publish a picture magazine in the first place?

I'll tell you why. The public *did* care for pictures, that's why, and, by God and by Jesus, if there was a market for such things they were going to set about supplying it, even if it violated all their basic tastes and natural instincts.

If you guessed all this, and suspected a lot more, it was easy to understand the whole original *Life* setup. Remember, in due time I got to know all the really responsible people in person, and I can assure you that the Westchester feudalism that these owners and operators stood for had no room in its cosmogony for any of the real graces of life. Not one of the owners or originators of *Life* magazine had ever cared seriously for any of the arts or sciences, and what's more, most of them were highly suspicious of anyone who showed any strong intellectual preoccupations.

"So what?" you say. "They weren't getting out a highbrow weekly. What difference did it make?"

Well, then, let me also tell you that some twenty-odd years ago when the magazine began and I worked there, the powers that manipulated its destiny cared even less for the so-called common interests of mankind. As far as I could see, the majority of them hated jazz, loathed popular entertainment, despised all sports, and couldn't abide any form of folk jubilation or festivity unless it was a political rally of some kind.

In fact, most of these Ivy League clothes dummies had reduced their interests to the collecting of money, to interoffice finagling, to name-dropping and to petty gossip.

The few really enlightened and civilized members of the staff were allowed to write only reviews of books, of movies and the theater, and the two or three jazz enthusiasts among them were given a half-dozen columns a year in which they were free to blow off on their special frenzies. But, believe me, not one of these lads was ever allowed to cast his shadow even fleetingly across the family cash register.

After a while I discovered that most of the powers that owned and purposefully manipulated the Luce enterprises had an absolutely metaphysical relationship to money. They sincerely believed that profit derived from invested capital was not only nice to have because it permitted you to wallow in the rich broth of immediate personal security; they were also convinced that it shed a beneficent effulgence on all those who garnered it—that, indeed, it had an aura more than probably derived from the pure radiance of the Holy Ghost itself.

So there you have it. These completely square country-club goofs proceeded to publish a magazine which was to reflect the most vital visual aspects of American living. How did they do it?

Well, they hired a few people like me, people who had lived their lives fully and loved it passionately, and, by filtering our enthusiasms through some of their fine-meshed editorial sieves, managed to arrive at an amazingly marketable sediment.

In short, I'm compelled to admit that they did have a talent, a talent whose exact nature I myself never quite fathomed. I only recognized that by macerating, adulterating, and attractively packaging our varied exuberances they at last achieved a product which had demonstrably wide sales appeal.

Maybe that's what editing really is. At any rate, it wasn't easy.

It wasn't easy on me either, because the powers in charge greeted most of my suggestions, if not negatively, at least with a sort of superior reserve. I never knew whether they were disdaining me, discouraging me, or dismissing me, until, in due time, I found many of my ideas, in one form or another, used in the magazine. In the beginning I settled for a technique of editorial collaboration in which I merely submitted long lists of ideas and at the end of each week quietly collected my enormous salary.

But let me tell you how I got my job there in the first place. As I said, I was living out in Greenwood Lake when their dummy came through the mails, and I was so disgusted with it I sat right down and wrote a long letter about it. I addressed this letter to Henry R. Luce simply because his name was on top of the masthead. I certainly pulled no punches in my criticism of his new magazine, and I finally wound up with a few ideas of my own which I thought might improve some of his future issues.

"Father's Day is coming," I said. "Why doesn't somebody on your staff dig up a picture of Whistler's father? So far, the old lady has gotten all the breaks; her silly profile has even been printed on a two-cent stamp, but I'll bet my neck not a single one of your readers has ever seen a picture of the old man. And yet he was a distinguished man on his own account; his name was George Washington Whistler, and what's more, he'd helped to build the Trans-Siberian Railroad. Also, there is quite a bit of evidence that his son, Jimmy, had liked him a good deal better than his mother. He had painted her famous portrait simply because it was an interesting arrangement in graduating shades of gray, and not out of any special sense of filial piety at all. So, in heaven's name, let's have a picture of Whistler's father, for Father's Day!"

I wrote a lot of other peevish balderdash in that letter, too, because I was sure no one was ever going to read it anyway.

Two weeks later I had a letter from Henry R. Luce asking me to call on him any time I happened to be in New York. So, a few days later, I went up to the Chrysler Building, where they were located at the time. I had been busy shopping all afternoon, and when I arrived up at *Life* I must have looked something awful. I was wearing an old sweat shirt, that's for sure, and I was certainly badly in need of a shave, when Mr. Luce's secretary let me into his awe-inspiring office. (Awe-inspiring because of the vast size, the cold climate and the inhuman modern furniture.)

Since this was something of a memorable occasion, this first encounter between us, let me tell you a few things about Harry Luce. He was a sparse-haired, pale, timber-wolf kind of man, quick in his movements, and very decisive in his speech, as frequently happens with men who are afraid they might fall into a stammer. He had shaggy reddish eyebrows and cold, pale-gray eyes that hardly ever participated in his rare smiles.

I felt at once that there was a great deal of dangerous integrity in the man. I mean, the sort of integrity I generally associate with the head of the Women's Christian Temperance Union. An almost unbribable pigheadedness. It was also instantly obvious that he didn't have a shred of humor to cover any part of his almost frenzied intensity. He was as serious as an overdue mortgage, and none of my witticisms roused the slightest blink of response in him. He was quite impervious to my charm and the only thing that interested him was the fact that I seemed to have definite ideas for improving his ghastly publication.

"Religion and education are deadly dull subjects," I told him. "They're quite unphotogenic."

"How would you tackle it?" he asked.

"Hell," I said, "Yom Kippur, the Jewish Day of Atonement, is coming the end of this month. Send a good photographer down to the Home for the Jewish Aged. Offer to

135

reshingle their roof, or something, and you'll get some great photos of old Jews; and it will also give your readers an idea of what Job and Jeremiah really looked like. In fact, you could remind everybody that the Bible's original cast of characters were not blond-haired, blue-eyed Anglo-Saxons. By the way, I think you might have a little trouble getting those pictures of those old people, because really religious Jews are against getting photographed. It is the ancient taboo against making graven images; but the right man can probably talk them into it."

"Will you go and do it?" Luce asked.

"I'm not working for you," I reminded him.

"Well, do you want to come to work here?"

"All right," I said. "Suppose I try it three days a week."

"How much do you want?" he asked.

I blurted out an absolutely insane figure, expecting to settle for a lot less, but Luce never batted an eye. He just wrote it down on a little pad, got up, and shook hands with me.

"Can you start tomorrow?" he said.

"I'll come in next Monday," I said. "Yom Kippur is still sixteen days away."

"And what about Whistler's father?" he asked.

"I've got him with me. It's a good glossy print, copied out of a biography of the old boy."

"Fine," said Luce. "You can leave it with me and I'll see that it gets to the proper people."

By the way, that picture of Whistler's father didn't get into the magazine until two years later. That's the way things often worked out up there. In some ways it was more mysterious than the goings on in Hollywood or Washington, D.C., and the real wonder was that they actually managed to hit the newsstands fifty-two times a year.

Of course, everything has changed a great deal since I last worked there. I know they have quite a few hep characters employed on *Life* now, people who really know something about photographs and who appreciate picture values. But one thing is sure, their aesthetics remains just exactly as stinking as it was two decades ago. They recently did a rehash of primitive human society, and by way of illustrative material they reproduced some fabulous prehistoric paintings from the caves of Altamira. Next to these incredible masterpieces the editors had tastelessly, and I might say shamelessly and unblushingly, printed the work of some modern hack cartoonists, whose inane crap was barely fit to embellish a halfway decent comic book. That's *Life* for you. Now, you know, they've got perfectly good art editors on their staff, people who know a lot better than to perpetrate such a solecism, but these editors haven't got a damned thing to say about what gets printed and how it gets laid out. That's one thing that hasn't changed up there in twenty-three years.

Anyway, I started in working on the Monday following my interview, and for a little while I stayed on the job just three days a week. But before long I was there most of the time, almost fifteen hours a day, simply because I found it so fascinating.

It may be dull as a treadmill up there right now, but in those early days, when the magazine's policy fluctuated from week to week and a man could really feel himself effective in the shaping of its character, it was an absolute delight to be part of it all.

It stands to reason that I was constantly at odds with the upper strata of *Life* executives, managers, and editors. But that was all right, too, because I knew just exactly where everybody got off. Nearly everybody was scared stiff of his job. Scared gall-green. So, since I didn't give a damn whether I got fired or not, since I had landed there by a fluke anyway and I didn't plan to make this my life work, I had an enormous bargaining advantage in any arguments that happened to arise. There weren't many arguments really, just conflicting spheres of influence. I just stuck consistently to my role of finding lively novelties to brighten those gruesome pages in which the political claptrap, for instance, had always had a tendency to take itself too seriously. In fact, the feudal barons who owned and ran the damned sheet seemed at all times to be chiefly concerned with their historic roles as mentors and monitors to this rich, bewildered nation. I tell you, I've watched them write their idiotic editorials in an atmosphere of momentous significance and compose their silly reactionary diatribes as if destiny itself were looking over their well-tailored shoulders.

Luckily, nobody read their goddamned crap anyway. All their readers really wanted to see was a worm's-eye view of a skating queen's crotch, and people went on buying the magazine for the pure shock value of its superb photographs. And that was that.

But Harry Luce is the son of a missionary, and preaching and adult education are part and parcel of his sales equipment. It works, too, to some extent. It certainly has deeply affected his editors and so you'll find that their captions are always freely larded with admonitory and informative tidbits.

The Luce enterprises did have an entirely original editorial policy. If for instance we happened to print a war picture showing four decapitated Bulgarians, we would, captionwise, point out to our readers that the foliage in the background was composed of native eucalyptus trees, and that the soil in which the victims had bled to death was alluvial, and predisposed to grape culture.

I notice that nowadays *Holiday* magazine claims to be devoting itself to promoting "Active Leisure." On that basis, sloganwise, *Life* magazine was certainly dedicated to "Informed Stupidity."

But don't let me minimize the gifts of the men who have built such a rich and powerful publishing enterprise. For, as I have indicated, they do have many mysterious endowments. For instance, they unerringly know how to reduce the violently exceptional to acceptable human proportions and to relate seemingly indigestible inorganic materials to the tastes and appetites of their audience. They know how to do this so successfully that even a reader with a double goiter, a vestigial tail and a harelip can look at a story in their magazine and have an immediate sense that the matter presented to him is peculiarly applicable to his special bias and condition. The editors of *Life* also knew enough about their business to print in the first issue of their magazine a photo story which was entitled "How to Undress before Your Husband."

So much for the gentlemen of the ensemble; now let me tell you something about some of my really interesting clients, the ones who, for one reason or another, troubled to come to my office to suggest publishable ideas to me. They were varied, often peculiarly accented, and almost always a little afraid of me. Not of me, personally, but of what I represented. You see, I was the keeper of the gate through which they might instantly pass from obscurity to fame, to sudden wealth or at least to pleasant notoriety. At the same time, who knows? There was always the danger that I might steal their valuable ideas from them and reap the benefit of their genius or cunning, myself. It was a tough setup for all concerned. You see, I couldn't possibly tell these poor schlemiels that the last thing in the world I was looking for was an idea; that I myself was lousy with ideas and didn't have the time to carry out half of them. No. The ordinary man who has one half-baked idea in a lifetime simply can't believe that this is a common, constantly recurring event in certain other lives. He's got to cling to the belief that if only he himself had the proper connections, or knew more about the various angles of the game, he could instantly achieve some astonishing stranglehold on destiny.

This is an old native superstition among us, and I think it is stronger now than ever before. Since the television giveaway programs have raised their ante to six figures, millions of people in the country are constantly searching for a gimmick with which to open a recalcitrant Sesame. Years ago, many poor Europeans used to think that the streets of the

138

New World were paved with gold. Nowadays the Americans themselves believe it. They feel that all they actually need is a snappy notion, a slick trick, a twist of the wrist at the right moment and they're in. They can retire to Cuba, and go fishing for sharks with Ernest Hemingway.

Not all the people who came to see me were daffy in that particular direction. Some were just natural buttinskies and some others were just public-spirited and had no profit motive at all.

At any rate, I was probably the most accessible editor that has ever worked on the damned sheet and that's how I came to meet a lot of strange and interesting people during my years among the Gentiles. Because I speak five languages and am sympathetic to all other tongues, it was natural that any visitor who happened to puzzle the receptionist by an over-production of gutturals or a too florid use of unfamiliar adjectives was automatically propelled in my direction.

Remember that a typical *Life* editor spoke a sort of constipated New England Americanese and automatically patronized not only all foreign languages, but all brogues and parochial speech devices which had not originated in his own bailiwick. I understand that this is no longer true. New England no longer predominates. It seems that now, after endless editorial shifts and shake-ups, a strong, open-spaced Midwestern bray has become the official fashion.

Before I start telling you about a few of my wonderful visitors, I just want to inform you quickly about the wives of some of my fellow editors. They were indeed a special and peculiar breed, and, if I were not now laboring under an oppressive sense of urgency, I would certainly devote a whole volume to these particular ladies alone.

A few among these gals, a very few, were no better or worse than a lot of others I had seen in previous exhibits of the domestic life of *homo americanus;* but by far the larger number did have certain strange common characteristics (I think they even had a certain generic physical resemblance), which makes it possible for me to say that our native magazine writers of that particular breed and vintage had, by means of some incalculable, fantastic gift, selected the most dreadful marriage partners available in the land.

Just recall that in my own lifetime I have already known the Gibson Girl, the Johnny Held Flapper, the Petty Girl and the Togetherness Calamity; but I must say that the American magazine writer's wife, whom I encountered for the first time in 1936, was surely the most complicated female disaster of all epochs and ages.

I realize now that even as long as two decades ago she already foreshadowed and set the fashion for the monster who, in recent years, has caused so much alarmed speculation among our more alert social scientists. I am, of course, referring to the woman who manages to smother her husband and her family in the idiotic but cozy minutiae of an elaborate and circumstantial domesticity.

Officially she was known as an absolutely up-to-date mother, which simply meant that her poor kids started to be psychoanalyzed in their cradles. Also, as a graduate of some flagrantly undisciplined liberal-arts college, she was naturally entitled to misquote all ancient and modern literature, and to enliven our conversations with long, pointless campus reminiscences.

I would sometimes watch with amazement, and concern, as some seemingly sane husband allowed his garrulous housemate to monopolize the attention of his helpless guests, who, in the meantime, had no alternative but to get defensively plastered.

I want you to remember that most of these ladies could easily outsmoke and outdrink any sailor on Sand Street, and that, in their relations with mankind in general, they were known to be tougher than a cold chisel. But if the occasion arose and any one of them found herself crowded into a corner by some tactless bastard like me, she would suddenly grow breasts and tear ducts right in front of your eyes and begin to weep helpless, womanly tears, just like her dear old grandmother back home in Winnetka.

In short, she had it both ways; sometimes she was a man, and sometimes she was a woman. But at all times she was an unmitigated horror.

Now, then, most of these creatures prided themselves inordinately on their roles as creative homemakers, in proof of which they were constantly inclined to hint and to gurgle about their many esoteric cooking secrets. I discovered, in due time, that with less than a little urging they could be persuaded to give you their formula for banana-peel jam; and one of them even disclosed to me the secret recipe for her own original soy-bean crullers.

As I said, I used to stare in amazement at their seemingly torpid husbands, who would just sit quietly by while all this nonsensical jabbering cycloned around them. It seemed almost as if these married couples had been bound together by some collaborative crime that made any protest entirely unthinkable. (Maybe that's what Togetherness really means, a silent partnership in a grotesque social pretense, an elaborate collusion in some sinister emotional swindle.)

Anyway, because I was a friend of their husbands I was saddled from time to time with these semidomesticated furies, and I'm convinced that it was at their dinner tables that I first

140

started to lay the foundation of my currently bleeding ulcers.

But I will consign these domesticated dragons to the lugubrious statistics on marital decay and rather tell you something about one of the most tantalizing visitors who ever came to see me on *Life* magazine. He was called Timothy Gilligan, and, believe me, he looked and sounded exactly like that, all the five feet two inches of him. It stands to reason that he was possessed of a fine brogue, and he also happened to have one of the loveliest voices to carry it. Let me further add that Gilligan stared at the universe through a pair of transparent blue eyes which were as beautifully clear as they were guileless.

He came to my office, unannounced, at ten-thirty one morning, just as I was about to tackle my huge, untidy bundle of mail. After coughing experimentally two or three times to attract my attention, he gently unloaded his fabulous brogue on me.

"I was told you'd be a most hospitable and understanding man to consult about my little problem," he said.

I turned around and took a long look at him and wondered how recently he'd come to the States; and yet, for all I could guess, he might have been born just around the corner. New York is full of such surprises. But he had a weird, old-country air about him, and not just his accent, either. His clothes looked odd, and, without the slightest change, he could have walked on in any one of Sean O'Casey's wonderful plays. He had shaggy, Airedale-colored eyebrows, and I noticed that he carried a huge, sloppily furled umbrella.

"I'll be with you in a minute," I said. "I'd just like to look at this mail first. Sit down, why don't you?"

"I will," he said. "I'm not aiming to disturb you at all. No indeed. But a man has to get some sort of counsel when things are coming to a head and he happens to be of a divided mind himself."

He sat down in my secretary's chair with his umbrella between his shanks and let loose such a deep sigh that he positively fluttered a sheet of paper that had been abandoned in a nearby typewriter.

While I'm about it, I might as well tell you something about my secretary, who was also my researcher and unofficial assistant. She was a very intelligent and beautiful girl whose name was Mary Jane and who looked like a smaller edition of Rosalind Russell, whose sister she was. I won't deny that Mary Jane did have certain minor failings, but I was only too glad to overlook them for the pleasure of her young beauty and for the delight of her many winning ways. At any rate, she was late that morning, and that's how it happened that my visitor had managed to move in on me without any previous warning.

"My name is Gilligan," he suddenly said, to my back. "Timothy Gilligan, that is my name."

Although we were quite a distance apart, he spoke softly and casually like a man who is sure of the carrying power of his voice.

"Glad to know you," I said, over my shoulder. "I'll not be too long, Mr. Gilligan."

"Take your time," he said. "Just take your own time. It is urgent, of course, for it goes 'way, 'way back, goes back thirty years, as a matter of fact, when, in a little forgotten place in Ireland called Bethlehem, a baby boy was born on Christmas Day."

Oh my God, I thought, here I go again! I took one last reassuring look at the RCA Building across the street, pushed away my unread mail, and turned around to face Mr. Gilligan.

"A place called Bethlehem, in Ireland?" I said.

"Yes, indeed, it's not likely you'd be finding it on any map at all. I myself was born within three miles of it, so you may well believe what I'm telling you."

"Well, what about this boy that was born there? Is it about him you've come here to tell me?"

"Aye," said Gilligan, "that it is. I've been told that it's a powerful lot of information you've got locked up in that head of yours, and I'm proud and grateful to avail myself of your famous gifts."

"Just a minute, Gilligan," I said. "Before we start swapping compliments let's have that story of yours, because I'm not so sure I'm really the man you ought to see about it."

"I'm not worried one bit about that," he said. "Wasn't it you who did the beautiful story of the Holy Mass in the last issue of the magazine?"

"I arranged it and supervised it," I said. "But it's the wonderful photographs that did it all."

"Oh well, I'm glad you have a lovely job here that pays you a handsome fee, for I can see your modesty is a full match for your great talents."

"Lay off me, Mr. Gilligan," I said. "Come on, now, what happened to the boy that was born thirty years ago in Bethlehem, Ireland? Is he still alive?"

"That he is. He grew up to be a strong, bright lad, too bright for his own good, maybe, and so his mother destined him for the priesthood."

"That's a strange way to dim his brightness," I said.

"Oh, destiny was in it from the very start," said Gilligan. "When the lad was only fifteen years old he got into a bit of a brawl with another pupil at the divinity school, and by

142

a dreadful accident he did the poor chap an awful injury. Aye, the poor gossoon nearly died of it."

"A fighter, eh?" I said. "Are you his manager now, or what?"

"You've gotten to the wrong end of it too quickly," said Gilligan. "His mother was frightened of the boy's temper, and so she sent him to a brother of hers in America, to be brought up as one of the family here."

"So he's in this country now?" I said.

"That he is," said Gilligan. "He's living with his uncle in a fine frame house out near Calvary Cemetery."

"From Bethlehem to Calvary. That's a strange coincidence," I said.

"Ah, and does a man of your power of mind, in a world full of wonders, believe in coincidences?" he said.

"Has he the signs of the stigmata?" I asked.

"He has," said Gilligan softly.

"And, of course, you've got his birth certificate showing he was born in Bethlehem?"

"I can see what you think," he said. "You think I've come to make a cheap story out of it. A story to entertain the silly multitudes."

"Just a minute, Gilligan," I said. "You know this is a picture magazine, don't you? Who sent you here, anyway?"

"It was Father Carlin's servant who told me you had done the Mass. It was he who steered me into your wake."

"Did you tell his servant your story, too?"

"I did. He was busy dusting Father Carlin's desk all the while I was telling him about it, and he never stopped his dusting even for a moment. Finally, he said, 'So, it's Jesus is back, is it? Is that what you're telling me? And why should He do that, when Father Carlin is tending to His business fine? Tell me that.' I could see he was just afraid of losing his little job. And he would hold on to his miserable little post even if all the seams of the whole mortal world were about to come asunder. Strange, what some people feel and think in an extreme moment."

I myself had just had a very strange thought at that very moment, I couldn't quite make up my mind whether my visitor was John, come to *announce* something, or Judas, come to *sell* something.

"But what do you want me to do?" I said. "Do you realize that you might be about to fall into a great heresy? Did that ever occur to you?"

"The truth must be spread abroad," he said. "The time is nearly ready. I feel it in my bones. Aye, it was easier in the old days. One could walk to the shore of a lake and tell the great news to the fishermen drying their nets of an evening.

143

Aye, sitting on a boulder while they would be sorting their catch, one could drop among them the eternal words, and their hearts would be opened to the shining truths that mankind had so long been waiting for. But now, is it likely one could go down to Fulton Fish Market, where there is never a blessed moment of silence, and find in the bedlam and noise even one minute's peace to make known the greatest wonder of wonders since this world began?"

"And how could *I* help you?" I asked.

"You're a man in a position of power," he said. "Your fingers are on the pulse of a great enterprise that reaches millions of people each week. You're a man with a heart, a man with ideas, and you wouldn't be frightened to launch a great truth even if it turned the whole earth upside down!"

"Thanks," I said, "but you're just kidding yourself. We couldn't touch a story like that. It's a delicate subject. Religion always is. No matter how you treat it, it always seems to offend somebody. I'll tell you what you do. Why don't you go to the Jewish papers with your story?"

"The Jewish papers?"

"Oh, I don't suppose he speaks Jewish, but . . . By the way, what *does* he speak?"

"English, with a fine brogue on it," said Gilligan. "And what's more, he writes a neat little Hebrew hand."

"Excellent!" I said. "The Jewish papers are the best outlet for your little tale."

"You mean, getting a lot of vulgar publicity out of it, is that your advice?"

"Well, you want to notify the world of your story, don't you?"

"Publicity!" said Gilligan contemptuously. "Yes, I can see it all now. The lame, the halt, the blind . . . the Communists and the whole WPA would gather around and smother him, smother him with their greed and their clamor. And is this the best you can tell me? Is it? Ah, well." He rose slowly and leaned heavily on his umbrella.

Poor fellow, he'd expected a lot more from me.

"I'm sorry, Mr. Gilligan," I said, "but how in the world did you get mixed up in this thing in the first place? You talk like, well, like . . ."

He smiled a sad little smile, and suddenly I felt deeply sorry for him.

"I know what you mean," he said. "You really think I'm daft, don't you? But, you know, I used to be a writing man myself, once. Yes, that I was. And once I even made up a profitable little slogan, for ale, that netted me ten pounds."

"A sales slogan?" I said.

"Yes. It was for Guinness Stout. It was a little Biblical pun

144

that got me the ten pounds. It said, 'He who is not with us is a Guinness.' "

A little later when he finally left my office, he nearly collided with my secretary, who had obviously just come from a beauty parlor. I suppose Mary Jane must have noticed that I was unusually thoughtful and preoccupied for the rest of that morning and she probably concluded that my peculiar condition must have been brought about by my diminutive visitor. At last she asked me about him.

"His name is Timothy Gilligan," I told her, "and he has the finest brogue this side of the water. I'm sorry you missed it."

"What did he want from you?" asked Mary Jane. "What's his business, anyway?"

"He's sponsoring somebody," I said. "I suppose you could call him a kind of an agent."

"An agent?" she said. "Did you fill out a card for him?"

"Yes," I said. "I've put it on top of your desk."

She went over, picked up the filing card I had filled out, and read it aloud.

"Decatur 6-5947, Jesus . . . care of Gilligan."

She whistled softly through her teeth. "Well," she said, "he's certainly got himself *some* client!"

During this period when I was trying to jazz up education and religion, I ran into some trouble with another strange little man. I had read about this one in a mimeographed parish paper that was gotten out in some obscure province 'way up in Canada. There was an item about a nineteen-year-old boy who'd just gotten baptized; what made this piece of news of special interest to me was that this young man, called René Braton, was reported to be only twenty-one inches tall.

Now, you just take a look at twenty-one inches on a ruler or a tape measure and then you'll have an idea how phony this whole thing really sounded. Still, it was certainly worth a try. I don't recall the name of the town where this all took place, but I do remember that the only telephone in the vicinity was thirty miles away. Also, it was some time in December when this piece of news first trickled through to me and the roads all around the critical locality were snowbound.

You can't imagine the agonies I suffered during the next couple of weeks until I finally got word from the priest, a Father Marquette, who had performed the baptism. Yes, René was twenty-one inches tall and perfectly formed in all respects. He came from a normal family and was, for his age, well educated and very well spoken.

Marvelous!

If you open up *Life* magazine and spread it out flat, it measures exactly twenty-two inches from trim to trim. That meant we'd be able to print a full-sized picture of a man in our center spread, and even have half an inch left on each end for captions.

How about that? It certainly paid to read the religious publications carefully.

I started mobilizing all my forces at once. I wrote the good padre a long letter in which I more than hinted that several tangible advantages would inevitably accrue to his parish if we could get to print a picture of René in our world-famous publication. I asked him if his church required storm windows, or a paint job, and begged him to tell me freely if his roof needed to be reshingled. That shingling offer was a standard gambit of mine that few rabbis, ministers, or priests were able to resist. I sent off my letter special delivery and anxiously awaited the return mail.

I didn't hear another word out of Canada for the next six weeks, during which time I naturally wrote twelve more letters.

Not a peep out of anybody.

Finally, when I'd practically forgotten the whole thing, a five-line note landed on me, in which Father Marquette informed me that René Braton was planning to come to New York sometime in April. René was expecting to stay only three days, and could I please arrange something about his transportation.

April was another six weeks away, but I realized those slow-moving Canucks had me completely bulldozed. By the way, there was not one word in the letter about painting the walls or reshingling the roof of the church, so I figured these characters were playing it straight; and perhaps, for all I knew, they just didn't give a damn about a lot of publicity. I'd heard about such people, too.

Well, anyway, I kept in touch. I promptly sent off plenty of travel money and advised René to phone me the minute he hit New York.

And now comes the crazy part of it. You see, one day René really did show up in my office in Rockefeller Plaza. I can tell you he caused quite a sensation, because he was surely the smallest human thing alive at the time, and I was absolutely jubilant as I lifted him up on my desk and prepared to measure him.

And then came disaster. He was *twenty-two* inches tall. My whole idea was out the window. The whole damned magazine was only twenty-two inches wide, and if I bled off his picture at each end there was always the danger that a faulty trim would either cut off his feet or half decapitate him. And, besides, where the hell was I going to put the caption?

I was so rattled that I'm afraid I was a little offhand with René, who seemed deeply touched by my disappointment.

"I was twenty-one inches tall at the baptism," he said, "because Father Marquette measured me that very morning. I suppose I've grown the additional inch since December from all the good things I ate from the money you sent me."

"All right, René," I said. "I'll try to figure out something. Meanwhile I'll have somebody take you over to the hotel. I've got a room reserved for you."

"If you don't mind," said René, "I'd first like to see a movie. It's called *Gunga Din* and it's playing at Radio City Music Hall."

"Well, you can't go alone," I said. "You'll be trampled to death. I'll have one of the boys go along with you and I'll phone you at the hotel later on."

"There is a boarding house in Brooklyn," said René, "that caters especially to small people, and I think I'd rather stay there, if you don't mind. The man's name is Blystone and he's sort of expecting me, too. I wrote him from home."

"Okay," I said. "You go to the movies and meanwhile I'll get in touch with Blystone and he can pick you up here later in the afternoon."

And that's how we did it. After a while, Blystone appeared in my office and, what's more, he brought along two of his miniature boarders, a couple of parchment-faced midgets from Austria, who were simply delighted when they learned that I also originally came from Vienna. These little men weren't anywhere near as tiny as René, and they certainly had none of his touching childlike vivacity. As for Blystone, he was simply a German, a former animal trainer with colorless eyes, bristly hair, and a thick Teutonic neck and accent. Anyway, I was so full of my disappointment about René's extra inch that I couldn't keep my trap shut about it to Blystone and his friends.

"It happens all the time," said one of the midgets. "I myself grew two inches in the last three years. There's something altogether wrong with this whole damned country."

I realized again that one's entire attitude toward the world depends mostly on the tiny horizon of one's own self-interest. This midget wanted to stay small because that's how he earned his living. Any form of growth represented bankruptcy and disaster to him. He thought we all drank too damn much milk and orange juice and spent entirely too much time out in the open air. Bad for midgets. As I watched these two fascinating little men, I noted that they wore bracelets, wrist watches, rings and even stickpins, and that their persons were loaded down with seemingly endless buckles, buttons, belts and doodads, as if they were desperately anxious to make use of all these punctuational tidbits just to circumstantiate their diminutive presence.

Anyway, in due time René returned from the movies, and, after a lot of cross introductions, some squeaky social palaver and some grim amiability on my part, Blystone finally removed himself and his clients from my office.

I was completely shattered.

The following day, the solution came of itself, unbidden and unanticipated, in the morning mail. In short, I had a letter from Father Marquette, enclosing a photograph, and its negative, which the good father had himself taken and developed on the very day of the baptism, at which time René had actually been only twenty-one inches tall.

No one will ever know why he hadn't sent me that precious artifact four months earlier and spared me a lot of needless waiting and agony.

By dumb good luck I had suddenly found a simple, logical way out of it all. We were just going to publish a belated news item, with an up-to-date illustration, about an unusual baptism in Canada, and, what's more, the unassailable truth of our story was attested by a man of the cloth. He *was* twenty-one inches the day he was baptized, wasn't he?

So it came to pass that the next issue of *Life* magazine contained the life-size picture of a living man.

A week later I got a raise in salary, and George Hamid, the famous carnival tycoon, signed up René Braton for a featured spot on his million-dollar entertainment pier out in Atlantic City. As far as I've been able to find out, I don't think René ever did go back to Canada, at all.

One thing is sure, though. Father Marquette's church was completely reshingled. I talked him into it.

A little later on, when I dropped religion and education, I devoted myself for a time to a department called "Speaking of Pictures"; that is to say, I had two and a half pages at the very beginning of each issue that offered one of the very few possible areas for humor in the whole magazine. But humor rarely happens of itself; at least, it hardly ever happens in photographs. So I began a series of elaborate schemes and devices that seemed to give promise of at least a mildly amusing photographic payoff.

Once, with the connivance of one of the guards at the zoo, I managed to sneak half a dozen cheap German cameras into the chimpanzee cage. The reaction of the monkeys was easily predictable; they examined the machines curiously for a while, and then they absent-mindedly started to chew on them. But, as I had hoped, in the process of manipulation a couple of the chimps happened, by sheer accident, to click the camera shutters so fortuitously that they got a few really good, printable snapshots of the spectators on the outside of the cage.

"This is what you look like to the monkey in the zoo!" was the name of that story. I knew it was no world-shaking idea, but it definitely set a pace that gave people some notion of our expectations for further contributions to this department. The baby who was constantly being photographed sitting on a chamber pot just wouldn't do any more, not even if he'd happened to turn the pot upside down on his head.

It was also during this period of my life that Morton Ploshkin floated into my orbit. He showed up in my office one Saturday afternoon, just when I was about to call it quits for the day. He, too, was very small, about five feet one or two, and about as big-nosed, hairy, and repulsive a young man as I've ever laid eyes on. He looked like some frightening illustration out of an old medical textbook, an illustration for virulent acne or galloping adenoids, for instance.

"I'm sorry," I said, "but I'm quitting for the day. Why don't you come back next Monday?"

"Because I'd like to use this weekend constructively," he said, "My name is Morton Ploshkin and what's more I have a brother, Gorton, who is my identical twin."

"No!" I said.

I didn't mean that I doubted his words, I simply couldn't bear to think that such a nose, such eyes, such a complexion and such a head, altogether, had a possible duplicate anywhere in that part of the world where I was likely to run into it.

"Yes!" said Morton. "My brother Gorton is waiting out in the hall for me, right now. We're going to have a big plastic surgery job done, both of us, and we thought you might be interested to photograph us before, during, and after. It might be interesting for your readers to see if we still resemble each other after our noses have been trimmed."

"What will it cost?" I asked.

"Six hundred dollars."

"Nonsense!" I said. "Your surgeon will get a lot of free publicity, so you won't have to pay him a dime. And, since you're getting the operation for nothing, where's the six hundred dollars come in?"

"Convalescence, hospitalization, bandages, wear and tear . . ." said Morton, as his voice trailed off.

"I'll give you a hundred dollars, just for the hell of it," I said. "But don't give any of it to the doctor. He'll take it out in free advertising. Okay?"

"Okay," said Morton. And we shook hands on it.

This operation actually did take place that weekend, but the pictures turned out so bloody and gruesome (all face operations, no matter how harmless or slight, are something awful to look at) that we were never able to print the story. Not wholesome enough. But, to keep in line with our promise to the doctor, we had to briefly mention the basic essentials of the case and to print two stamp-sized pictures of Morton and Gorton, before and after their blood bath.

You see, not everything I tried turned out successful or usable. I had plenty of headaches on that goddamned job.

I'll tell you a lot more about it a little later on. I'm particularly anxious to recall one of our very serious editorial meetings, and I must certainly give you a detailed report about my various collaborations with Clare Boothe Luce, my boss's wife.

It shall all be done in good time.

## CHAPTER SEVENTEEN

WHEN I BECAME eight years old, my Uncle Leopold, who owned a bookshop in Saxony, sent me a batch of books for my birthday, and among them were two enormous illustrated volumes called *Mann und Weib,* Man and Woman. This work, comprising several thousand pages, was a typical German compendium, delineating the physical, psychological, sociological, anthropological, historical, cultural and political history of man and woman, beginning with protoplasm and winding up with Bismarck. The text was a little beyond me at the time, but I just loved the pictures, the majority of them reproductions of famous paintings, which I clipped out at once to paste in my special scrap book. What made my scrapbook special was that it contained the most famous nudes in all of ancient and modern art. As a matter of fact, I belonged, at the time, to a little informal society of boys who met exclusively for the purpose of swapping their duplicate pictures.

So, with the arrival of *Mann und Weib,* I became, overnight, the wolf of Schoenbrunn—that is to say, of the park where we used to forgather. I achieved at one stroke a corner on all the most desirable nudes extant.

But all this is really beside the point. I particularly wanted to talk to you about the *text* in *Mann und Weib.* Since the pictures I had clipped out were mostly full-page illustrations with no printed matter on the back, the text had remained undamaged, and when my family migrated to the States those two volumes came along with us. In the ensuing years I dipped

150

into them quite often, and I assure you that if anyone wants to get hep to the true nature of the German mystique, they simply have to read *Mann und Weib*. *Mein Kampf* is much too personal, too paranoid and megalomanic, to render the peculiar timbre, the all-pervading aura, the proper critical wave length of *homo teutonicus* disporting himself in his prehistoric tar pits.

Now, all these articles in *Mann und Weib*, although written by many experts from various fields of special research, were activated by only one ideological circulatory system, which pumped the blood of their bias through the whole calcified body of this circumstantial work.

All those *Professoren* and *Privatdozenten* who had contributed to this opus simply stank with unscientific prejudices against any foreigners who had happened to make important contributions in their realms of endeavor. Not one of these learned Heinies was able to suppress his patronizing sneer for Frenchmen, for Englishmen, for Americans; and as far as the Italians were concerned, they managed to dismiss Marconi with a five-line footnote on wireless telegraphy. Only Deutschland seemed to have made any significant contributions to human awareness, and you could easily visualize how their boneless, saber-scarred faces must have puckered into contemptuous pustules as they squinted at Asia, Africa, and the Near East.

So, what about these arrogant meat loaves? Just this. When I first came to the States, I was for a long time homesick for the old country. Of course, as a Viennese, my loathing for Germany was practically my inalienable birthright; but in those distant days I still had the earnest, unshakable belief that Europe was, somehow, the true home of all real culture.

I was entirely too young and too dopey to take stock of what had actually happened there. I overlooked completely that even my dear Austrians, those great music lovers, had allowed Schubert and Mozart to languish into pauperism and to sicken out of this world in their early thirties, and that those great art lovers, the French, had failed to buy a single painting from either Van Gogh or Cézanne during the forty long years those two geniuses had labored among them.

Through all of my visits abroad, I came to the bittersweet knowledge that our Columbia has one proud jewel in her diadem, whose duplicate you may seek in vain in all the other countries of this earth, and that jewel is Generosity. I've been all over, and I've been all over it with everybody, and let me tell you that from that day long ago when the first poor stonecutter had started to cough out his lungs in the quarries of Egypt, until this morning in New York, when somebody served me Crunchy-Cracklies for breakfast, there has never been a people more generous, more openhearted and more careless of its money than the overly washed, too heavily insured, insecure, lovable people of this country.

Naturally, this makes for great hatred of us among all the chronically penurious bastards in the world who squat in sham reverence amidst their noble ruins and glower enviously at our good clothes and our expensive cameras.

Just remember that there are signs posted all over the holy temples of Asia and the sacred cathedrals of Europe warning people not to pee up against their ancient walls. You know damned well that those signs weren't placed there for the benefit of visiting American tourists. We don't do such things even to the walls of *new* churches, which are sometimes so hideous that there would be plenty of excuse for doing it.

And so I lost my homesickness for Europe the very first time I went back, and I've never felt another twinge of it since. Certainly I would like to see Chartres, and Carcassonne, and Salzburg, and Venice, again, but I'm not a bit anxious to meet the petty, stingy, money-hungry leeches who, unfortunately, infest these landscapes.

If you think the above sentiments seem to contradict what I've said earlier about the more favorable artistic climate that obtains in Europe, then please let me clarify my point.

At this juncture, you are still better off in the old country if you are involved in any of the arts, because over there they don't set the artist any financial standards. They've got *that* on us, definitely. Since almost everybody is equally on the bum, the painter, or the poet, or the musician doesn't have to live up to anybody. They ignore him and his efforts, and they don't think that just because he doesn't own the latest television set or drive the slickest motorcar he is necessarily bad at what he is doing. But *we* do. We definitely measure every form of accomplishment by only one standard. Cash! And that's surely a boneheaded way to judge people, excepting, maybe, manufacturers of laxatives. If those boys aren't raking in millions, then what the hell are they doing, anyway? Just covering us all with crap? Well, this is not exactly the artist's mission in life, though too many Americans seem to think different.

When I took my family abroad for my first memorable visit, in the mid-twenties, a friend of mine, DeHirsch Margules, decided to come along with us. I have known this two-hundred-thirty-pound boychick for some forty-three years now, and during all that time we have never mislaid each other for more than six months. He has, in fact, often lived with me, and a few years ago my wife and I were his guests until he found us our present apartment, right around the corner from him in Greenwich Village.

152

It is very hard for me to do justice to DeHirsch. First of all, he was not always as mountainous as he is now, although even as a child he was a pretty substantial bundle. As a boy of fifteen he was already too rugged for most ordinary needs, and his appetite was always like a stupendous exaggeration.

Let me try to describe him for you. On top of his wide, solid frame there blooms the face of a gigantic, amiable Pekingese who has decided to grow himself a pair of virile, luxurious eyebrows. His mouth is permanently set in a generous pucker; his eyes are dark, penetrating, somber, and full of incipient laughter; and his strong chin is deeply cleft by an anomalous, girlish dimple. He still has lots of dark, curly hair, which now, alas, is turning gray.

I think the outstanding characteristics of my friend's personality are affirmation, emphasis, and overemphasis. He chooses to express himself predominantly in superlatives, and the gestures which accompany his utterances are sometimes dangerous to life and limb. Of the bystanders, I mean.

And this is about as adequate a description of DeHirsch as if I told you that the Jungfrau is a tall mountain that has snow on top. How can I convey to you my friend's alarming ebullience, his faunlike high spirits, his overly resonant speaking and singing voice, his decent angers, and his truly overpowering coyness? How can I ever do justice to his capacity for aggressive sleep and his facile gift for dozing off in the most unsuitable places on the most unlikely occasions?

DeHirsch is quite a good cook, and if he should ever invite you to dinner he may serve you a hamburger with onions, in his kitchen-living room, with such an air of gastronomic protocol, such mysterious hints and ogling innuendoes, as if César Ritz and Brillat-Savarin had sneaked out, only a moment before, with his secret recipe in their pockets. If there is wine, it will be served at room temperature, and even if it is the crappiest bottle of California disaster, DeHirsch has some decisive, cogent reasons for having selected that particular vintage of half-fermented dribble.

Before I forget, let me tell you that DeHirsch is a very gifted painter. I think he is one of the truly talented watercolorists in the country, and, I'm pleased to say, his work is owned by several distinguished museums and has also been purchased by some of the most discerning private collectors. This two-hundred-thirty-pound behemoth can, when the occasion arises, spread his washes with such acute regard for the most subtle nuances of color that one would swear that these results had been obtained by some bird-boned, half-translucent Chinese in Szechwan province.

If I meant to deal exhaustively with DeHirsch's origins, his beginnings, and his becomings, I could easily cover five hundred pages telling you only about his adolescence in New York, when he had been apprenticed to, of all things, the cloak-and-suit business. Just imagine him as a young man, trundling those awkward, unpredictable dress carts through Eighth-Avenue traffic. Imagine him, a little later, as a leg man for the moribund City News Association, covering the Bowery, Chinatown, Bellevue Hospital and the morgue; observe him in his spare time in a leprous, latrinelike room, playing poker with his soiled colleagues, and playing to such good purpose that he eventually wins enough money from them to pay for his transatlantic trip abroad with us.

I hope that from this last glimpse of DeHirsch as a leather-faced card player, you have gathered still another dimension of his character—namely, his astonishingly high survival potential.

Just by way of illustration I will present two facets of his character as they happened to manifest themselves during the long years of our curious communion.

Shortly after we landed in Paris on this our first visit to the old country, we happened to run into George Antheil, the American composer, who at that time was also on Donald Friede's dependency list. Because Antheil had, all his life long, been on a chronic North Africa kick, he emphatically advised us to get out of a lousy tourist trap like Paris and to go at once to Tunis, where life was still colorful, mysterious and cheap.

He also pointed out to us that the American Legion was about to descend on Paris for one of its yearly get-togethers, and I must say that the prospect of all those practical jokers footloose in France, without their wives, finally decided us to get out of it all and seek peace and refuge among the heathen. DeHirsch, of course, was coming along with us. Antheil, who had to stay in Paris for business reasons for a while, promised to shake his obligations in short order and assured us that he and his wife Böschke were definitely going to join us in Tunis within a month. It was George, also, who strongly advised us to avoid the French hotels in Africa.

"Get the real feel of the place right off," he said. "You can't do that by staying in those phony posh places; besides, it will cost you a fortune and only separate you from the real life of the people."

I must say I was suddenly quite enchanted by the whole idea of the trip. It came to me as a pleasant shock what a romantic voyage we were about to undertake, sailing off on the blue Mediterranean, the classic *mare nostrum*, where the triremes of Rome and Phoenicia had crossed before us. I was

154

simply delighted by the feeling that I was about to sink ass-deep into the beguiling tides of ancient history.

I loved Africa long before I ever laid eyes on it, when we were still far out at sea and the odor of Tunis, a mixture of jasmine, charcoal and camel dung, floated out to us on the morning breeze. I was particularly thrilled to be visiting fabulous Carthage, because, long ago, I had read and loved *Salammbo*, and it was my secret hope that some day I would have the privilege of illustrating a new edition of Flaubert's masterpiece.

I eventually did do the book, for George Macy, but in time it became such a costly collector's item that I didn't own or see a copy of it for many years. Only recently, however, Sam and Bella Spewack made us a present of the book, which had been originally given to them by Jean Arthur.

It stands to reason, that on our arrival in Tunis we followed George Antheil's advice without the slightest misgivings. First of all, we moved at once into an Arab hotel, which was called Ramona but which otherwise certainly proved to be a real down-to-earth native article. This caravanserai was a sprawling pink ruin with enormous vaultlike rooms, and if you accidentally happened to lean against any of its porous walls a lot of loose mortar would at once crumble right down your neck and into your ears; also, if you happened to pull a doorknob with any sort of normal vigor, the chances were that this cracked glass fitting would cut a bloody memento into your hand.

But it was the toilet arrangements at the Ramona that I found most astonishing of all. It seems that in this choice hostelry they had nothing but indoor outhouses, which did have special entrances for the different genders; but, once inside this cubicle, men and women would find that there was not even the shred of a dividing wall between them, and that the management simply expected them to squat down back to back, over separate holes in the ground. In due time I couldn't help but notice that no matter how flagrantly they happened to expose themselves, the modest Arab ladies would frantically clutch at the concealing shawls that covered their faces. The face was obviously taboo, and their caution was far from superfluous, since none of the doors to these ramshackle shelters could ever be properly fastened. In fact, it was unavoidable that any passing stranger should hear, if not observe, the varying states of intestinal travail that agitated the different guests in their condition of semiretirement.

On my particular floor, as a possible concession to our pampered tourist status, they seemed to have added a special feature to the toilet facilities; a bearded nonagenarian, called Machmoud, was permanently in attendance and always oc-

155

cupied a neutral corner *inside* the toilet enclosure. I can only tell you that, unless you were extremely alert and knew how to anticipate him with deftness and decision, Machmoud would assist your final ablutions by swishing a ratty, long-haired brush quickly across your naked bottom—a brush which he had first carefully immersed in an ice-cold, powerfully corrosive antiseptic. Let me tell you that the first time this happened to me I actually hit the ceiling with the sheer shock and horror of it.

So, you see, it was really Africa with all its color and mystery. Nothing was lacking in this picture except a sudden incalculable illness, and I got that at four in the afternoon on the very first day we landed.

Right after we got off the boat and had registered at the Ramona, we all went for a long, crazy walk through the native markets. The sun didn't really hit us too often because the *souks* of Tunis are mostly sheltered, overhead, by carpets and latticework, but I suppose a couple of times during the afternoon, several billion tons of sunlight must have managed to land on me just the same, because I suddenly got dizzy and started to yoik up some of the native delicacies that I had most injudiciously imbibed, on the way.

Luckily, a kindly Frenchman who was passing in a carriage and saw me painfully spraying the neighborhood stopped and offered us his help. He took the lot of us back to the hotel at once and promised to send up a doctor. (By the way, this Frenchman became a good friend of ours later on, and eventually he told us that most of his Arab friends considered the Ramona a pretty swanky enterprise.)

Back in our rooms, Nettie at once put me to bed and got the kids quietly occupied with some toys in an adjoining alcove. Meanwhile, DeHirsch piled all the available blankets on top of me, because I was having the shakes so badly that my teeth were chattering like castanets.

It took a hell of a long time before the doctor arrived, because it was the *apéritif* hour. When he finally did show up, he looked a lot like Charles Laughton in an old film about the Belgian Congo. Although Tunis was a French protectorate, this doctor turned out to be a fat, florid Englishman, with a huge wet mustache and a cracked, terribly soiled topee.

This blimp never did enter our rooms completely, he just hovered in the doorway and looked suspiciously around, as if he were in mortal terror of catching something from us. In fact, he was about eight feet away from my bed when he said, "Will you stick out your tongue?"

I did. He stared at it for a few seconds and gave a big sigh.

"Nawsty! Very nawsty!" he said. But he still showed not the slightest intention of budging out of the doorway.

"Do you know what's wrong with him?" Nettie asked.

"Any number of things in this blawsted climate. I'll leave a prescription at the Ferrière pharmacy and they'll send up some tablets for him." At this point he gave a great big yawn. "You owe me one guinea," he said.

Nettie gave him five dollars and a quarter, and the conscienceless son-of-a-bitch waddled off.

No matter how you looked at it, it was certainly a serious moment in our lives. Here I was, down with God only knows what kind of deadly malady, a million miles away from home, with a wife and two small kids, living in this hideous Dracula layout, and we were obviously surrounded by a lot of heartless swine, if the doctor was any example of the local population.

But little Nettie always shone in a crisis. She at once commandeered Machmoud from his post in the privy and sent him to fetch a bucket of ice; she made DeHirsch move my bed into the shadiest corner of the room; and she proceeded to busy herself purposefully with all the things that had to be done for my comfort.

After I was settled in the twilight of a windowless corner and was just beginning to study the pattern on a spectacularly mildewed wall across the room from me, DeHirsch gingerly sat down on the edge of my bed. I could see that he was deeply moved. He took my burning hand into his two perspiring ones, swallowed a couple of times, and said, "We're certainly in a very tough spot, aren't we, kid? If you should happen to die here, it would cost us a fortune to get you back to the States. I know that the transportation of a stiff by boat or train costs a hell of a lot more than just a ticket for a live person. You know that, don't you?"

It must have been due to my lightheadedness, caused by the fever, but I must say his lugubrious chatter didn't strike me as terribly out of line. After all, he was our closest friend and full of deep concern for my family's welfare. In my condition it even made some kind of sense.

"I'll tell you what," he continued. "I've got an idea. See what you think of it. If you should happen to kick off here, God forbid, why don't I just quietly incinerate you out on the beach, and then, without anybody being the wiser, we can take your ashes back to the States in a small suitcase, or a satchel."

I was prevented from giving DeHirsch an opinion on this ingenious suggestion because Nettie just happened to overhear the last part of it, and, as she was carrying a portable typewriter at the time, she ended our conversation by dropping it down on his noggin.

All this happened thirty years ago, and I just recently remembered and told this story to someone who dropped in on us one evening, while DeHirsch was also present. As I unfolded my little yarn, DeHirsch kept nodding approvingly in my direction, because he's a great stickler for accuracy in stories that concern our common past.

When I finally finished, my guest looked quizzically at DeHirsch and said, "Well, luckily Alex recovered, and you didn't have to bring him back in a paper valise."

"That's not the point," said DeHirsch. "I want you to realize that I was just a young punk in those days, but in an emergency I always did have my wits about me. Always!"

That will give you a rough idea of one aspect of his character. Here's another:

Some forty-two years ago when we went to grade school together, we were already close friends. DeHirsch and I and another boy called Henry Lilling formed an inseparable triumvirate. Although the three of us attended different classes, we spent all our free time, the late afternoons and all of our weekends, in each other's company.

In my youth such close associations were quite common among adolescents; but in those days it didn't necessarily portend juvenile delinquency, or that the three of us were preparing ourselves to be pansies.

At any rate, after grammar school Henry and I went on to high school together, while DeHirsch, whose theatrical family was scattered all over the land and was not prepared to make any further provisions for him, had to go to work. And so, quite suddenly, we altogether lost track of him.

I must candidly admit that Henry and I were so greatly preoccupied with all the new doings at De Witt Clinton High School that we soon forgot poor DeHirsch as completely as if we'd been just a couple of successful, heartless grownups. It happens sometimes.

About half a year went by this way when, one day after our favorite biology class, in which we were the responsible monitors, Henry and I accidentally dropped a microscope.

We were absolutely horrified.

You see, our biology teacher, Mr. Landis, not only was our favorite teacher, but the two of us simply idolized the man. I remember that we even used to imitate his way of speaking and of walking, and I'm quite sure we had both of us privately resolved to pattern our whole future existence on the example of this paragon.

So you can understand that the dropping of the microscope was not just a casual accident to us, particularly because, by a quite natural exchange of sympathy we, in turn, had become the two class favorites of Mr. Landis.

158

What could we possibly do? What in the world were we going to do?

"We've got to get it fixed up without telling anyone about it," I said.

"How?" said Henry. "It might cost a lot of money. How're we going to pay for it?"

"We'll have to find an optical-goods store and see what the damage is," I said. "We'll have to do it this very afternoon."

"I passed a store like that on Forty-eighth Street the other day," said Henry. "It's between Fifth and Sixth Avenue, and they had a lot of microscopes and reading glasses in the window. Let's try there."

And that's what we did. We carried the damaged instrument down to this shop on Forty-eighth Street, and the man who listened to our story turned out to be a really sympathetic and nice guy.

"Luckily it isn't an expensive instrument," he said, "and the damage isn't too bad. Seeing that you're in such a jam, I won't charge for the labor, I'll just charge you for the glass."

"How much is that?" I asked.

"Five dollars," he said.

"Five dollars!" I repeated. "Where in the world are we going to get five dollars?"

"It can't be done for less. Go home and empty your piggy banks," the man said. "Or, better still, tell your teacher what happened. After all, you didn't do it on purpose. I'm sure he'll be very decent about it."

But, even without consulting Henry, I realized that it was out of the question; that we couldn't possibly confront our idol with this terrible evidence of our clumsiness.

So, after we left the store, we walked silently and aimlessly about the hostile streets, unable to nerve ourselves even to go home. We took turns carrying the injured microscope and I can tell you that each of us sheltered the wounded apparatus under his coat as if it had been a living thing in mortal agony.

Where, in God's name, were we going to get five dollars? Five dollars was a lot of money. And let me tell you, it really was a hell of a lot of money back in 1915.

"You know what?" Henry suddenly said. "Maybe De-Hirsch has five dollars! He's working. He's been working about six months now. I bet you he's got five dollars and what's more he'll give them to us."

It was a marvelous idea! It was a stupendous idea! It was the idea of ideas! DeHirsch was a wage earner and he was our friend. Our closest friend. A great wave of affection for our old comrade suddenly welled up in us.

"He works down at 200 Fifth Avenue," I said. "That's

down near Twenty-third Street, and if we get a move on we can talk to him about it this very afternoon."

New life, new energy, new hope had suddenly come to us. We practically ran the whole distance down to Twenty-third Street; and, as we ran, we had not the slightest misgivings about DeHirsch's reception of us. We had no fear at all that he would resent our neglect of him; we knew for a certainty that if he had five dollars he would give them to us without qualms or reproaches.

At 200 Fifth Avenue we ran into some sobering information. Since we were just a couple of dopey kids, we confided at least part of our story to the elevator starter.

"If your friend works in the Mobile Skirt place," this worldly man said to us, "you'll have to wait for him till he comes out, on the Twenty-fourth Street side."

"On the Twenty-fourth Street side?" I said. "Doesn't he come out here?"

"No. He has to use the service entrance," said the elevator starter. "And he can't have no visitors during working hours, neither. But it's nearly six o'clock now, anyway, so you won't have to wait more than twenty minutes for him. Just go around the corner and you'll see the sign, Service Entrance."

And it was there, at the grim hole of that service entrance, that all my misgivings came to me in a sudden rush.

First of all, the idea that DeHirsch wasn't good enough to be allowed to go in through the front entrance was an awful blow to me. And who knew how he would receive us, after our long, callous neglect of him? Who knew if he was even inclined to be friendly with us? It was certainly crazy to expect five dollars from him when he probably had to work, God knew how hard, for his money; and, anyway, he probably had new friends now with whom he spent his evenings and his weekends; and we certainly had no right to expect anything but a cold shoulder from him. Maybe he wouldn't even care to recognize us. What then?

Although I said nothing at all to Henry about my thoughts, I could tell by his pallor and his pinched expression that he too was suffering from bitter forebodings.

At last, a few minutes after six, DeHirsch emerged from the drafty darkness, and for a moment I wasn't even too sure it was really he. He seemed to have aged a good deal since I had last seen him, and, although he was only a year older than we, he seemed badly in need of a shave. His ill-fitting clothes, all covered with stray cotton threads, appeared unbelievably shabby and even pathetic to me.

Luckily, he caught sight of us just then, and he certainly recognized us at once. A smile like morning sunlight spread

160

across his face, and his eyes grew misty with happiness as he impulsively put his arms around us.

It was the old DeHirsch, and I had been cruelly wrong to suspect him of possible rancor or indifference. Although I was very young and hadn't as yet had much experience with human emotions, I felt, instinctively, that his joy at our encounter was not far removed from real tears, or even a mild form of hysteria. I knew so much about his feelings because I was, at least partially, affected the same way at sight of him.

At any rate, with his arms still around our shoulders, DeHirsch steered us purposefully to a nearby cafeteria.

"We'll have some coffee," he said. "After all, this is an occasion, isn't it? I haven't seen you guys for ages."

I must say I was deeply impressed by his casual air of worldliness—by the way he fetched us huge stone crocks of coffee, and particularly by his self-possessed manner, which clearly demonstrated how completely he was finished with all schools and all petty scholastic concerns. He belonged in this cafeteria and I knew that this rakish, somewhat sordid milieu had no secrets or terrors for him.

After he had further provided each of us with a glass further water and piled a plate high with huge, sugary doughnuts, he finally sat down at the table and simply beamed at us.

Forty-two years have gone by since that dreadful moment in the Biloxi Cafeteria, but I still get the authentic goose pimples when I think about it.

It was awful.

My toes still curl up inside my shoes when I remember DeHirsch's glad, unsuspicious expression, and how he never for a moment suspected that any sordid or ulterior motive might have propelled us down to his place on Twenty-third Street.

God!

Luckily, we were so artless, both Henry and I, that the whole gruesome bundle came out very suddenly and all in one piece. Let me tell you, it certainly put a damper on our festivities. I had never seen DeHirsch so glum and so thoughtful before, and I was bitterly sorry we'd ever told him about the whole mess. He was absolutely quiet for almost two whole minutes, an alarming amount of time for him, and I had to struggle like hell against the impulse to grab the crippled microscope and to run out into the goddamned street with it.

At last DeHirsch gave an enormous sigh and started talking.

"So, you've got to have five dollars?" he said. "Well, I earn five dollars a week down here, but I've got to give three-twenty of it to my aunt. The rest of the money is for carfare and lunches and so on. You see what I mean?"

"Oh, we should never have come to you," I said. "We didn't realize . . . We're just a couple of saps."

"No, no, I'm glad you came to me. Why shouldn't you?" he said. "I'm the most logical guy, ain't I?"

And, let me tell you something, there was really not the slightest trace of a reproach in him. He was simply distressed by the fact that he earned so damned little money he couldn't help us out now when we were in a jam.

"It's getting late," said Henry. "We'd better start for home before it gets real dark."

"Just a minute," said DeHirsch. "I think I've got an idea. I really don't know . . . I don't know. Still, it's an idea. . . ."

His voice trailed off, and he seemed suddenly lost in some dark conjectures of his own. For a moment or two he even seemed unaware of our presence; and whatever the thoughts that so deeply engrossed him, he had to free himself from his deep absorption with them.

"I may be able to help you out, after all," he said slowly, "but we'll have to go uptown for that, up to Ninety-sixth Street and Fifth Avenue. Come on, fellers. Let's get out of here!"

So we rode up to Ninety-sixth Street without exchanging another word. We even avoided looking at each other, simply because we were too stirred up inside for any sort of trivial palaver. I know grownups manage such things much better, but we just stood side by side in the Fifth Avenue bus and kept up our mulish silence until we arrived at our destination.

When we got off, DeHirsch told us to wait for him on a bench right inside the park entrance; then he took one more long, serious look at us and beat it.

Of course Henry and I felt terribly small and cheap, and now that DeHirsch was gone we also felt somehow frighteningly exposed and forlorn.

"I'm going to come and see him every weekend, from now on," I said. "He's the best friend anybody ever had."

"I feel awful," said Henry. "Do you think he's gone off to hock something for us? I hope not. I hope he doesn't get into any trouble on account of us."

"He hasn't anything to hock," I said. "He only gets five dollars a week. Five dollars, for a whole week, just think of it!" And because we were young and still rather tender, unsoiled packages, we felt genuinely sorry at the sadness we had brought into the life of our friend.

Meanwhile we waited, nor did we have to wait very long —only about fifteen or twenty minutes altogether—before DeHirsch's head appeared again above the park wall. I noticed that he was walking very slowly and that his face had the translucent pallor of someone who has just recovered from a severe illness. Henry and I were so frightened by his looks and by his manner that neither of us even got up as he approached our bench. So DeHirsch sat down silently between us, and I could sense that he was struggling with feelings and emotions too profound for immediate utterance.

The three of us sat that way, in absolute silence, for quite a long while.

"I've got the money for you," DeHirsch suddenly said, into the evening stillness. He stretched out his hand toward me, and in it was a five-dollar bill.

"Take it," he said. "It's quite all right."

"We'll save up and pay it back to you," I said.

"No," he said. "You don't have to. I don't have to return it either. It was given to me as a present." He got up. "You better go home now," he said, "or your folks will start worrying about you."

And that's how that particular day ended. But our lives were definitely altered from that evening on, and, as you see, for the intervening four decades I've never been too long out of hailing distance of DeHirsch's voice.

Of course, he absolutely refused to tell us where and how he'd gotten that money for us; and, what's more, he stubbornly kept his trap shut about it for the next twenty-five years.

But one day in the early spring, when he and I had been strolling out in the country together, and we had somehow drifted into a particularly reminiscent and nostalgic mood, I did finally manage to make him cough up his little secret.

"Come on," I said, "it all happened a quarter of a century ago. Whatever it was, it's all dead and buried now. Come on, cop out, why don't you? How did you get that five spot for us, and who in hell ever gave it to you?"

"Okay," said DeHirsch. "You're quite right, twenty-five years is long enough. I imagine everybody who was concerned in it, except Henry and the two of us, is dead by now, anyway. Yes, you might as well know the whole bloody story.

"It all started one afternoon in March when I had a lot of heavy packages to deliver and I'd just taken the East Side subway up to Fifty-ninth Street. I was loaded down like a jackass; I was carrying half a department store on each arm and everybody in the train gave me plenty of room. Now, as I was standing with my load out on the car platform, I noticed an elderly, well-dressed man suddenly slide off his seat and fall lengthwise into the aisle. I don't have to tell you how the goddamned New Yorkers react to a thing like that, do I? Everybody steered clear of the old guy. They were afraid he might be drunk or dying or dead, or that they might have to testify in court about it, or whatever, but they certainly wanted no part of him. Well, I just couldn't let him lay there like that, could I? I asked a colored boy who was standing out on the platform beside me to keep an eye on my bundles, and I went in to see what was wrong. Luckily he wasn't unconscious and I managed to get him back on his seat again. 'It's my heart,' he whispered to me. 'Please try to get me home. My address is written inside my breast pocket.' So I looked, and his name was Frank Liebkind, and he lived up on Fifth Avenue in the Nineties. At the next station I give the colored kid a quarter to carry my bundles after me, while I helped Mr. Liebkind out of the subway. Out in the street we got a cab, and after I'd piled my crap in front with the driver we got in and took the old man home.

"Luckily his wife was in, and I can't tell you the fuss she made over me for the trouble I'd taken over her sick husband. After she'd paid off the cabbie, she took a twenty-dollar bill out of his purse and tried to shove it into my pocket. But I wanted no part of it. 'You owe me a quarter,' I said, 'and that's all I'm intending to take.' Of course she tried pretty hard to make me take the money, just the same. She kept telling me they were very well off, and that I deserved some recognition for my kindness. But in the end she realized I wasn't that type of guy and that I wouldn't take her twenty dollars, and so she finally let go of me.

"And that's how it was. And that's how it would have stayed, from then on, until you and Henry showed up, about three weeks later, with that busted microscope; and I didn't have any money to pay for the repairs. I saw only one way out—I'd go up to the Liebkinds and ask them for a five spot. Believe me, it cost me quite a lot to get myself to do that, and I had nightmares about it for a long time afterward. Even now, I get the willies when I remember the way she opened the door and looked at me. You know what I said to her? I said, 'I'm sorry to bother you, Mrs. Liebkind, but I'd appreciate very much if you could please let me have just five out of those twenty dollars. It's something terribly important and very urgent,' I said, 'or I wouldn't think of bothering you.' I guess I'm never going to forget the look on her face when she finally recognized me, and without saying a single word, she quietly handed me that goddamned fin."

But don't let this little story mislead you, and don't you jump to any hasty conclusions. As I told you before, I've known DeHirsch for nearly half a century, and, in all that time he was never, never anybody's gladsome fool.

✱

# CHAPTER EIGHTEEN

IT WAS NOT until early in 1948 that I finally got around to committing suicide.

I was living up on the West Side at the time, in a newly remodeled hotel called the Remlick. I'd decided to get away from my old haunts, the flea bags around Times Square, and to get a fresh start among the respectable bourgeoisie. I'd had enough of Tritons and Nereids, pixies, Cyclopes and kobolds for a while. I'd just come out of Lexington for the second time, I was off drugs, and, by a lucky fluke, some member of the Turkish legation had given me a thousand dollars' advance to ghost-write his autobiography.

So I decided to set myself up among new sets, new lights, new costumes, and new scenery. I was really anxious to function once more among sensible people and to make an honest try at a so-called normal existence.

It proved to be a mistake. At least, it proved to be a mistake to move into the Remlick. Most of my fellow tenants looked like retired supermarket managers, and the women were a lot of dumpy widows or divorcées who seemed to live exclusively for the benefit of their cats and dogs. I discovered, after a while, that these pudgy, sexless dolls had hardly any feelings left for people at all. Whatever rheumatic twitchings still agitated their vitals were chiefly transformed into goo-goo talk for their revolting pets. I suppose it is common knowledge that domestic animals tend to take on the habits and afflictions of their owners, and so most of the beasts in this hotel suffered from asthma, from hemorrhoids, from bad breath, and God knows what else. And, do you know, the owner of one particularly disgusting cocker spaniel told me gloatingly that her shivering bundle of disaster had to have his prostate massaged twice a week.

Also, a couple of times I made the terrible mistake of eating in the hotel dining room. The food tasted as if it was catered and served under the auspices of a licensed embalmer.

So, what with my depressing neighbors, the hideous plywood furniture, the arty wallpaper and the boring, uneventful life story of my Turkish patron, it will not surprise you that within ten days I was back on drugs again.

But I was hitting absolute bottom this time, because even

sizable doses of morphine failed to lower a really effective curtain of indifference between me and all the unbearable realities of existence.

"Well," I said to myself one evening, "it's been a good life, on and off, and I've had plenty of laughs in my time. I'd better cut out now, while I still have the guts left to do it."

There was an upholstered window seat in my room that looked right out on Central Park; so, just as the light was beginning to fail, I lay myself down on it, shot fifteen grains of morphine into myself, and quietly drifted off.

When I opened my eyes I realized that I was dead, because I was confronted by an absolutely magical vision. Everything outside my window—the roadways, the bushes, the trees— was white with morphine.

Imagine me kicking off as a skeptic, I thought, and then I wake up right in the heart of never-never land. Even the wall across the way had ten inches of white powder on top of it.

I just lay there quietly and let it all happen to me, because this was surely the grooviest moment I'd had in many years.

The world is finally all covered with dope, I thought, and, believe me, it certainly never looked better. Yes, this is paradise, at last. No more chasing around after prescriptions, no more blackmail to a lot of crooked druggists, no more narcotics squad. The rat race is over.

There was enough "schmeck" lying out there to keep all the archangels in heaven doped up for all eternity.

I didn't move for a long, long while. I really didn't dare to move, because, faintly, ever so faintly, a nasty little cricket of doubt had started his frozen chirping, 'way back in the dark recesses of my mind.

Finally, when I did somehow get to my feet, my whole body felt so sore and so feeble I was barely able to stagger across the room. Also, I couldn't take my eyes off that goddamned window, because I couldn't get myself to part with that enchanting dope mirage. I finally had to turn away, because I felt so thirsty I wanted to drink at least a bathtub full of water, just as a starter.

Then I suddenly got sight of myself in a mirror. My eyes had shriveled down to mere mongoloid slits, and I certainly had at least a three days' growth of beard on me.

I tottered under the shower, where I let the water run freely into my mouth until, finally, my belly got to feel like the inside of an aquarium. Afterward, I fell helplessly on my bed and rang for a bellhop.

So I hadn't died after all. No, nothing good ever happens to a junkie, I thought. It's no use, I'm back with the plywood furniture and the licensed embalmer cooking. What's more, I'll have to hustle around to get myself some junk right away, before I start puking.

When the boy showed up I gave him some money for cigarettes and a paper, and I asked him what time it was.

"It's about a quarter of eleven," he said. "Shall I take the Don't Disturb sign off your door?"

"Do that," I said, "and bring me about five or six buckets of ice water, too."

Later on, when he brought me the paper, I realized that it was Thursday morning, and that I'd completely knocked myself out just two and a half days before. There was also a lot of crap in the paper about dangerous roadways and stalled cars, on account of the sudden ten-inch snowfall.

Funny that my suicide attempt hadn't worked. Fifteen grains of morphine all at one shot was certainly enough to kill anybody. Anybody but a hardened drug addict, maybe. Well, I was right back again in the old hustle-bustle with the built-in permanent tailspin. What a drag!

And yet I'd never in all my life thought much about suicide before. Bill Seabrook used to talk to me a lot about it, around 1929 and the early '30s. Of course, he was always fascinated by death because he was something of a necrophile. I think Bill was a born investigator; he certainly never missed a chance to try anything, and I mean *anything,* at least once. So it was natural that he should have wanted to catch just one authentic glimpse behind the final dark curtain, because this was one of the very few things he hadn't done and afterward written about.

Well, in the end his reporter's curiosity seems to have gotten the better of him, because about ten years ago he finally did commit suicide.

Not a word from him since then.

I have very mixed memories of Bill, most of them uneasy and a few of them even decidedly unpleasant. I had illustrated his book *The Magic Island,* which was the one that made him famous and certainly earned him the most money. That, in fact, was the basis of our friendship, but it was also the equally strong foundation for a certain definite animosity on Bill's part. You see, various critics had given a good deal of praise to these illustrations, and everyone concerned knew perfectly well that the blatant shock value of my drawings had had a decided influence on the quite phenomenal sales.

Bill Seabrook, who was a huge, stub-nosed, fleshy man, sometimes liked playfully to impersonate a sort of slow-witted Georgia cracker, and in the course of these charades he would invariably come to make sly, falsely humble references to our successful collaboration.

"I'm sure lucky as all get out," he would say. "Yes, I get the breaks every time, don't I? Where would my poor little book be now, if it hadn't attracted the interest of an honest-to-God celebrity, who graciously let himself be persuaded to illuminate my clumsy efforts?"

And so on.

But sometimes he wasn't quite so harmless.

One day he and I were visiting a friend of ours out along the Jersey coast somewhere, and late in the afternoon Bill and I decided to go down to the bay for a dip. When we got there we found a raft anchored offshore, quite a distance offshore, as a matter of fact, but Bill at once suggested that we swim out to it. I told him that it looked a little too far for me and that I was afraid it might be too much of a strain on me.

"I'm not a terribly good swimmer," I said, "and recently my wind hasn't been any too good."

"Nonsense!" said Bill. "You can make it easy, and if you get tired on the way, you just hold on to my shoulders."

So we tried it and I somehow managed to make it to the raft without any of his help. We lay down on the warm boards and talked for more than an hour out there, and finally, it seems, I must have fallen asleep for a while.

When I woke up, Bill was nowhere in sight, and it was only too evident that the incoming tide had added a hundred feet to the distance between the raft and dry land.

Now, don't get panicky, I said to myself. Just lie flat on your back and paddle yourself slowly into shallow water. Come on, you have no time to lose, this tide is running higher every minute.

Of course the water felt very much colder to me now, but I quietly turned over on my back and started paddling. I kept this up for quite a while, too, but at last I couldn't resist flopping over just to take a quick look to see how I was making out.

Well, it seemed to me that I was as far away from shore as ever, and I tried not to notice that a stabbing pain had begun its persistent throbbing somewhere in my appendix region.

So now I decided to try a breast stroke; that's the stroke I had first learned as a kid in Austria and it sometimes used to rest me. Naturally, I began very slowly, but after a while I was working and puffing at it until my eyes nearly hung out of my head—and yet, I tell you, that goddamned beach kept right on receding from me.

So I turned over once more and again tried paddling on my back. I was frightfully exhausted and I had long ago given up any sort of normal breathing. I was gasping in hysterical spasms and was just about to gather my last strength to scream for help, when I felt my hand entangled in some blessed seaweed.

I stood up. It was still pretty deep, but the tips of my toes did manage to rest for a moment on the shifting sand. So I kept bounding frantically along the insecure bottom until, at last, I finally managed to stand up, with my head freely out of the water.

But by now I had grown frightfully heavy to myself, and only my desperate, deadly fear gave me the frenzied strength to crawl out onto the sparse foliage that fringed the shore at this point. I tottered a few steps along the sand and then suddenly fell on my face and started retching. After a while I pulled myself together and looked around.

Bill Seabrook was sitting quietly on a little knoll right above me. He'd been watching my whole desperate maneuver all along, and he'd never made the slightest move to give me a hand.

I must say I wasn't really too surprised by his behavior, because I'd come to know him quite well by then. I suppose he'd only wanted to see how a so-called intelligent man would look and comport himself in the act of drowning. Bill was a born reporter of lurid tales, and that's what he was chiefly capable of. It was this very talent of his which also made him terribly unhappy, which turned him into a pathological drunkard, and which, in the end, finally caused him to take his own life.

I know what I'm talking about on this subject, because I'd had quite a little experience with Bill and because I've given the matter a lot of thought. You see, Bill Seabrook had had his original start as a writer on one of the sensational week-end supplements that the Hearst papers have specialized in for years. You know the type of crap—"Secrets of the French Sûreté" or "Does the Kokoringa Palm of Sumatra Consume Human Virgins?" That sort of informational tutti-frutti. I daresay Bill was very good at his job.

There was just one thing wrong with the picture. Bill loved good writing, real prose and real poetry; he was absolutely mad about Joyce and Proust and Eliot and Pound and he was even quite laughably intimidated by that compulsive non-sequiturist, Gertrude Stein.

And that's where the big rift occurred in him. He too would have loved to be a man alone—a man aloof and bitterly misunderstood. But Bill was surely the most accessible of men and his aims and his means could be fathomed and easily appreciated by any child.

I recall that during those years *Finnegans Wake* used to appear in installments in a magazine called *Transition*. Bill would often ask me to read aloud to him some excerpts of this work, which was predominantly obscure but which quite frequently was charged with marvelous poetic images and alliterations.

One particular section seemed to have him quite bulldozed; it was called "The Mookse and the Gripes," and I'm sure that we read this piece at least a dozen times together.

"I wonder what it must feel like to write stuff like that," he said to me one day. "You're not just talking to the butcher and the grocer on the corner, or to your sweetheart, or to the lady next door. You're just looking right over everybody's head, straight into the eyes of posterity. I sure wonder what that is like. I suppose that's what you'd call . . . immortality."

That's how Bill felt about it. But he didn't address himself only to the lady next door; eventually he even came to address himself to *The Ladies' Home Journal*.

These good people had recklessly contracted with him for the advance installments on his next book, which turned out to be *Jungle Ways*. They paid him something like thirty thousand dollars for the stint, and I know it was really one of the high points of his life.

You may perhaps remember that it all ended in a sort of debacle. If you've ever read *Jungle Ways*, you know that in it he tells of living for quite a spell with a certain cannibal tribe a little south of Timbuktu. Well, it seems that a few of his friends had concluded a successful raid on one of the neighboring tribes and were now busy preparing some of their human victims for the festive table. The ceremony, you understand, had no religious or fetishistic significance at all, it was just a little matter of local gourmandizing. It stands to reason, doesn't it, that Bill certainly didn't intend to miss any part of it.

He tells us in his book how he stopped smoking a couple of days before the banquet, so that his palate would be clean and receptive to the novel taste sensation. He finally tells what the human chop looked like as it slowly broiled over the flames, and in conclusion he reports that the flavor was not entirely unlike the taste of roast veal.

Well, he sent back his little report to the States, but somehow the people at *The Ladies' Home Journal* didn't seem to care for it. Not really. In fact, they decided to skip the installment altogether.

Of course Bill was furious. He was all for suing and making a great big fuss about it. He complained to me about it at the Brevoort one day.

"It's an arbitrary dictatorship over man's mind!" he insisted. "Who knows where all this will stop!"

"You can't really blame them," I said. "After all, they're

a kind of family magazine, don't you see? I know that in each issue they do print some cooking recipes, but . . ."

He didn't see it that way.

I personally date the decline in his popularity to this event in his life. Americans are a notoriously hero-worshiping people, and in his own way Bill had become a sort of public idol. But, as he discovered, Americans, despite all their famous tolerance, do seem to draw the line at some things— at cannibalism, for instance.

All I can tell you is that Bill Seabrook was never again a popular best seller, and he honestly never quite understood why.

Come to think of it, I don't know why I was so patronizing about Bill's early jobs, since in the course of my life I've certainly worked for some pretty strange outfits myself.

In fact, around 1917, before I went off to Oswego and Syracuse, even before I was married, I worked for about a year on a Jewish joke paper called *The Big Stick;* I was one of their cartoonists. Because it appeared only once a week, the editorial office was open only on weekends. This office was located in an old-fashioned railroad flat on East Broadway, and among its memorable equipments was a huge round-bellied coal stove, a brass samovar in working order, and an office boy named Mottle, who was seventy-eight years old and an uncle of the owner-editor, Jack Marinoff.

Here is where I first learned to speak my flavorful Yiddish and where I first came to understand the true meaning of a real Jewish joke. Believe me, it isn't as simple as you think. A joke is not necessarily a Jewish joke because the protagonists are called Abie and Jakie. No sir, that has nothing whatever to do with it. In nine out of ten cases that's just a facile device for putting across a rabidly anti-Semitic point.

Jewish humor, as I learned at one of its very sources, was a racial antibiotic whose original cultures the children of Israel had carried out of Egypt, more than two thousand years ago, and whose health-preserving properties had been nurtured through the centuries in all the ghettos and outposts of persecuted Judaism.

I remember only a couple of the jokes that we printed in *The Big Stick*, and I must tell you again that everything loses a lot in translation. Here's one of them:

One Sunday afternoon a couple of culture-bound young Jews, a brother and a sister, were determined to drag their poor old father to the Metropolitan Museum of Art. They nudged and maneuvered him from room to room, until the poor old guy, who had spent most of his past life standing over a pressing iron, nearly passed out from boredom and exhaustion.

171

But his daughter, determined to rally his flagging strength and attention, suddenly pointed to a large canvas of the Nativity, and said, "You see that painting over there, Papa? You know what the museum had to pay for it, last year? It paid three quarters of a million dollars for it."

The old man raised his eyeglasses higher up on his nose and took a long, tired look at the canvas. "It's a family, eh?" he said.

"Yes," said his son.

"And this," said the father, pointing at St. Joseph, "this is the papa?"

"Yes," said the daughter.

"And this," he said, pointing at the Virgin, "this is the mama?"

"Yes," said the son.

"And this is the baby, eh? And why are they all sitting in this stable? And why are all those animals sniffing around them?"

"Because," said the daughter, "they were terribly poor people and they had no place to stay, except in a stable. You understand?"

The old man sadly shook his head from side to side and gave a great big sigh. "That's gentiles for you," he finally said. "Here they are, without a cent to their name, but they go and have their pictures taken."

Now, then, you may believe me that in all these years I have never seen a Nativity, either at the Louvre, or the Prado, or the Metropolitan, without at once remembering this story. After all, it's easy to understand the old Jew's attitude. He felt that no matter how dismal the circumstances might be, the gentiles always acted as if they owned the world.

What makes the story particularly useful as an illustration of Jewish humor is that it makes its point by indirection and that its motivating dynamics is based on an error.

You see, a great many Jews have always believed, or learned to their cost, that life actually proceeds much better by misunderstandings. That's why their humor often has a surrealist quality, in which the *non sequitur* is frequently the perfect answer.

Let me give you another example:

One day a rich Jew is compelled to lay over for a few hours in a small Russian village, because his car has broken down. When, in deep irritation with the delay, he happens to consult his watch, he notices that the minute hand has become detached. So he decides to look around the main street of the town for a watchmaker who might make the necessary repair for him. He walks nearly the whole length of the street before he finally lands in front of a shop window where half a dozen assorted watches are displayed.

The door is a few steps below street level, and when he finally enters he finds an old and venerable-looking Jew sitting at a lectern and quietly reading in what is obviously the Talmud.

"I have to stay in this town for a few hours," says the visitor, "and this minute hand has somehow gotten loose. I wonder if you could repair it for me?"

The old Jew looks up, slowly shakes his head, and without a word returns to the reading of the Scriptures.

The visitor, thinking the old man may be a little deaf, now says in a much louder voice, "My minute hand has fallen off, and I'd like you to fix it for me. Will it take very long?"

The old man again looks up, once more shakes his venerable head, and again proceeds to immerse himself in his sacred tome.

Now the visitor is really getting quite irritated with him. He puts his hand on the old man's arm and says at the top of his voice, "Why don't you answer me? Are you going to repair this minute hand for me or not?"

The old man looks up benignly, and says, "I can't possibly do it for you."

"Why not?" shouts the visitor. "Don't worry, I'm able to pay you for it."

"That's not the point," says the old man. "I can't do it because I'm not a watchmaker."

"You're not a watchmaker?" says the visitor, stupefied. "Then what in heaven's name are you?"

"I'm a mohel," says the ancient. "I only circumcise the village children."

"You circumcise children?" says the visitor. "Then what, in the name of God, are all those watches doing in your window?"

The old man looks at the intruder speculatively for a moment, and says, "So what would *you* put in the window?"

Anyway, the people who invent such jokes are certainly a peculiar breed, and Jack Marinoff, the editor, was like an experienced wild-animal trainer who knew exactly how to keep them all in line.

He would also stand right in back of my chair as I was drawing my cartoons, and he would not only illuminate but *dictate* the various symbolic aspects of my drawing to me. Since we were, even forty years ago, already avowed Socialist-Zionists, our political attitude in world affairs was not always quite as clear-cut as other people's. Also, because engraving was a big expense to us, we had to get a hell of a lot of meaningful stuff into each of our pictures.

Once, Marinoff entrusted me with a particularly important cartoon, one which was going to carry the whole weight of our journalistic authority. "I want you to start with the picture of a handsome Jew," he said to me. "I want him to sit right down front, you understand? And in back of him I want you to draw the Spirit of Jewish Consciousness, and she has one hand on his shoulder and says to him, 'Get Up And Build!' Well, in the background I want you should make the ruins of Palestine in all their sorrowful desolation. A lesson in horror and neglect, you understand? And then, up in the sky, among the clouds, I want you to show how the class consciousness of the working people is knitting a sweater—"

"Just a minute, Marinoff!" I interrupted him. "How big are you planning to make this cartoon, anyway?"

"Three inches by two and a half inches," he said.

"And how in God's name is all that stuff going to fit in there?" I asked him.

"That," he said, "is not my business. Remember, young man, I'm not the artist."

Well, I obviously wasn't either, because I had a hell of a lot of trouble with that cartoon. First of all, I had to ask another cartoonist for certain basic advice.

"Tell me," I said, "what does the Spirit of Jewish Consciousness look like, anyway?"

"Have you ever been to City Hall?" he asked.

"Yes, of course," I said. "So what?"

"Well," he said, "you know all those statues of big women they have down there—Peace, Justice, Liberty, and so on?"

"Yes," I said, "so what about them?"

"Well, for the Spirit of Jewish Consciousness you draw just such a woman," he said, "and then you put a good, solid Jewish nose on her, that's all!"

I had other difficulties. Marinoff didn't care for the handsome Jew I had put in the foreground. "That's not a Jew," he said, "that's an Italian."

"What are you talking about?" I said. "Just look at his nose, that's a real Jewish nose."

"You know nothing about it," Marinoff said sadly. "Your man is a member of the Mafia. You have never studied the Jewish nose. The Jewish nose, in its full florescence, is like a tower of beauty looking toward Damascus."

What's more, I knew in my heart that this was an entirely fair and objective pronouncement, because Marinoff himself was a tall, gray-haired, athletic-looking man whose own nose was so modestly unobtrusive it could easily have passed for gentile.

174

So, you see, I discovered at a very early age indeed that there were a lot more angles to this cartooning game than the average man ever imagines.

# CHAPTER NINETEEN

I HAD TO GO out and visit my doctor this afternoon and, during my absence, my friend Sidney Stewart dropped by my house and happened to read a few random pages out of my last two chapters.

When I got home I found a note from him stuck in my typewriter.

"Of course," he says, "you are perfectly right in pointing out the specially angled and highly biased writing in *Time* magazine. But if I were you, I would give at least a token example of their 'sail-trimming' and 'crow-eating' for the less initiate."

I suppose it is high time for me to make clear, at this point, not only that this book is crammed with the facts and fancies of my life, but also that it carries the rich distillation of my carefully considered hates and prejudices, which, after a great many difficulties and annoyances, I have finally managed to accumulate.

Unlike the editors of *"Time,* The Weekly News Magazine," I'm not at all interested in giving the false impression that I'm trying to be fair to anybody. Nonetheless, I am going to back up my distaste for this particular publication by telling you how I came to distrust it so intensely.

Long before I ever came to work for the Luce enterprises, I had noticed, for instance, that photographs of Leon Trotsky printed in *Time* magazine, would very frequently bear the caption "Leon Trotsky (nee Bronstein)."

On pictures of Lenin, Stalin, or Molotov they rarely ever bothered to give the real names. Now, then, everybody knows perfectly well that all of the Russian revolutionists used to perform their various functions under a whole series of assumed names. It was mostly a futile but understandable camouflage device on their part, or, if you like, it could even be interpreted as a romantic cloak-and-dagger affectation among these Slavs.

But it seemed to me that the editors of *Time* particularly liked to single out Leon Trotsky by his real name because it tended to expose him as just a cheap little Jew who, in the manner of his breed, had, for devious, shady reasons, decided to change his monicker. It not only reduced his status as a world figure, but, because every Jew is, unfortunately, responsible for all Judaism, it cast an inevitable aspersion on the whole race.

I can just imagine what the responsible parties on *Time* would answer me at this point. They would tell me, with a great deal more restraint than I am displaying, that to print the "Trotsky née Bronstein" caption is informative journalism which tells a simple fact that the public is certainly entitled to know.

As for printing the facts, all I can tell you as an example is that in a good many private conversations with some of my fellow editors, they used freely to concede to me that Senator Bricker of Ohio, for instance, was a real dead weight of reactionary ballast to the more enlightened membership of the Republican Party. Nevertheless, when Bricker was running for Vice-President these same truth-obsessed, objective editors simply foamed at the mouth with ecstasy and could barely control their joyful convulsions, in enumerating all his talents.

I assure you that one could easily have found higher standards of ethics and nobler principles of truth displayed at that well-known house that unpretentious old Polly Adler once used to keep.

Apropos of Trotsky—when he first sought, and found, asylum in Mexico, the foreign-affairs editor of *Time,* a man called Laird Goldsborough, claimed to have special inside information on this move. He loudly maintained that Leon Trotsky was nothing but the pliant tool of wily old Joe Stalin, and that Trotsky's presence anywhere in the Americas was tantamount to having a revolutionary time bomb right in our own back yard.

I want you to know that *Time* kept repeating this patent balderdash in issue after issue for nearly half a year. I know that they finally dropped Goldsborough for pulling this and other boners on them, but remember, he wasn't the only news-blunderer throughout the years who had the free run of their pages simply because he happened to chirp the sort of nonsense that was dear to their hearts.

Just think, for example, of the embarrassing twaddle that John Chamberlain has written for them, in *Life,* on the subject of our native literature. I recall one piece in which he simply stamped his little dimpled legs and tore up his perfectly clean diaper in a blind rage with our practicing novelists, because they were inclined to believe that all too often the American businessman was just a greedy, flatulent hypocrite. In soulful, doleful tones, Mr. Chamberlain admonished these writers to mend their pens before it was too late.

Too late for what?

Oh, I suppose, before the American businessman, wrapped in his wounds and his profits, silently folded his factories and stole away to more hospitable shores.

Chamberlain's reproachful litany to the literateurs went on and on, for a whole long editorial section, and you would never have believed it possible that the man who was dishing out this nauseating, predigested tripe had once been a really promising, and even brilliant, young book reviewer for the *New York Times*.

But all this is really beside the point at the moment, because what I originally intended to tell you about was the time when I was finally arrested for passing a forged prescription in a drugstore up on Seventy-first Street and Broadway.

I had, as usual, gathered an indiscriminate armful of cosmetics from the display tables and, loaded down with this debris, had stepped up to the counter and placed my phony scrip before the attending clerk, when a tall, gangly, country-type gent quietly stepped alongside me and flashed his goddamned badge.

Well, I'd been expecting something like it for quite a while, because for almost two years I'd been flooding the town with hundreds of forged drug prescriptions. But still, when Uncle Sam's boy suddenly stood there beside me with that bronze onion in his hand, the jolt of it nearly knocked me on my can.

Nevertheless I took a good, close look at the legend embossed on his badge, not because I was so calm and self-possessed about it all, but because, in a crazy town like New York, even some members of the public library and the Sanitation Department are liable to flash some kind of badge on you. I wanted to make sure I was in for the real thing and not just being pushed around by some ash-can supervisor.

Well, he was a narcotics agent, all right, but, I tell you, he looked and acted less like a cop than some of the doormen I've seen around this town. He looked like a sort of untalented Lincoln, and I also noticed that he had a very nice, quiet voice.

"Why didn't you go back to Lexington?" he said to me. "Why didn't you go down there and give yourself a chance?"

"I've been there twice already," I said.

"But you just stayed a month each time," he said. "A month ain't enough. Why don't you go back there and stay for a while?"

"Well," I said, "you've got me now. I don't see where I have much of a choice in the matter, have I?"

"Where do you live?" he asked. "Is it far from here?"

177

"No," I said, "it's just a block and a half."

"You mind if we go up there?" he said.

"Not a bit of it."

It was raining like hell that day, so when we got outside he opened his umbrella and we sloshed over to my place near West End Avenue. I happened to have a fine big room in a brownstone house at the time, and, as a matter of fact, I'd just a few days before gotten through furnishing it.

I naturally expected him to frisk the joint and see if I had any "schmeck" concealed anywhere about the premises, but he just planted himself in a comfortable armchair and looked around the place with obvious approval.

"You've got it real nice here," he said. "You must have spent quite a bit on it."

"I spent four hundred dollars on it, " I said, "and now that you've grabbed me, you can have it all for forty cents."

"I'm sorry to hear you say that," he said. "I don't intend to make things seem brighter than they are, but you ought to store all this stuff with some friends for a while and go back down to Lexington and get yourself straightened out, once for all. Go down and blue-grass yourself, why don't you? Turn yourself in, get yourself sentenced. They'll only give you the minimum—four and a half months, that's all."

"Just a minute," I said. "You mean, you'll let me put all this stuff in storage and let me go down to Lexington by myself, without handcuffs?"

"Sure," he said. "You're not a bad guy. You're just in a jam. One of your doctors told me that you *are* pretty sick. So go on down. Only, don't take too long about it. Let's see, today is Friday. Why don't you get off the beginning of next week? By the way, you didn't cash your scrip this evening, so how are you fixed for stuff?"

"I'll need a shot pretty badly in a couple of hours," I said.

"Okay," he said. "You go to any doctor in this neighborhood and if he doesn't want to write for you, just tell him to call me up. I'll give you my home number and I'll see that he puts you straight until you can get out of town."

In short, he was an absolute prince.

And how did I react to this prince? Like a typical drug addict. I sold all my furniture the very next day and took it on the lam. I moved over to Brooklyn, and for the next six months I scraped and cheated and scrounged and finagled. And then, when I was at last completely strapped and couldn't even raise a quarter, I finally landed down at 90 Church Street, with the narcotics squad.

I'll say one thing for those boys, nobody reproached me, nobody was disappointed in me, and nobody had a grudge against me.

By the way, I had purposely landed with them on a Tuesday because I'd heard, through the grapevine, that addicts were generally shipped out every Wednesday. This information proved to be quite wrong. Actually, shipments to Lexington were made at various odd and unpredictable times and, as it turned out, I was stuck, good and sick, over in West Street jail for the following three weeks.

In case you don't know about West Street jail, it is the Federal House of Detention in New York, and from the moment you enter it you become aware of its extraordinary atmosphere of almost festive corruption. It reminded me of the Marshalsea Prison out of *Little Dorrit*, because here too each floor was like an aviary, in which the jailbirds chirped and fluttered about under the guardianship of a lot of garrulous, paternal turnkeys.

In other words, if you're planning to devote yourself to a life of crime, implying all its incipient risks, I advise you to confine your activities to the specially selected areas where you are likely to be faced by only a federal rap. A federal house of detention is definitely the only place where the officiating personnel seems to be remarkable free of moral ascendancy or personal rancor. Also, I'm told, the food is much better.

At any rate, even though I was deathly sick over in West Street, because I got only one shot of morphine a day for the first four days, I can't say that I found myself in company that was either boring, despairing, or depressing. Of course it wasn't all beer and skittles, by any means, but it seems that most of my fellow prisoners had, by common consent, decided to face their desperate dilemmas in a spirit of rakish bravado.

There were exceptions, of course. Particularly, right after a man got sentenced and had, perhaps, landed a ten-year stretch at Leavenworth. He was then inclined to be moody and uncommunicative for a couple of days. But before long he was again likely to join in the noisy, nightly card games, and even to try his hand at stealing some canned fruit out of the jail warehouse.

It was hard to resist the devil-may-care spirit that permeated West Street, and I thought it was entirely possible that the really shattering sadness of their situations probably came home to most of these people only some time afterward, when they finally had to settle down to serving their long, solemn years in the various federal prisons all over the country.

I was sentenced for a cure to Lexington, Kentucky, which at that time meant only four months and fifteen days. Meanwhile, I languished in a chronic state of nausea on my bed in

179

West Street, hoping vainly from day to day that I would be shipped out with a contingent of other addicts from the Manhattan area.

But, despite my debility and my illness, I did partake in some small measure in the life and activities around me. First of all, I met a six-foot-four-inch Negro named Jonathan Bell, who was doing time for being a conscientious objector. Since he was a Jehovah's Witness he had gotten only eight months for refusing to bear arms; and so he was serving out his short term in the West Street kitchen, and in his spare time he tried to make converts to his peculiar denomination. Although he was only twenty-one years old, he had a great deal of quiet dignity, and, because I found him unusually handsome, I had made a little pencil drawing of him. So we became friends.

Jonathan soon noticed that I skipped all my meals and that I drank only the milk that was served twice a day, so from then on he somehow managed to smuggle me some precious stewed fruit out of the officers' mess, and every once in a while he would even manage to bring me a box of salt-free Uneeda Biscuits.

Sometimes I used to talk with Jonathan about the only man in our midst who was facing a possible death sentence, Julius Rosenberg, the single prisoner in West Street who was locked in a cell all by himself, and to whom none of the rest of us were permitted to talk. I told Jonathan that one day I had been taken to court along with the Rosenbergs, and that I was sure, from the couple of hours I'd spent with them, that it was Mrs. Rosenberg who was the strong and dominant person in this team. He seemed more like a bewildered, chuckleheaded Talmud student, who'd somehow gotten adrift in tides that were entirely beyond his understanding or control.

"I often hear him talking to the guard," said Jonathan, "and he seems to be more worried about his dry cereal for breakfast than about the death sentence that is on him."

"Well," I said, "you can't judge a man just by the way he talks. God only knows what really goes on in his heart."

"You sure got that right," said Jonathan. "By the way, do you know how to play chess?"

"Yes," I said. "Do you want to learn?"

"It's not for me," he said. "It's for Mr. Alger Hiss, who's looking for a game, particularly tonight, because they're sending him off tomorrow morning. If you don't mind, I'll bring him around here, later on."

So, I played only that one game of chess with Alger Hiss, because they did take him away the very next day to serve his five-year sentence for perjury. I might as well admit that the game we played that evening was a pretty stinky one;

180

chances are we both had a hell of a lot of other distracting matters on our minds.

Although Hiss had been convicted of a very serious crime, all the inmates in West Street were uncritically courteous to him. To most of these men, who had been counterfeiters, bank robbers and hi-jackers, he was just a frozen enigma. Lacking the profit motive, it was all somehow completely beyond their understanding and, consequently, beyond their condemnation.

There were three or four small-type Communists also in West Street awaiting trial, and I noticed that they were a pretty well-disciplined, closemouthed lot who hardly ever had any traffic with the other prisoners.

The greater my surprise, when, one morning right after breakfast, the least attractive of them, a man called Lennie Stone, came over to me and sat down at the foot of my bed.

"How you feel?" he asked.

"Terrible," I said. "I should be down in Lexington where they would take care of me."

"I want to talk to you about something that's happening here," he said. "Something that concerns all of us."

"What is it?" I asked.

"You know," he said, "that the day after tomorrow is the Jewish Passover, don't you? Well, they always hold some kind of a service downstairs on the first Seder night. Jewish restaurants all over town send all kinds of food and pastries, so that the people in here can also have a holiday celebration. You understand?"

"Fine," I said. "You sit next to me at the Seder, and you are welcome to my share of the grub. I'd only throw it up, anyway."

"That's not the reason I'm talking to you," he said. "I want you to realize what is happening here, right under your very nose."

"What is it?" I said. "I'm so sick most of the time, I hardly notice anything."

"You know, of course, that Rosenberg is a Jew," he said. "Well, then, the authorities here have flatly refused to allow him to participate in the Passover festival. He can't come to the dinner."

"Well," I said, "don't forget that the jailers here are responsible for the maximum security of his person. His cell is lit up twenty-four hours a day, and he's the only one in the place who's under constant surveillance by the officer who is in charge of the receiving room."

"That's got nothing to do with it," said Stone. "He's a Jew, isn't he? Passover is a sacred Jewish holiday, isn't it? He has his rights, hasn't he? Well, I'm getting up a petition that we'll boycott the Passover dinner unless Rosenberg is permitted to participate in it."

"Just a minute," I said. "Are you trying to get me agitated about the fact that Rosenberg is not going to have his share in a service that he probably hasn't even thought about in a quarter of a century? What are you trying to tell me? That he's a religious Jew whose Passover rights are being violated?"

"Are you just a typical, selfish petty bourgeois?" said Stone. "Or what are you, anyway?"

"At the moment," I said, "I happen to be a drug addict. But whatever the hell I am, unlike some other people I could name, I've never confused my private calamities with the public welfare. That's why I'm not a Communist. You understand?"

"So you won't sign," Stone said, as he got up, absolutely pale with rage.

"No," I said, "and what's more, if you don't move your ass out of here pretty fast, I'm even liable to puke all over you, besides!"

As a matter of fact, I did go to the Seder, which proved a very festive occasion if only for the fact that all the Irish prison guards in attendance wore rabbinical skullcaps during the services. The Jewish restaurants in town had given their lavish best, and even I had two matzo balls and some breast of chicken, which I had cause to regret deeply, later on. It might interest you to know that Rosenberg was given a dinner identical with ours, in his cell. There was no boycott.

Another creature on trial for treason at the time was a peculiar enigma called Sergeant Provoo. When I first met him he had already spent more than five years in various prisons and detention homes, and he was now back in New York because his case was again being appealed in Foley Square.

I ran into him about four days after I'd landed in West Street. For some unfathomable reason, the powers in charge had decided to move me to another floor, and, in my condition, I can only say that those goddamned stairs nearly finished me off. When I finally did manage to totter up to the next floor, I fell onto the first bed that was planted right alongside the staircase, and I just lay there for a while, like a dead lox.

About half an hour later a tall, blue-eyed, well-spoken, football-playing type came over to me and said, "I'm sorry, friend, but this bed is already occupied."

"I'm terribly sick," I said, "so I just had to plump down here, because I simply couldn't drag myself any farther."

"Oh, you poor darling!" said the blond giant. "You just stay right here, and I'll run and get some clean linen for you."

Well, that was Sergeant Provoo. He was the official trusty

on my floor, and let me tell you that his hands were nearly as cool and his manner almost as soothing as Gertrude's, down in Lexington.

He did have a couple of things over Gertrude, though. He knew *The Love Song of J. Alfred Prufrock* by heart, and at one time, before he'd gotten into trouble, he had owned a copy of *The Emperor Jones*, with my illustrations.

Specifically, Provoo was accused of having perpetrated some really shocking actions of a treasonable nature while in the custody of the Japanese prison authorities. His many trials had already dragged on for five years, and since he had no money of his own, it was Uncle Sam who had been footing the bills for his numberless appeals, and who had also been digging up the carfare for the various witnesses that had to be conveyed from Japan and other far-off, outlying places. I think Provoo enjoyed going to court every day, because he certainly had a ball regaling me with dramatic accounts of the many legal skirmishes that were provoked during his trial.

All I can say is that, throughout my stay in West Street, he was enormously kind to me—brought me fresh ice bags, clean linen, warm blankets, and behaved altogether like a real pal. I don't know how well he would have worn in a Japanese prison compound, but in the Federal House of Detention he was an absolute Florence Nightingale.

Every day he read the gossip columns in the New York papers and kept me thoroughly informed of the latest goings on in all the literary and theatrical circles.

"Here's one about Clare Boothe Luce," he said to me one morning. "Seems like she's planning to write another play. It says here she's going down to Charleston to work on it."

"She's probably going to Mepkin," I said. "Mepkin, South Carolina."

"You wrote a play with her once, didn't you?" said Provoo. "Whatever became of it?"

"It was never produced," I said, "but I think she managed to unload it on some movie people, because I remember getting a few thousand dollars out of it from somewhere. It was called *The Yohimbe Tree*."

"She must be quite a gal!" said Provoo.

"She is," I said.

She is, indeed!

A lot of people have written, and a great many more have talked, about Clare throughout the years, but the basic essence of her personality has somehow always managed to elude both her adulators and her detractors. Some of them have claimed that she is a sort of psychological praying mantis, a reincarnation of Lucrezia Borgia, or a female version of

183

Niccolò Machiavelli. Others have compared her to Marguerite de Navarre, George Sand and to Mme. de Staël.

After knowing her for more than a quarter of a century, I must confess that some kind of reasonably convincing case could certainly be made out for each of these comparisons. And yet the truth, the absolute truth, resides, enigmatically, still somewhere else; because all of these people, the Borgias and the de Staëls, and all the rest each had organic identity, like wood, and wool, and silk, and cotton. There was certainly nothing synthetic about any of them. But Clare, whatever else she may be, is definitely a completely modern invention. For all I know, she may indeed be the basic archetype for the future rulers of the impending American Matriarchate.

Remember, she is no mere Oveta Culp Hobby or Dorothy Thompson. Oh, no! She seems more like the next development in a frightening fruition whose seed was dormant in those terrible dames who used to slip me their secret recipes for soy-bean crullers, more than twenty years ago. But while those ladies permitted themselves to be quagmired in their dull domestic activities, Clare has added to their diamond-hard effrontery and insectlike persistence her own stupendous, all-encompassing ambition.

Well, at any rate, for quite a number of years I was completely fascinated by her cavortings, and during most of that time I had a very active social and working relationship with her. I think it is significant, however, that when I started to work for her husband neither he nor anyone else on *Life* suspected that I had known Clare for quite some years before. It would have been no recommendation, and certainly no help to me, if anyone had suspected it.

The boss's wife is a kind of a nightmarish figure, anyway, wherever the hell you happen to be working, but Clare Boothe Luce was such a potent ogre on her own account that the staff on *Time* and *Life* practically crossed themselves whenever her name was even accidentally mentioned.

By the time it finally leaked out that I'd known her for years, and that I occasionally visited with the Luces up in Westport and on their plantation down in Mepkin, I was so soldily entrenched as a helpful idea man in every department that my camaraderie with our employer and his awe-inspiring wife seemed like a pardonable, if somewhat nerve-racking, eccentricity.

I went down to Mepkin a couple of times to work with Clare on our play, and, believe me, I was properly impressed by the air-conditioned dilapidation of their baronial layout.

When the Luces had first purchased that Southern plantation of theirs, there was considerable speculation among their employees as to what this gambit could possibly signify.

After all, there was nothing in the past of either of them that gave any clue that the fulfillment of their aspirations required half a dozen gardeners to drape Spanish moss from their ancestral trees every morning before sunup. One saturnine spirit among us suggested that they had gone down below the Mason-Dixon line for the sole purpose of reintroducing slavery. This was not only a palpable libel, but base ingratitude besides, since both of the Luces were notoriously considerate and generous employers.

Mepkin puzzled me, too. I could understand Westchester or even Palm Beach, but the magnolia trees, the sunken gardens, and the duck blinds somehow didn't quite connect with the image I had in my mind of Harry Luce as a landowner. But there they were, entertaining their peers and their dependents with a grace and an aplomb that could hardly have been bettered by the past.

One evening at the dinner table there did occur a slight contretemps, the memory of which becomes wakeful in me whenever I happen to overhear a couple of children quarreling in the street below my window.

There were nine of us at table that night, and it was indeed a remarkably nondescript group that was flatteringly illuminated by the pale-yellow, windproof, nondrip candles. As I remember it, Iris Tree and Dr. Kommer and I were being obligingly multilingual for the benefit of some quite undistinguished recent arrivals from abroad. A very mixed bag, as you can see.

Now, then, as is only becoming on these occasions, Clare, beautifully dressed, was holding forth at one end of the table, while Harry quite properly was seated opposite her, at the very far other end of it. The rest of us, since we were all of equal unimportance, were scattered helter-skelter in between them.

And then we noticed that our hosts, while carving the wild duck and deftly passing the various dishes on to their guests, continued with an animated discussion which had obviously been started before any of us had arrived in the dining room.

As far as I'm able to recall, there was some disagreement between them about the merits of the star system in the movie industry, or maybe it was something even more trivial than that; but, as their contention grew gradually more personal, and even acrimonious, a certain unavoidable pall of embarrassment began to settle on the assembled company.

And then, suddenly, in a moment of complete silence, Harry decisively put down his carving tools. I watched him as he leaned slightly forward in his seat and said, in a voice so cold that it seemed completely bereft of vibrations, "You're sure you're right, aren't you? You're quite, quite sure!"

"Yes," said Clare, "I'm absolutely sure!"

"Well," said Harry, "if you're really so certain, are you . . . are you willing to bet a million dollars on it?"

Now, let me tell you something, it was so still in that room at that moment that you could hear the stuffed fish over the mantelpiece flapping his gills.

Clare had become very pale and had turned suddenly, fiercely angry, and, I suppose, was just on the verge of answering him when she probably happened to catch a sobering sight of some of our stupefied faces.

You see, even the foreigners among us had clearly understood that these two contenders were not just a couple of show-off kids doing some exaggerated boasting in a corner candy store. Our hosts were two honest-to-God millionaires, and one of them had quietly but firmly challenged the other to bet him a million American dollars, right across our dinner table.

I haven't the slightest doubt that the most obtuse among us knew that Harry was in dead earnest; and, what's more, I'm convinced that Clare was prevented from accepting his challenge only because, as a socially perceptive person, she must certainly have become increasingly aware of the frozen bewilderment, and even fear, on the faces of her seven impecunious dinner guests.

# CHAPTER TWENTY

I HAVE THE CURIOUS feeling that in the next few chapters I'm going to lose the last few friends I still have left, because I'm about to relate some of my adventures and misadventures in show business. I think I have mentioned somewhere before that for a time I was managing editor of *Stage* magazine; and so, in the very nature of things, I couldn't help but get mixed up with a lot of theatrical people.

It is strange how fond I am of nearly all actors when I'm watching them perform on a stage, or even when they're just going through their paces at rehearsals, and how odious I find most of them when I happen to encounter them socially. And yet I suppose it is understandable, too; you see, after a while an actor gets to play so many different parts, in such a variety of plays, that somewhere along the line he can't help mislaying his own identity. And if you don't know who in hell you really are, it certainly is very difficult to be yourself.

186

There are exceptions, of course. Take an incorrigible, sugar-cured ham like Charles Laughton, for instance; you'd swear he hasn't a shred of identity left, by now. But you'd be wrong. He is a wonderfully straight, uncontaminated hombre, once he steps out of the spotlight. I know about half a dozen others like that, but by and large my depressing generalization holds only too true.

Another thing I've noticed—that nobody in all creation talks more persistently and more exhaustively about his Art than an actor does.

How come?

I suspect it has to do with a desperate fear that the whole art of acting resides in the keeping of about two dozen people the whole world over (including Bali and Sumatra) and that all the rest of the practicing mummers one encounters are just so many examples of acute, ingrown vanity and compulsive exhibitionism.

A terrible thought, isn't it?

It makes me think of those two Austrian midgets I mentioned a while ago, who had encompassed their small persons with endless cuff links, tiepins, wrist watches, and other tangible details, just to make sure that they existed at all; well, it seems to me that Melpomene and Thalia are, very likely, the midgets of the Muses, and so their servitors can't ever stop their stultifying controversies and expositional discourses on the subject of technique.

There was one person I knew who had a truly wonderful relationship with all actors, at all times, and that was Mr. Alexander Ince, the publisher of *Stage* magazine. Mr. Ince simply talked *to* them and *about* them as if they were all a bunch of ever so attractive, slightly crippled children.

In the course of a few years I learned a great deal from Mr. Ince, and I place him, unhesitatingly, at the very top of my long, long list of favorite Hungarians.

My affectionate relationship with this particular ethnic group is really quite surprising when I recall how, when I was a small boy, my mother had always gravely admonished me to be most careful about my various social relationships.

"Remember, my child," she used to say to me, "that everything east of the Danube is Asia."

I knew perfectly well what she meant; she meant Hungary.

And yet, although I was deeply attached to my mother and often took great stock in her teachings, I must confess that I have been involved one way or another with all sort of Hungarians for the better part of forty years, and that I have rarely savored the rich juices of life with greater awareness than in the company of these particular Asiatics.

Mr. Alexander Ince, my publisher, was about ten years

older than I, but he always managed to look a hell of a lot younger than his age. I used to think he resembled one of those slant-eyed, ruddy-faced Tibetan bonzes that are always grinning out of the pages of the *National Geographic*.

Ince proved in many, many ways an almost ideal employer for me. I had certainly had a wonderful time working for Frank Crowninshield, too, but even he quite definitely lacked the cheerful, tolerant skepticism that seems to be the basic birthright of every Hungarian.

Yes, I owe Mr. Ince not only a greater understanding of the theater, and the affiliated skills which are employed in its service, but by sage words and astonishing examples he definitely managed to increase my not too lavish fund of human tolerance as well.

I'll tell you the kind of guy Alex Ince was.

When I'd been working for him for about three months, I said to him one afternoon that I was going to quit a little earlier because it was my sweetheart's birthday. I told him I'd bought her a couple of fine Victorian bracelets, and that I wanted to stop off at the store to pick them up before I went uptown.

"You are going to the jeweler's right now?" Ince asked.

"Yes," I said. "It's over on Madison near Fifty-sixth Street."

"Excellent!" said Mr. Ince. "Would you mind very much if I went with you?"

"Not at all," I said, "but I'll have to go straight up to my girl's afterward. I hope you won't mind."

Actually I was a little annoyed that he wanted to come along with me. I couldn't see the point of it at all, but as long as he had asked I couldn't very well refuse him. So we left the office and took a cab up to Fifty-sixth Street.

The jeweler had promised to attach some safety catches on my little bracelets. Before finally wrapping them up he showed them to me once more, and so Ince also got a look at them.

"How do you like them?" I asked him.

"They are nice," he said, taking them into his hands. "Quite nice. And is this the best that you were able to find in this store?"

No matter how you looked at it, it was a hell of a tactless question, and I didn't quite know what to make of it.

"You see, she likes Victorian jewelry," I said, "and she is particularly fond of trinkets that are made of gold and black lacquer. You understand?"

"I'm sorry," said Ince, putting the bracelets back on the counter. "I think you are making a big mistake."

I was stunned. What did the old goat mean, anyway?

188

"A mistake?" I said. "What kind of a mistake?"

"You must forgive me for what I'm going to tell you," he said, "but I'm sure, I'm absolutely sure, you ought to get your sweetheart something much nicer."

I felt myself suddenly getting quite sore at him. I hadn't wanted him to come along with me in the first place, and now that he had crowded himself into my goddamned afternoon he was making soap bubbles out of my birthday gift.

"I'm sorry," I said, "but these bracelets are exactly what I was looking for. They cost me nearly two hundred dollars, and that's a lot more than I actually can afford right now."

At this moment, as if obeying a sudden, irresistible impulse, Mr. Ince took my hand in his, and, as I looked into his shining obsidian eyes, it came to me with a shock that, for some mysterious reason of his own, the old Chinaman was deeply moved.

"Please don't be angry with me," he said, "but, believe me, this is not the time to think of money. You must get your little girl a real surprise. I'm sure she will like these bracelets very much, too, but be honest about it—in a certain way, she is really expecting them. It will not be a great surprise, a surprise that one likes to bring on a birthday. Will it?"

Let me tell you, there was something so compelling, almost hypnotic, in the way he said all this, that I felt a good deal mollified by his earnestness.

"Unfortunately," I said, "everything else I looked at cost a great deal more money than I can spare right now, so I've settled for the best and most attractive gift within my means."

"Then you must let me help you!" he said. "Let us look at some other things in the shop and see if we can't find something that would be more suitable. Please, please let us do that!"

I don't have to tell you that the goddamned jeweler had overheard every word we'd said and had for more than five minutes been jittering in back of us like an epileptic ventriloquist. Before I was even able to raise a protesting hand he was flashing a couple of jewelry trays under our noses and making clucking Madison Avenue noises over them.

"Just a minute, Mr. Ince," I said. "If you're planning to put out a lot of money for me this afternoon, I want you to know that I won't be able to pay you back any part of it for God knows how long. Never, probably. I just want you to know that."

But Ince had turned completely aside from me and was already fishing around critically in those black-velvet jewelry ponds.

To tell you the truth, I didn't quite know how to take this presumptuous, buttinsky performance of his. In fact, I was so

189

puzzled by my own feelings that I hardly paid any attention to him, until he finally lifted a necklace off a tray and held it in the air right in front of me.

"Now, this is more like it!" he said triumphantly. "This is really beautiful, and it will look just wonderful on your little friend. How do you like it?"

"How much is it?" I said to the jeweler.

"Only four hundred dollars," said the brigand. "It's a real museum piece and worth at least double that amount, any day."

"Put it in a nice gift box," said Mr. Ince. "Make a nice package, and we'll wait for it."

While he was fumbling in his pocket for his checkbook, I felt myself getting sore at him all over again. What the hell did he think he was doing, anyway? He was either off his nut, or he had some angle that I hadn't figured out yet. I was certainly determined never to give him back a penny of his two hundred bucks, that was sure.

I walked over to the other end of the store and stared moodily out the window. After a couple of minutes, Ince approached me and put his hand on my shoulder.

I can tell you one thing, if he had been a younger man I would certainly have bawled the crap out of him at this point. As it was, I just made a gesture of impatience and continued to stare stonily out into the street, where a soft spring drizzle had just set in.

"My friend," Mr. Ince said softly, "I want you to understand why I have done this thing this afternoon."

I turned around and looked at him sternly, and, by God, the crazy old Tibetan positively had tears in his eyes.

"You see," he said, in a shaky voice, "I know that you like this young lady very much. You do, don't you?"

"Of course," I said. "You know I do."

"All right," he said. "And I also know that you are very happy with her. You are, aren't you?"

"Yes, yes," I said impatiently.

"And I'll tell you what else I know," said Mr. Ince. "I know that you have many, many friends in this city who are very fond of you. If you had to have sudden money for an operation, hundreds of people would lend it to you, if you didn't have it. If you couldn't pay your rent, or your telephone bill, everybody would be ready to lay it out for you. I'm sure of that. Whatever bad luck would come your way, they would certainly help you. Well, then, at this moment in your life you are not having such bad luck. You're in love with a beautiful young woman who also is very much in love with you. That is so, isn't it? Well, then, Mr. King, I want you to remember that Alexander Ince once stood by you, not in misfortune, but in your *happiness!* You see, I, too, was once very much in love, just like you, quite a long while ago, and after some strange happenings I lost not only my girl but my position, too; and everything in that life ran through my fingers and came to nothing. You know, I have since wondered many and many a time whether it might not have been of great help to me, and to the whole situation, if I could have found anyone in all of Budapest who would have stood bravely by me in *my* happiness. . . ."

By the way, the young woman whose birthday I was celebrating was called Marjorie Belle, not to be confused with Margie Lou King, my present and final wife.

Marjorie Belle was a diminutive ballerina whom I had first encountered in southern California some two years before, when *Life* magazine had dispatched me out to the West Coast on a rather amusing scouting job.

You see, Walt Disney's first feature-length picture, *Snow White and the Seven Dwarfs,* had just been released, and I had told Mr. Billings, the managing editor, that each cartoon character in the picture surely had a human prototype who had served as a model for the artists. I had long known that the animators at the studio preferred to make their drawings after watching films of live actors going through the various motions that were essential for their cartoon sequences.

"You mean," said Mr. Billings, "that there are real people who posed for the seven dwarfs and all the rest of them?"

"Certainly," I said. "I have friends who are working out at Disney's and they have assured me that their sketches represent a synthesis which is based on the movements of living models."

"Good!" said Mr. Billings. "Obviously our Hollywood office is never going to get any of this stuff for us, so why don't you fly out to the Coast and see if you can dig up some of this photo material for our next issue? *Snow White* is getting more publicity and public attention than any other film is likely to get this year, and it would be a real scoop for us to print the original human cast of characters, wouldn't it?"

So the following morning I flew out to Hollywood, and the day after I'd landed at the Beverly Wilshire I had photographs of all the seven dwarfs, of the stepmother, and even of the prince; the only one who still eluded me was Snow White herself. You see, for some mysterious reason Disney wanted to keep her identity under wraps for a while, and no one, outside of a small group in the studio, had the vaguest idea who she really was!

But, as I said before, I had some old friends working out at the plant, and in another couple of days I was able to inform their publicity department that I knew the identity of the model for Snow White. Disney finally gave his consent for us to take some photos of her, which we couldn't have done without his agreement because, as it turned out, she was married to one of the head animators at the studio.

Her name was Marjorie Belle, and she was a ravishing eighteen-year-old ballerina. When I got my first gander at her, it gave me such a jolt that remnants of the atomic fall-out stayed with me for the next five years.

But I'm nobody's gladsome fool, either, and after taking a good look at little Marjorie Belle I went right out and bought myself a plane ticket back to New York. The *Life* office in the East had expected me to stay a month or six weeks on the Coast, but, when I considered the high potential for incipient mischief and disaster that was hovering all around me out there, I decided to cop myself a fast walk.

What would have been the sense of hanging around, anyway? She was married, and I was married, and it was obvious that I was going to get an awful crush on her, so I did the only thing that made sense, under the circumstances. I packed up my bundle of scoop photographs and beat it back East.

And that's the way the land lay, until about a year and a half later, when little Marjorie called me on the phone at my office one afternoon and told me that she was in New York. Alone!

I took her to the theater that evening, and later we went up to dance at the Savoy Ballroom, in Harlem.

What an evening!

The lights were rosy and subdued, the girls looked enchanting, the band wasn't just swinging, it was wailing. And Marjorie Belle told me she was separated from her husband.

"And what are your plans now?" I asked her.

"Well, now I'm going back to California," she said. "I only had a chance to come on East because I was on the road with a Hollywood variety troupe that played its last date in Boston day before yesterday. In fact, I have a ticket for the Chicago train that leaves here tomorrow morning at ten-forty-five."

"In God's name!" I said. "You only just got here, and it certainly seems silly to dash right back, particularly since your marriage is on the rocks anyway. Why are you in such a mad rush to get back?"

"I'm not," she said. "But the company I danced with has paid for my ticket, and I really don't know how I'd get along here in New York. I'd just love to stay here. Believe me, I'd like nothing better than to stay here."

If you are interested, and want to read an exhaustive account of this emotional safari in all its lush detail, you can find it in a collection of stories called *The Vogue Reader*, which is a potpourri of stuff out of *Vogue* magazine that was published by Julian Messner a few years ago. Meanwhile I'll give you a brief topography of some of the salient peaks, promontories and quicksands of this romantic landscape, so that you will at least be able to follow my hegira with understanding, if not sympathy.

"Listen, Marjorie," I said, "there is a man called Einar Skobeleff, who has recently started a dancing group named the New World Ballet Company. Well, then, this character has been after me for weeks to get him some kind of publicity in *Life* magazine, but, frankly, until this minute I didn't quite see what I possibly could do for him. Another thing, he has also been begging me to write him the story for some sort of new ballet he wants to produce, because, it seems, he has a whole roster of young composers on hand who are in desperate search for likely ballet material. So this is what I've decided, Marjorie. I'm going to go home this very minute, and I'm going to write Mr. Skobeleff a brand-new ballet, in which you are going to be the leading danseuse. Get it?"

"What kind of ballet?" she said, and I could see her face clouding over with uncertainty.

"Don't worry," I said, "I'll think of one in the taxi, on the way downtown. You mustn't be worried, and you've just got to believe me. You know I don't drink, and the stories you've probably heard about me were just gotten up by people who've never even met me. Do you know what I read about myself in a column just recently? Somebody claimed that I didn't even exist; that I was just a hoax, a phony rumor, a practical joke, a phantom deliberately invented by a couple of Hungarian journalists on a rainy Sunday afternoon in a coffeehouse in Budapest!"

I said a lot of other stuff to reassure her, and finally I could see that she started to believe that I was serious about writing a ballet for her.

Half an hour later I dropped her at her hotel. "Don't you leave tomorrow morning," I said to her. "When you get upstairs, you just phone your company manager and tell him to turn in your railroad ticket, because you're going to stay here for a while. Promise?"

"I promise," she said.

So I took a small kiss as a down payment and went home to write a ballet for her. By six-thirty in the morning I was finished with it, and it really wasn't such a bad job, considering.

I'll tell you a little about it. It consisted of two scenes, the first of which was located on top of the Empire State Building.

As the curtain goes up, a radio announcer is just finishing a commercial for a cough medicine, and when this is concluded, he says, "Ladies and gentlemen, we are on top of the tallest building in America, to give you an eye-witness account of a most unusual event, an event which has never before been brought in front of a microphone. My friends of the radio audience, we are about to bring you the voices of all the winds of the world, who are having their annual board-of-directors' meeting right here on this terrace, this very night. Just remember that this extraordinary report is brought to you by the makers of Lick-a-Cold, who have spared no expense to again bring into your homes a phenomenal, an epoch-making radio sensation."

The announcer goes on to tell about the first arrival, the West Wind, who climbs over the side of the roof in typical Western getup—goat-hair chaps, six-shooters, etc.—and is quickly followed by the South Wind, who is dressed as a Southern colonel; and, of course, the East and North winds also eventually arrive, rigged out in appropriate attire. It stands to reason that all these characters make their appearance to the sound of suitable music, to which they perform their varied choreographic evolutions. After these major protagonists we have a few minor breezes, and even a few ill winds, who come onto the scene accompanied by fitting Hebraic dirges of an *oi-weh* nature, the theme of which is chiefly carried by clarinets and oboes.

The meeting is at last called to order, and, as happens at most important board meetings, the powerful big shots just pass every motion that suits themselves and vote everybody else out of order.

Suddenly, the music goes completely haywire as a frantic late arrival leaps crazily upon the board-room table. His hair stands on end, and he is obviously too obsessed for any form of rational behavior.

Who is he?

Through a wild cacophony of sound, the announcer finally manages to get it straight and tells the listening audience a truly shocking piece of news. It seems that this highly dependable little wind, who for centuries has blown the drapes of public statues proudly across their genitals, has suddenly suffered a nervous breakdown and insists that from now on he means to blow *in the other direction!*

You can imagine the racket and the consternation caused by this announcement. Of course the staid, respectable winds try to reason with him. They remind him of his grave responsibility to the public. They appeal to his sense of chivalry. It is all hopeless.

What? Will he bring a blush of shame to the cheek of innocent American womanhood?

Yes, he will! He's off his rocker and he doesn't give a damn what happens. And so, with a last maniacal scream, he leaps overboard, and all the other assembled winds follow him in a crescendo of hysterical rage and alarm.

That's the end of Scene One.

Scene Two takes place in that sunken part of Rockefeller Plaza which in summer is spotted with beach umbrellas and in winter pretends to be a skating rink.

When the lights go up, two song writers down on their luck are bemoaning their sad fate in typical Tin Pan Alley doggerel. It develops that they have just been evicted from their hotel and are obliged to spend their night out of doors. In the midst of their little dirge, they hear someone approaching, and, afraid that it might be a policeman, they quickly hide behind a stone pedestal.

It proves that they have been alarmed about nothing. It is only a long line of long-legged Rockettes, tripping their way home after the last show. They walk sideways, of course, two steps forward and one step back, exactly in rhythm, as they do on the stage. Just as the song writers are about to emerge from their hideout, other footsteps are heard, and this time it turns out to be a couple of lovers, who playfully cavort down the long staircase until they wind up right in front of the fountain. In short, they are standing in the very shadow of the huge Golden Boy who, for reasons best known to the Rockefellers, stands like a gargantuan paperweight at the back of the plaza.

And then the young girl, very girlishly and therefore unaccountably, gives signs of being desperately smitten with the beauty of this piece of athletic plumbing. Of course the boy tries, good-naturedly, to divert her from her debasing aberration, but the young woman, consistent with the manner of her species, is quite unable to stop her mad compulsion, which seems fated to bring their rendezvous to a disastrous conclusion.

In the final stages of her unreasonableness, the girl at last charges her lover with being insensitive to Art and the Higher Things in Life and flatly accuses him of being interested in nothing but necking. Goaded beyond caution by her cruel words, the young man gives her some deliberately low-brow answers and finally accuses her, in turn, of snobbery and affectation.

At this critical point of our little drama, the alarming figure of the wind with the nervous breakdown can be seen stag-

195

gering along the parapet. The music is loaded with ominous implications as he proceeds to cavort frantically across the midnight scene.

Our heroine has instinctively frozen up against the protecting arms of her lover, and it stands to reason that they are both stunned into immobility by this strange apparition. Then, suddenly, the rampant psychopath takes a long and delighted look at the golden Prometheus, or whatever the hell it is, and gives an ear-splitting shriek of wild ecstasy. The lovers watch with growing fear and alarm as he inflates his cheeks to enormous size and blows an absolute cyclone of a blast right across the statue's midriff.

Slowly the enormous drapes begin to move aside, as if they were supported on gigantic hinges, and suddenly there is disclosed to our view a crotch which is so blindingly illuminated by neon lights that all we can see is

THE PAUSE THAT REFRESHES.
DRINK COCA-COLA!

And now our little heroine gives a loud scream on her own account and falls senseless to the ground, with her nose caught in her lover's trouser cuff.

Luckily, at this point all the other winds have finally arrived, and, after a brief, energetic struggle, they manage to overpower their demented colleague and lead him gibbering off into the wings.

And now at last the song writers gaily emerge from their hiding place. It is years since they had actually seen lovers of opposite genders going through their amorous paces, and they observe with pleasure how affectionately the young man occupies himself in reviving his still-unconscious inamorata. They have found a wonderful title for a new song, and, after just a few preliminary bleatings, both the lyrics and the melody seem to be ready for a first run-through. It is called "Serenade to a Statue."

As the two song writers are busy auditioning their new material for each other, our heroine suddenly opens her eyes and impulsively embraces her ecstatic lover.

In the finale, the young couple perform an enraptured *pas de deux* up and down the Rockefeller Center staircase, and at last the curtain falls, to thunderous applause.

At ten-thirty in the morning I submitted this little opus to Mr. Skobeleff, and of course he was enchanted with it.

"There is only one stipulation I have to make," I said to him. "The girl who is going to play the sweetheart is somebody I am going to choose."

Skobeleff's nose turned so pale that I was sure that it had once been frozen. "Is she a dancer?" he asked.

"Her name is Marjorie Belle," I said. "She's an accomplished ballerina, and what's more, she was the original model for Disney's Snow White. And that's also our big publicity angle. Get it?"

Skobeleff phoned Marjorie at her hotel and offered her three hundred dollars in advance, on a contract to dance for his company. When he called her up, I looked at the clock. It was eleven-fifteen.

Her train was gone, but she was sleeping like the princess in the fairy tale, not only because she believed in magic, but because she had absolute faith that when the occasion arose I was going to perform miracles for her.

And don't think I didn't.

Well, as I told you, I was editing *Stage* magazine later on, and one day I had occasion to go to Central Islip, Long Island, to visit a friend who had managed to land himself in a mental hospital out there. Marjorie was going to come along, and Mr. Ince also wanted to be of the party, so on a sunny afternoon in late September the three of us started out.

When we were about halfway there, Marjorie suddenly decided that we ought to buy our sick friend a carton of cigarettes. I stopped off at a drugstore and she quickly jumped out to make her purchase, while Ince and I parked ourselves under some old elm trees across the way.

"This Marjorie is an adorable girl," said Mr. Ince, looking smilingly after her.

"Yes," I said, "she's one of the best."

"Such girls are very rare nowadays," said Mr. Ince.

"That's true," I agreed. "You know, I'm very seriously thinking of marrying her."

Mr. Ince was suddenly frozen with consternation. "Oh my God!" he said. "You're not really going to marry her? Please, say that you're joking. It will be the biggest mistake of your life—the biggest!"

Well, I was absolutely stupefied. The old guy had always been crazy about her, and he'd just a few seconds ago gotten through raving about her. And now, suddenly, without rhyme or reason, he was warning me against marrying her.

"What in the world is wrong with her?" I said. "You told me yourself she's one in a million, so what has happened all of a sudden?"

Ince gave a great big commiserative sigh. "Oh, Mr. King, Mr. King," he said, "you are in some ways such a very, very young man."

"Come on," I said, "you give me one good reason why I

should not marry this attractive, talented girl, who is, incidentally, very devoted to me. Come on, now," I said, "trot out your reason."

"Just think, for a moment," he said, "when this beautiful young girl now comes to visit you at the office, how the switchboard operator quickly gets you on the line, and with a little laugh of pleasure she says to you, 'Mr. King, your lady friend is here!' Right?"

"So what?" I said. "What are you trying to tell me?"

"I am trying to tell you that when once she is your wife, and drops in on the office, nobody will be so terribly glad to see her, not even you. The telephone girl won't even call you, she'll come right into your office in person, and, out of the corner of her mouth, she is going to say to you, '*Mr. King, your wife is outside.*' Don't you understand, when Marjorie comes to see you now, it brightens up the whole place. I kiss her hand, we all admire her new hat, she makes the dreary place *look* good and *smell* good for the rest of the day. But, believe me, with a wife it is quite different. A wife appears at her husband's work place either to spy on him, to reproach him, or to serve him with divorce papers. Whatever her reason for coming, it is bound to embarrass him and to put a damper on the whole office force. No, Mr. King, you must think carefully about this. For example, I know that you are even now planning to send Marjorie's father an airplane ticket, so he can come East for the Christmas holidays. Just think what a surprise this will be for her; think how ecstatic she will be when the old man suddenly arrives here. Her gratitude to you will know no bounds. But if you are married to her, and she is your wife, she will look reproachfully at you on Christmas morning and say, 'Well, big shot, where is my father?' No, Mr. King, you are about to put an end to a wonderful pattern of existence. I'm surprised that a man as intelligent as you should sometimes be so terribly reckless and foolhardy. But I suppose you will not listen to me, because I can see it in your eyes, you are one of life's hopelessly chronic bridegrooms. May God help you!"

That was Ince for you.

Before I forget, let me tell you that the inmate whom we went to visit at the booby hatch in Long Island later wrote a book about his experiences, which even became something of a best seller. There is a villain in this book of his, a man called Max, who, the author claims, was largely responsible for driving him off his nut.

Now, then, you may well believe me, that throughout the good many years that I had known him I had done nothing but favors for the teetering wretch who wrote this dizzy book; and yet the scoundrel, Max, who is supposed to have driven him balmy, not only resembles me physically, to the last detail, but quite obviously makes free with some of my most cherished prejudices, besides. So there you have it.

And to think that we took the trouble to bring a carton of cigarettes to this toothless werewolf.

Pfui!

## CHAPTER TWENTY-ONE

WHEN I LANDED at Lexington for my third cure, great changes seemed to have taken place down there. For one thing, the psychologists and psychiatrists were high in the saddle, and the tough custodial forces were definitely on the defensive. It didn't last very long, but, while it lasted, it was possible to demonstrate that doctors, and only doctors, could ever achieve any worth-while and effective methods of coping with the problem of drug addiction.

For instance, I attended innumerable meetings at which group therapy was practiced, and there was no question in my mind that individuals otherwise inaccessible to any form of social approach or co-ordination became, in the course of these sessions, voluntarily co-operative and even self-critical to a really astonishing degree.

I saw no miracles performed, but I witnessed the next best thing. I saw and heard drug addicts who, finally, freely confessed to themselves and to others that their addiction was just an inadequate but desperate cover for their failure to accept the responsibilities of grown-up men. Now, then, this admission is so grimly basic a requirement for any reformation, that no conceivable cure can ever be achieved without it.

They had some damned good psychiatrists at Lexington during that short spell of purposeful rehabilitation, and the best of these, a Dr. James Thorpe, has since become one of my very dearest friends. In fact, he is the only psychiatrist in the country to whom I would dare to disclose the shaky state of my mental equilibrium, if I ever decided to do such a thing.

You won't find Dr. James Thorpe down in Lexington any more; no, he flunked out into private practice, and so he now makes himself a pot of money attending some well-heeled psychopaths around Washington, D.C. However, his over-developed social conscience causes all his spare time to be consumed by endless derelict intruders who are still in search of postgraduate help, after all their years in Lexington.

Incidentally, the third time I went down there for a cure my roommate was a twenty-two-year-old kid from New York City. He was of Yugoslav descent, his name was Mirko Pavlic, and he was a first offender doing a "deuce" for pushing junk.

Also, I soon discovered to my cost that he was chronically afflicted with the screaming nightmares. It was awful. I sometimes had to wake him two or three times a night, but he was always so contrite and so grateful to me, I didn't have the heart to move out on him, as a couple of other people already had done. Besides, he was obviously in some kind of bad jam, and I hoped that I'd eventually manage to talk him into getting some help from the local psychiatric staff.

But Mirko didn't seem to care too much for the "nut-crackers" around the place, and I think he was even convinced that consistent exposure to their ministrations might drive a man permanently off his rocker. I wasn't too sure that he was altogether wrong about this, but still even I had to admit that my young friend was haunted by devils that certainly required to be exorcised by some form of authority superior to my own.

Another reason why Mirko was especially leery of most of the people in Lexington arose from his quite remarkable good looks. He was a pale, dark-haired, almost somber-looking youngster, who was constantly being waylaid and propositioned by long-term, sex-starved prisoners, as well as by the dozens of professional pansies that flitted all over the joint. It wasn't easy for the kid.

Well, one night when he'd again made an unusually loud racket in our room, I woke him up and told him to get himself a couple of aspirins and to drink some warm water.

"I'm sorry, Mirko," I said, "but you just gotta get yourself straightened out, because, if you're gonna keep this up, I'll just have to cut out on you, too. You can see how sick I am, and, God knows, I need every minute of rest that happens to fall on me. You just gotta go and see a croaker tomorrow, that's all!"

"It's got nothing to do with a croaker," said Mirko. "If you wanna come out to the day room with me, I'll . . . well, I'll tell you what I think is bothering me."

"What's wrong with telling me right here?" I said.

"No, I don't like to talk about it in the dark," he said. "Put a blanket around you, so you won't catch cold."

So we trudged out into the day room, where a feeble little night light was burning all the time, and after Mirko had lit cigarettes for himself and for me he started to talk.

"Did I ever show you a picture of my kid sister?" he asked.

"No," I said. "I saw a picture of your mother once, but not your sister. Not that I remember."

He took a picture out of his shirt pocket and handed it to me. "Her name is Theresa," he said, "but we call her Tessa. She's just turned fifteen."

I looked at the snapshot of his sister for a long while, and I suddenly pitied the Hallmark people, and all the other sterile unfortunates who are manufacturing and consuming ready-made greeting cards, because, even among their choicest items, among their most expensive numbers, they had never been able to corner a Christmas angel that deserved to hold a candle to little Tessa Pavlic. She was a darb.

"She's very beautiful," I said, handing him back his picture.

"She's just turned fifteen," he said, "and you know how it is, the boys are just starting to notice her; and she's getting so that she watches her hair, and her clothes, a lot more than she used to. You know what I mean?"

"She's a doll," I said.

"Well, I'm her older brother," said Mirko, "and she always used to look up to me. Always. Even when she was just a little twerp, she used to like to sit on my lap more than anybody else's. And, later on, she hardly ever did anything without telling me about it. Even about her homework, and her girl friends, and all that stuff—everything. You dig?"

"I'm hep," I said.

"And then, when I started to get hooked on junk, it sure made an awful rip in her. She never talked to me about it, you understand, but she used to bawl her head off whenever she heard my old man lacing it into me. She'd just go into the next room and bury herself in the bedclothes, and bawl by the hour. Man, it sure shook me."

"Well," I said, "that's what junk does. Poor kid, you'll have to make it all up to her, some day."

"That's not the whole of it," said Mirko.

"It never is," I said.

"You see, my people are strictly square," he said, "as square as they come. My old man has been working for the same brewery for twenty-six years, and my mother cooks and washes and irons all of Tessa's dresses and stuff, and a couple of times she even knitted some fancy socks for me. You know what I mean?"

"Real, solid old-timers," I said.

"That's right. Well, lately, Tessa started to baby-sit for some of the neighbors, and the reason for it was she'd seen a pair of high-heeled red shoes in Beck's shoe store on our corner, and those shoes cost eight ninety-five or eight ninety-nine or something, and Tessa just made up her mind she wanted to buy those shoes for herself, see? Well, finally the kid had saved up five dollars already, and she used to keep the dough in a little brass box that I'd once gotten for her down in Chinatown. You can't imagine how the kid was looking forward to getting herself that pair of shoes. She'd never owned a pair with high heels before, and so she was getting an awful big bang out of the whole deal."

Mirko suddenly stopped talking and seemed to lose himself for a moment in reveries of his past. Meanwhile, I felt a painful stab of intuition goading me to a most unpleasant conclusion to his story.

"What happened to the five bucks?" I said.

"You know what happened," said Mirko. "You're a junkie yourself. One day, when I was hard up for a fix and my connection wouldn't let me have it on the cuff, I just took the five bucks out of her brass box and laid it on the line."

"You should have told her," I said.

"Yeah, but I was gonna put it back, before she got wise to it. I never had a chance, though, 'cause that same night my old man asked her how much money she had saved up. She told him five bucks. 'All right,' he says, 'I'll give you the other four dollars, so you can go down and get yourself the shoes to wear for next Sunday.' I could hear everything they said, because I was lying down in the next room, sort of halfway on the nod, from the shot I'd taken. I just lay there and listened to them. Then I heard the kid go into her room and fumble around with the box for a minute . . . and then it suddenly got awful quiet. I guess my old man must have followed her into her room and seen in a flash that the dough was gone. And then he started to curse like a son-of-a-bitch, in Yugoslav, and then he smashed the box down on the table and screamed, 'We got a thief in the house! Nothing in this house is safe any more. He'll steal the mattresses off our beds and the gold fillings out of our teeth, while we're sleeping— that's what's gonna happen to us. But I'm gonna put an end to this, once and for all. Yes, I'm gonna skin him alive while he's still in the reach of my hand, before the cops get after him, before he disgraces us in front of the whole neighborhood!' And then you know what happened? My kid sister suddenly starts screaming on top of her lungs, too, and bawls out that she's made a terrible mistake, that it's all her fault, that she's really given the five dollars to her club, for a party they were planning for Easter. I tell you, that kid kept talking so fast and she made such a racket that in the end I think she even managed to convince my old man that it was all the fault of her own forgetfulness."

Mirko was silent again. Indeed, he put his hand across his mouth as if he regretted having spoken so freely, and so much, on a matter of such secret desperate concern to himself; on a matter which obviously embittered all his waking hours and was certainly making a wild devastation of his sleep.

"It was damned white of the kid to cover up for you the way she did," I said "She sure acted much older than her age, and, what's more, she certainly still cares a hell of a lot about you, don't she?"

Then Mirko started to cry, the way a very small child cries, with water running out of his eyes and his mouth and his nose, and I think he didn't mind so terribly much making such a mess of himself in front of me, because I was more than twenty-eight years older than he, and, even so, I was only a junkie like himself.

"Don't worry, you'll make it up to her," I said. "You'll hit the street again, and in a few months you'll get yourself a job and that five bucks won't seem like nothing at all to you. You know that."

"No," said Mirko, drying his face. "No, no, no, it don't work out that way, and you know it. I'm her older brother, don't you get it? She used to look up to me all the time. And then I went and took the dough she'd saved for herself by baby-sitting for the neighbors. And then she went and covered up for me to the old man. Don't you see? How in hell am I ever going to straighten that out? Suppose I give her fifty dollars when I get out of here, or five hundred, or even fifty thousand. What the hell difference does it all make, now? You know that I can't never straighten this thing out for myself. Never! 'Cause you know damned well that some things just have to go on and on and on, and they can't never, never be straightened out. Not in this goddamned world, anyway."

I tried to occupy myself purposefully during the four months and fifteen days that I stayed at Lexington this time. I helped to edit the institutional paper; I made weekly cartoons; I did endless illustrations and decorations for their quarterly magazine; and I even ran some English and French classes for the inmates.

Besides all this, I wrote a play about Casanova called *The Good Gray Wolf*. I had long meant to write such a play because years ago when I visited the castle of Dux in Bohemia, I realized with horror and sympathy how painful it must have been for old Casanova to end his days in such a rugged inhospitable pile of stones. It was a refuge, of course, and, nominally, he was the librarian, but I knew from his diary and many of his extant letters how desperately this poor, exiled southerner had longed for another sight of the canals and lagoons of his native city. His most rapturous outbursts were inspired, not by his mistresses, but by the Adriatic Sea, whose bosom he saw eternally bejeweled with her greatest treasure, Venice.

At any rate, I decided to write a play about his exile as the librarian at Dux, and, since I naturally took it for granted that he still had some sort of love affair going even there, I supplied him with the ideal subject of seduction, for both the novice and the old roué, a chambermaid.

Of course this particular maid was very young and very pretty, and Casanova managed to beguile her innocence, mostly by the magic of his facile verbosity and the wonder of his many daring and outrageous tales.

Three pages of my manuscript have recently turned up among my threadbare and scattered effects, and, if you want to know what I did in Lexington in 1951, here is a small sample of my activities.

(Someone has obviously accused Casanova of being an atheist and even an unfrocked priest; in short, a renegade to the Church, and so Casanova now defends himself.)

> No, my dear prince,
> I am a faithful son of Mother Church.
> The Holy Office never proved me otherwise.
> I'm conscious that my naked soul
> Is constantly in sight of God,
> And yet, I do not dare reduce
> All visible creation
> As footstool to my kneeling.
> Are there not morals in rainbows?
> And homilies in buttercups?
> I think it shows great vanity
> To give so much concern
> To one's salvation;
> To give up all the glories of the world,
> And see God's generous handiwork
> Only in terms of venial temptation—
> I would not so demean the universe,
> Merely to save my measly soul.

(Later on, the young chambermaid, Anna, wonders whether he is not going to find her a little too coarse for his taste, since she is just an ordinary girl of the people.)

ANNA

> Am I not much too simple for you,
> After all?
> I am like common bread,
> To one who's used to feasting on roast fowl.

204

CASANOVA

You are like bread fresh from the oven,
With smells of wheat and milk,
And good things of the earth,
Coming through crusts of crisp perfection.
It takes an epicure to properly appraise
Of such a toothsome loaf.

ANNA
(*in suppressed excitement*)

Say on!

CASANOVA

You are like honey from the comb,
The wax of youth still clinging to
The sweetness of your treasures.
You are the firm and fleshy grape,
Bursting with pure and unfermented savors.
Even a jaded appetite would wake anew
To feed on fruit as succulent as yours.

ANNA
(*excitement still growing*)

Say more . . . Giacomo!
Say more!

CASANOVA

You are my life's one ultimate reward,
A prize I have not earned;
But no man could deserve, more properly,
Because I truly know your worth.
A king could find no greater treasure in his bed.
Dressed, to deceive,
You could seduce the titled lechers of the world
And, in your white and soft resilience,
The remnants of their libido
Would gather for a last assault
On ecstasy.

ANNA

Please, tell me more. . . .
Please, do not stop . . . I beg of you!

CASANOVA
(*holding her in his arms*)

Between the firm and mystic pillars of your loins
Live such frail secrets
As might easily beguile
The caution of a cardinal
And bring belated blushes of regret
To the pale buttocks of a Turkish eunuch.

*(They embrace and kiss passionately.)*

Well, anyway, I wrote three acts of it, with lots of plot and subplot, and I must say I found it more satisfying than getting psychoanalyzed.

And, in the long run, it was a hell of a lot cheaper, too.

# CHAPTER TWENTY-TWO

AFTER ABOUT a year up at *Life,* I was starting to grow very restless to get the hell out of the New York office for a while. I kept a sharp lookout for some possible out-of-town news break of so peculiar a nature that my special presence might instantly be required in Kamchatka or Lusinpicollo. I read about twenty papers a day, always hoping to find something interesting and photogenic that would be worth the expense and the bother of a good long trip.

As a matter of fact, a couple of journeys that I did make paid off very handsomely and got us some wonderful stories, but most of the time I was just hung up, because so much of the junk that gets printed in the daily papers can't stand being seriously investigated, much less photographed.

For instance, I once read a very promising little paragraph in one of the Hearst papers about a most extraordinary scientific experiment that was supposed to be going on in Scotland. It was a piece printed, or reprinted, by a Hearst science editor called Gobind Behari Lal, who certainly must have had himself a hell of a time digging up sufficient sensational items to attract the attention of his adenoidal readers. Remember that it is quite rightly assumed by the publishers of all mass-circulation sheets that the average man is interested only in aspects of science which are astonishing, monstrous or unbelievable, or, better still, all three of these.

So, as I was saying, I read in Gobind Behari Lal's column one day that a scientist in Scotland had completed a truly epoch-making experiment. It seems that this Scottish savant had taken half a dozen rats from the same litter and had, for the duration of several months, fed them consistently on varying national diets. He had, for example, fed one of them exclusively on spaghetti with marinara sauce. Another on nothing but sweet and pungent shrimp, and so on.

Result? After a while the rice-fed rodent had started to

develop definitely Asiatic characteristics—high cheekbones, slanty eyes, etc. The rat that had been given nothing but chopped liver and gefüllte fish displayed marked Semitic attributes—a big schnozzle, a tendency to argue over trifles, a decided gift for mercantile finagling.

Well, you've got to admit that here, at last, was a hell of a photogenic science story. I won't deny that I read a good deal more into that paragraph than actually was printed there, but I'd never been to Scotland and I was certainly willing and anxious to go. Also I hadn't contributed a good science item in a long time.

So I put through a long-distance call to the scientist in Aberdeen, and that at once proved to be a terrible mistake. There *was* something going on about special diets for rats in Aberdeen, of course, but nothing like the staggering little yarn that I had sunk by eyeteeth into.

And then I realized what a true sap I was, and how, in my eagerness to travel, I'd bitched up a perfectly good story. I could have framed the whole thing right here in New York. I should just have run the Hearst story as it stood, and, with a little putty and theatrical make-up, I could have fixed up the rats myself. We wouldn't have had to falsify anything either; it would just have been a dramatic re-enactment of some interesting, distant phenomena. What's more, all the picture services would have bought reproduction rights from us, and it would certainly have paid off very handsomely all around.

But another story which also had a rather fantastic beginning did work out very well for me, and that one happened to develop out of some private information that came to me one day, to the effect that a fierce but secret massacre had taken place somewhere on the border between Haiti and Santo Domingo. At the time I heard of it the newspapers had carried only a few skimpy accounts of this trouble, because it seems that most of their native correspondents in these two countries had suddenly been put under arrest.

My information came to me from a close friend of mine in Port-au-Prince, a famous *hungan* (witch doctor) called Cicerone Mayeux. He wrote to me that to his certain knowledge fifteen thousand Haitians had already been killed in the last three days, and that he was sure that the slaughter was still to proceed for the rest of the week at least.

"Our own government suppresses the news," he said, "not only because it is afraid of provoking the Dominican dictator Trujillo into invasion of our land, but it is equally frightened of our own population, which would certainly rise up in bitter indignation if it were conversant with the true extent of our disaster."

By the way, all this information proved subsequently to be quite correct, and the Haitian government had indeed jailed everybody who might have leaked any accurate news of the massacre out of the country. Let me say that the killing of Haitians by the hired assassins of Trujillo was nothing particularly new. It was just the scale of the slaughter that caused consternation and, finally, brought it to world attention.

Let me take just a moment, at this point, to define and deplore the whole gruesome state of Central and South American politics. Surely everybody who reads the papers must be aware that most of the banana, coffee, and sugar republics to the south of us are predominantly under the leadership and domination of out-and-out brigands. For centuries now, murderous generals and greedy juntas have exploited the poor populations of these lands with a ruthlessness and a brutality that no single colonial power has ever surpassed.

Now, then, if you ever listen over WNYC to the broadcasts from the United Nations, you can hear some of the delegates from Central and South America thundering vociferously against the repressive measures that obtain in Poland, in Rumania and in Hungary. As you listen to their demands for liberty and justice for these downtrodden populations, it will be helpful for you to remember that the last honest-to-God patriotic leader south of the Rio Grande who lived and died for his people was the bitterly disillusioned Simon Bolivar.

You might also recall that the presidents, the generals and the juntas who run these countries must, during their hazardous tenures, fill their pockets with the utmost haste, so that when they finally have to run away, accompanied by their wives and mistresses, they can at last afford to live like retired gangsters and pimps in countries where they are reasonably safe from native reprisals.

In short, Central and South America have, since their very origins, been the consistent breeding grounds for every form of brutal dictatorship and tyranny known in this hemisphere.

That much is surely axiomatic.

And that also explains how for over thirty years an unspeakable creature like Trujillo has been able not only to terrorize the people of his own land, but also to murder off something like twenty thousand Haitians with complete impunity.

Incidentally, I don't know whether you are aware that Haiti and Santo Domingo occupy just one island between them, and that the countries are separated only by a narrow, turbulent watercourse, most appropriately named the Massacre River. Now, it stands to reason that the differences and difficulties between these two peoples are manifold; but one of the deliberately false and manufactured reasons for trouble between them is the feeling among the Dominicans that the inhabitants of Haiti are Negroes, while they themselves are of pure Castilian breed. Nothing could, of course, be more absurd and untrue, and therefore nothing could possibly be more irrelevant. Both peoples are certainly a mixture of Carib and Afro-Latin stock and there probably isn't a single pure-blooded person of exclusively French or Spanish origin to be found in the entire island, unless they happen to be very recent immigrants to these countries.

Nevertheless, it is perfectly true that the Dominicans are, by and large, of lighter pigmentation than their French-speaking Haitian neighbors; and it was on a basis of nothing more than this disgusting piece of color snobbery that a cunning megalomaniac like Trujillo was able to launch his ghostly auto-da-fé.

You see, Haiti is enormously overpopulated and very poor, and so, when the sugar cane is ready to be harvested in neighboring Santo Domingo, a great many Haitian laborers are recruited for this work. This means that sometimes twenty or twenty-five thousand field laborers are invited across the border to help with the gathering of the crops.

Now, then, when the work is finished, a good many of these Haitians like to stay on in Santo Domingo for a while, in the hope that some other work might be coming along their way. Also, quite a number of them have brought their families with them, and they are likely to settle down to do a little truck gardening just for their own use.

But Trujillo didn't want them to stay, once their work was done. He claimed that if they intermarried with his own superior native stock they were eventually bound to darken the skins of all his beloved Santo Dominicans. At any rate, that's the bill of goods he managed to sell his people in 1938, when the recruited Haitian laborers proved somewhat slow in moving back to their own country.

And then, one night the dirty bastard gave a murderously ambiguous order to his soldiers. "All Haitians must be evacuated from Santo Domingo within one week," he said, "and the means must be drastic and memorable! Don't shoot, but get them out of here!"

Well, his men were armed only with machetes, and they did the best they could under the circumstances. They killed and mutilated about twenty thousand people, and at least a quarter of these were women and children. I brought back photographs for *Life* of some of these victims, photographs which showed children with saber wounds all over their heads and arms, and, although the Dominican Consulate protested violently against these libels, after the pictures were printed their government finally did pay some sort of cabbage indemnity to the Republic of Haiti.

I must say that the ruling powers in Haiti certainly did their goddamnedest to keep Rex Hardy, my photographer, from getting any sort of pictures of this slaughter. And that is understandable, too, because quite a few of their presidents have, in the past, been torn limb from limb, skinned alive, and split open like cordwood by an impulsive and indignant electorate.

I'm not planning to give you a blow-by-blow description of our battle with the frightened Haitian politicians to get those incriminating pictures out of their country. We simply took it for granted that after Hardy had shot all those photographs of the dead and the wounded, our hosts were going to frisk us down to our very skins and just confiscate the films, in the name of national security, if you like.

The fact is, we would never even have reached the border where the massacre had taken place if the ordinary Haitian peasants, who had heard about our mission from my *hungan* friend, hadn't supplied us with food, water, and gasoline and handed us carefully on, from village to village, until we finally managed to reach the scene of the actual disaster, near Fort Liberté.

And, once we got there, we were up against the Haitian Army, and, take my word for it, it was a damned well disciplined army, too, one that had been trained by the United States Marine Corps, and you can be sure that those boys didn't want any part of us. After all, they were there especially to protect the interests of the political ruling clique in Port-au-Prince, and, although one or two individual officers would have loved to help us and certainly sympathized with our aims, the first thing the colonel in charge ordered them to do was to confiscate our cameras.

We were prepared for that, of course. Luckily, we had already taken our pictures, and we had just one worry now: How the hell were we going to get these hot films out of the country?

Let me tell you at once, we could never have done it without the help of an elderly, nondescript American consul who happened to be stationed at Cap Haitien at that time.

He lived in a good-sized stone house right near the seashore, and when Hardy and I, dirty, unshaven and unslept, finally arrived there, we saw with considerable alarm that the entrance gate was guarded by an enormous, saliva-dripping mastiff. We were in a big hurry, too, because we took it for granted that the colonel had already issued orders to pick us up on some trumped-up charge or other, just to curtail our activities in that territory. We certainly had to get into the consulate damned fast, in the hope of stirring up a little friendly protection for ourselves, at least.

And there we were, wasting precious time, staring at the sinister hound for a full minute, while the miserable beast was staring right back at us without even once blinking his goddamned eyes. There seemed to be no visible bell in the neighborhood of that gate, and neither Hardy nor I was in the mood to rassle with the monster.

And then God suddenly was very good to us.

The hound yawned. And do you know what? He didn't have a single tooth in his sloppy head. He must have been a hundred years old, by the looks of his gums, and I tell you, we shoved that fourflusher out of the way so fast, he fell right over on his side like a top-heavy bundle of dirty laundry.

When we finally got into the house there seemed to be nobody around, but we could hear a radio playing, out toward the back somewhere. So we just followed the sound and came out on a glass-enclosed porch that had been built right over the sea.

By the way, I forgot to mention that when we made our entrance it was a Saturday afternoon in late November, and so, naturally, Mr. Hiram Smith, the consul, was listening to the Army-Navy game on his short-wave radio. Luckily for us, half time had been called and he was just then listening to the band music.

He was the sort of harmless, sandy-looking man you might reasonably expect to find in any hay-and-feed store in the United States. Of course Hardy and I looked something awful, and, by contrast to us, Mr. Smith was not only neat, he even had his coat and necktie on, although he was quite alone in the house at the moment.

Anyway, he toned down the racket on the radio and then got up and shook hands with us. What's more, he acted as if there was nothing unusual in our appearance at all, and as if our showing up at his house on that special Saturday afternoon was something that he'd been expecting for quite a while.

"Well," he said, after we'd all sat down, "I'd been wondering since this morning what had become of you two boys."

"Oh, so you knew we were around?" I said.

"You can't keep any secrets from the houseboys in Haiti," said Mr. Smith. "The progress of your trip was drummed all over this landscape, and so I knew that the Army must have been expecting you, too. I'm surprised they turned you loose."

"They took our cameras," said Hardy.

"I expect they would," said Mr. Smith. "Did you get anything on film before they took them away from you?"

"We've got sixteen rolls of film in our pockets," I said. "We're very much afraid that they'll lock us up and take them from us."

"Well," said Mr. Smith, "you boys better wash up a little, and, for the time being, I think you'd better leave those films in my medicine chest. . . . Yes, you'd better do that."

We all got up.

"Mrs. Smith has gone visiting this afternoon," he said, "but I'll dig you up a couple of towels, if you'll excuse me for a minute."

When he came back he also brought us a razor, a fresh cake of nice-smelling soap and a long narrow box to put our films in. After we'd cleaned ourselves up, he gave us a couple of cups of strong black coffee, and I could see he was very pleased that neither of us asked for, or expected, any hard liquor.

"And now," he said, "I'd like us to go over to the local hospital, and I'll introduce you to some really nice people."

It seemed like a screwball idea to go in for a spell of socializing at that particular moment, but Mr. Smith certainly represented some kind of safety for us, so I saw no reason for not humoring the old boy a little.

The hospital turned out to be a really remarkable structure, and, as it developed, Mr. Smith had almost singlehandedly conceived it, designed it, and even financed most of it. No wonder he was proud of the place. He introduced us to the various nuns and sisters of charity who formed the nursing staff of the establishment, and it was quite obvious that everybody in the hospital just doted on Hiram Smith. He was on particularly understanding and amiable terms with the elderly head nurse, called Sister Elizabeth, who seemed to be absolutely radiant with energy and laughing good cheer.

"I've been here twenty years," said Mr. Smith, "and I still don't talk any French. You know, I was twenty years in Mexico, too, but I never learned any Spanish, either. Just the same, I have no trouble at all making out Sister Elizabeth, and, what's more, I'm sure she understands me just fine, too."

In the midst of all these amiabilities a staff car suddenly pulled into the hospital yard, and half a dozen military cops poured out of it and instantly descended on us.

What happened next was exactly what I'd been expecting for the last three hours. Hardy and I were taken into an empty hospital room and frisked with a thoroughness that was matched, in my life, only by the narcotics guard down in Lexington some years later on.

Of course they found nothing, and after apologizing to us,

to Mr. Smith, and, of course, to Sister Elizabeth, the Army cops piled into their car again and beat it back to Fort Liberté.

"Well, that was the first installment," said Mr. Smith.

"What will they do next?" I asked.

"Oh, they'll take apart your luggage, they'll cut the extra corners off your suitcases, they'll pull the heels off your sneakers, and they'll put knife blades between the soles of your shoes."

"You mean, in our hotel back in Port-au-Prince?"

"Oh, they've probably been through all that already," said Mr. Smith. "But they'll start all over again the minute you get back there. You can be sure of that."

"So what are we going to do?" said Hardy.

"Don't worry," said Mr. Smith. "I think the world ought to know about the terrible things that have been going on down here, and you can count on me to do my share to get those films back to the States for you. You just go along and let them frisk you and search you all they want. Just tell me this: How, and when, are you planning to go back home?"

"I thought we'd go next Wednesday on the *Veendam*, out of Port-au-Prince," I said.

"Okay. You just arrange your business to leave on that day. Don't write me, don't phone me, and don't do anything to make them any more suspicious. You understand?"

"We'll do just as you say," I said. "Shall we try to get back our cameras?"

"Certainly," said Mr. Smith. "You go straight to the police when you get to Port-au-Prince, and insist that they return your property! And now, boys, you'd better start out before it gets dark. Where is your car?"

"We parked it in front of the Pension André," I said.

"Good. Bring it around to my house and we'll fill the tank with gasoline and give you some extra gallons to take along in tin cans, so you won't have to stop off anywhere on the road."

And that's how it was done, and that's practically where our adventure ended. That is to say, we were searched three times more before we left on the *Veendam*, but the police gave us back all our photo equipment, and nobody tried to molest us when we finally embarked.

Of course, we had no films. At least, we had no films until the boat was well out to sea and the ship's purser handed us Mr. Smith's oblong box.

"How did it get here?" I asked the purser.

"A nun brought it yesterday afternoon," he said. "Her name was Sister Elizabeth, and she looked so tired, I made her take a little milk punch with me in my cabin."

"That was very kind of you," I said.

"Not at all," said the purser. "She had just finished walking a hundred and ten miles with your package, and she told me, quite cheerfully, that after leaving the ship she was starting right back home again. Wonderful people, some of these old girls, aren't they?"

"I don't believe they make them like that any more," I said. "But let us all thank God that a few of them are still around, for the help and comfort of poor mankind."

Of course, the Haiti story got duly printed in *Life* magazine, and it certainly proved a three-day sensation. Rex Hardy went off to California to get married, and I again returned to my search for an interesting photo essay that would require me to go to Outer Mongolia or to Nepal, at least.

It was shortly after this trip to Haiti that one day Harry Luce invited the liveliest members of his staff to a really momentous editorial get-together.

It seems that the Franklin D. Roosevelts had asked both the Luces to come to luncheon up at Hyde Park on the following Saturday. You can easily imagine the extent of the F.D.R. popularity on the *Time, Life,* and *Fortune* enterprises during that period; still, he *was* the President of the United States, and, what is more, he stemmed so evidently from the real landed gentry, from a long line of influential and monied people, that, despite his renegade behavior to his class, our monitors and bosses couldn't ever quite escape a certain reverence for his inherited position.

So now, when Harry was getting himself ready for his visit to Hyde Park, he had asked a few of us in to advise him and consult with him on the various possible questions that he might tactfully and reasonably bring up during this unusual meeting.

Well, you can be sure that before this session was over, the gang of us had loaded Harry down with about as much sly and purposeful interview material as it was possible for any one man to carry. I can tell you that when he finally left that editorial confab, his pockets were simply bulging with hundreds of clever notes and suggestions. After all, it wasn't every day that the President of the United States asked anyone to drop in to break bread with him in the casual setting of his family home.

There was another point to be considered, of course. The President must surely have been aware that the Luces were not exactly among the greatest admirers of his various political and economic policies, and it was our consciousness of this very ticklish situation that led some of us to believe that a really shrewd manipulator of people like Franklin Roosevelt might, just for the hell of it, disclose a particularly amicable

214

and conciliatory side of himself to these two notoriously prejudiced visitors.

At any rate, since the party was going to take place on Saturday, Harry tentatively scheduled another editorial meeting for the following Monday afternoon, to give us the results.

Well, Monday came and went, and Tuesday and Wednesday also passed uneventfully into oblivion, but not a one of us received a word or a sign that would give us any hint as to what the hell had finally happened during that historic luncheon up at Hyde Park. As a matter of fact, we never did have that second editorial meeting at all, and most of the people who had been present at the first one were sufficiently experienced jobholders never to refer to the subject again. At least, not within my hearing.

But about six weeks later, when I happened to be visiting the Luces at their place in Westport, I just asked Harry point-blank what, if anything, had come of that friendly social call.

Harry wasn't in the least bit put out or embarrassed by my question. I think he looked more bewildered than anything else.

"The darnedest thing happened," he finally said to me. "I still can't quite figure out whether the whole thing was just an accident, or whether those two hams had framed it all carefully in advance."

"The Roosevelts?" I said.

"Yes," said Harry. "You see, it all started off all right. Only about ten people were present at the meal, and everything looked pretty auspicious for a more or less intimate couple of hours with our hosts later on. And then, just as we were having our coffee, the old man cocks up his cigarette holder, in that rakish way of his, and he says to Clare, 'You know, Mrs. Luce, you are the subject of quite a serious controversy in this family.' Clare looked a little puzzled, and flattered, I suppose, and she naturally asked him what it was all about. 'It is about your play, *The Women*,' he said. 'You see, we saw that play a few months ago in Washington, and, I must say, I enjoyed it immensely. My wife, on the other hand, was simply infuriated by it. She insisted that your play was a deliberate slander and libel on all of American womanhood.'

"At that point Eleanor, who was busy serving cake at the other end of the table, suddenly dropped everything and started to defend herself against this accusation. That is to say, she more or less agreed that she had a very poor opinion of *The Women*, she just reproached the old man for bringing up the whole subject when the author was present at the table; anyway, she pretended to be very sore at him for his tactlessness. At the same time, you could see there wasn't any real rancor between them at all. As a matter of fact, I wasn't

215

too sure whether he really cared a damn for the show himself, or whether this whole discussion hadn't just been trumped up to give them a chance to take a big wallop at Clare's play.

"Well, whatever the hell was prompting them, they kept up their little performance for the next hour and a half, and the others at the table seemed to be enjoying themselves immensely over this amiable family squabble. I must say, Clare carried it off with her usual aplomb, but meanwhile the time for any possible serious discussion was certainly passing by, and in the end, when he finally wheeled himself out of the room to take his siesta, I still hadn't had a chance to say one purposeful word to anybody. So we just went on home and tried to figure out the real meaning behind their little performance. We finally decided that they'd rehearsed the whole crazy charade long before we came up that morning, or maybe even the day before. Funny, isn't it? You can't really ever tell about people, can you?"

And, just a little while after this visit to Hyde Park, Clare opened her next play, *Margin for Error*, at the National Theater in Washington. While it was still in rehearsal, she phoned me at my office in New York and told me that she was having trouble with her third act, and would I come down and take a look at things and maybe make some helpful suggestions. So I took a leave of absence from my job for a couple of weeks and joined her down in Washington the following day.

Now, then, positively endless and numberless are the lies that have been told about the help that I'm supposed to have given her, or not given her, with her playwriting. Just let me say this, Clare surely has certain staggering attributes that have made her the famous woman that she is today. These attributes do, occasionally, lie quite fallow, or perhaps just expectant, a little below the surface of her complete awareness. For these intangibles to come to their proper effectiveness, it may be helpful and even necessary that they be seeded and fructified by some potent, outside stimuli. And, that's about the size of it. As a matter of fact, now is the very time for me to dish up for you a not particularly relevant, but amusing, parable for this whole situation.

It seems that in the old days, in Budapest, the famous Hungarian playwright, Ferenc Molnár, used to have a sort of literary stooge and man of all work, who was constantly to be found in attendance whenever the master was busy with the writing or the producing of a new play. This man's name was Kerekes, I believe, and he was so much taken for granted as an essential literary factotum of Molnár's, that hostesses who happened to invite the great author to dinner would automatically set an extra place for Kerekes.

216

This had all been going along amiably for quite a few years when, late one afternoon, just as Molnár was having his breakfast, Kerekes came into the room and suddenly announced that he was leaving for Vienna.

"Nonsense!" said Molnár. "You can't leave now, we're still busy with the third act of my new play. After it's produced, we'll both go and take the waters in Karlsbad. But that won't be for another six weeks, at the earliest."

But Kerekes was obdurate and kept on insisting that he wanted to leave for Vienna at once. And then, at last, it dawned on Molnár that his friend was using the proposed trip merely as an excuse to acquit himself for some fancied slight to his feelings.

"Come on," said Molnár. "You're obviously angry about something. You'd much better tell me what is bothering you, and, whatever it is, we'll try to straighten it out. After all, we're old friends, aren't we?"

"That's just it," said Kerekes. "For years now you've let me help you in all of your work, and not once in all that time have I ever gotten even one measly sliver of credit from anybody. Have I?"

Molnár lifted the monocle from his eye and a look of genuine astonishment came over his round pink face. "I don't understand you," he said. "What sort of credit are you expecting, anyway, and who is supposed to give it to you?"

"*You* are supposed to give it to me," said Kerekes. "You know how much I have helped you with all your work, so wouldn't it be right and fitting that you should put my name alongside yours on the program, as a co-author? I certainly think I deserve it."

Molnár replaced the monocle in his eye slowly and clucked several times commiseratively over his freezing eggs Benedict.

"I'm sorry you brought the whole thing up," he finally said to Kerekes. "You see, you completely misunderstand the real importance of your role in my life."

"I do?" said Kerekes.

"Yes, indeed, you do!" said Molnár. "Don't you understand? When I put on a new play nowadays and it gets good reviews, do you know what all the important people in Budapest say after the opening? They smile knowingly over their coffee cups and say, 'You know who really writes Molnár's plays for him, don't you? It's a man called Kerekes, to whom he has to pay enormous blackmail.' That's what everybody says."

"I didn't know that," said Kerekes. "And besides, it isn't true."

"That's quite unimportant," said Molnár. "A legend doesn't

217

suffer in its public appeal just because there are some demonstrable errors in it."

"And why are you telling me all this?" said Kerekes. "If you know what people are saying anyway, why do you go on denying me the little credit that I'm asking you for? Why do you begrudge it to me?"

"Why? For your own sake," said Molnár, with a smile that was like a benediction.

"For *my* sake!" said Kerekes. "But you'll forgive me, Mr. Molnár, if I tell you that I don't understand one single word of your reasoning. I'm afraid it's all a little too subtle for my limited mental powers."

"Not subtle at all," said Molnár, wearily. "It is as obvious as the palm of your hand. Don't you see, if I really listened to your foolish clamor and did what you ask me, I would, at one stroke, destroy your whole reputation. Just think about it! Suppose I did put your name right next to mine on the program of my next production. You know what would happen? Every moocher in every coffeehouse in Budapest would laugh at you. 'Did you see what happened?' they would say to each other. 'That silly, presumptuous ass Kerekes has pushed his name up beside Molnár's on the last playbill. Could anything be funnier? Imagine that clown inflating himself to such importance, at the expense of Hungary's greatest playwright. Could anything be more presumptuous and absurd?'

"That's what they would say. Believe me, I really know those swine. They would singe off every single hair on your head with their burning witticisms. No, no, my friend, your position is enviable only as long as they don't see your name printed around anywhere, because then they assume, as a matter of course, that I am quietly picking your brains and hogging all the credit for myself. That's human nature for you. I'm sorry, but that's how it is, Mr. Kerekes, and neither you nor I are powerful enough to change it."

It goes without saying that Kerekes was deeply moved by this profoundly shrewd analysis of his enviable position and, quietly and anonymously, continued in the service of his great master. And, from that time forward, whenever the friends of Mr. Kerekes expressed any sort of sympathy for his dubious literary status, he would just look at them knowingly and give them a slow, superior, Molnár smile.

Of course, Clare did not have Molnár's high gift for dramatic writing, nor was she endowed to perform the breathtaking casuistical acrobatics of that astonishing Hungarian mind. What she did have was a wild talent for purposeful acquisitiveness and a fantastic gift for merchandising her accomplishments.

218

Take the original idea that inspired her to write *Margin for Error*, for instance. It must be plain to anyone who is at all theater-wise, that such a play, founded on such a plot, couldn't possibly work before an audience. At its best, it was just a mediocre after-dinner anecdote, with some dubious murder-mystery overtones; and let me assure you that some of the smartest people in show business, who came down to see the preview of it in Washington, assured me confidentially that our little disaster didn't have a chance in the world.

Well, when it opened in New York it got rave notices; it ran for over a year and a half on Broadway; and it was finally sold to the movies for a nice piece of change.

And there you have it. Whatever help I gave to this production I gave with the greatest misgivings, and with the almost certain conviction that it was all doomed for an early smashup, anyway. And then, on the opening night in New York, which Clare was too frightened to attend, I heard the audience all around me laughing and responding in so obvious an atmosphere of electric mass participation, that I called her up at the Waldorf after the very first act and told her she had nothing to worry about, that the play was surely a hit.

What I'm trying to tell you is this, that just as I couldn't have made *Life* magazine into the staggering success that it had become, no matter how brilliant an idea man I might have been in its service, I could, on the very same terms, never have been able to put over Clare's childishly contrived dramatic absurdity either, for the very simple reason that I didn't believe in it.

But *she* most certainly did.

Also, in order to write a successful Broadway play, the author himself must definitely be stage-struck, which Clare, of course, was. In fact, I know that if she does suffer from one unfulfilled ambition, it is her desire to be a successful stage actress. She has made several tries at it, some of them pretty disastrous, and yet I'm quite sure that she is never going to give up this dream, no matter what other great honors and distinctions may come her way. And the reason she can't give up trying is that she believes implicitly in her own perfectibility. She has already managed to triumph over so many handicaps and limitations that the one thing she seems quite unable to make room for in her life is a possible Margin for Error.

There was one curious aspect to my life during all those years, from 1917 to 1948, which I have somehow or other forgotten to mention to you before—that for more than thirty years I wore only pink neckties. Not ever any other color, under any circumstances. It finally got to be an identifying

219

trademark for me, although, heaven is my witness, I never intended anything of the sort when I first started wearing them. In fact, I got into this pink-tie addiction when I was only seventeen years old, and believe me, any boy or man who was willing to wear such an unorthodox color back in those dark days of somber men's attire had to have plenty of guts or plenty of stupidity, or plenty of both, to get away with it.

Of course I stumbled into it all, as I fell into most things, by strictly minding my own business, and by just carefully putting one foot in front of the other.

I was working on the New York *Sunday World* when I was seventeen, and I was also doing some cartooning jobs for the *Big Stick,* a Jewish joke paper that I already told you about. My salary on the *World* was twenty-five dollars a week, and I generally took long, leisurely walks every Friday afternoon, just to give myself, and those twenty-five bucks, a luxurious airing. These walks often included window-shopping tours ranging from Nassau Street and lower Broadway to Forty-second Street and Fifth Avenue up as far as the Plaza.

Well, then, loaded as I was, one of those Friday afternoons I happened to stop in front of Sulka's window, somewhere in the Forties or Fifties, and I noticed that they were having a sale of neckties. Six dollars a tie. I wondered what in hell they could possibly have charged for them before the sale. I felt myself getting even a little indignant about the whole thing. However, in spite of my simmering annoyance I found that I was deliberately walking into their cool, expensive-smelling store.

It stands to reason, doesn't it, that I wasn't planning to buy anything, and the clerk, whose face looked just like a shinbone with eyebrows, knew this as well as I did. But, like two idle dogs of the same gender who can't resist their pointless browsing, this clerk and I forthwith proceeded to give the stock a judicious fingering; which means that I sneered disparagingly at the tie-racks, while he kept on constructing smart four-in-hand knots in mid-air, just to show off his really stupendous manual dexterity, and also to make me feel like a cheap piker.

This went on for about twenty minutes or so, and I was just about to call off the whole silly ballet by making my exit, when the clerk, who was obviously a pansy, suddenly said to me, "You know, we have some colors that are much less popular, and those ties cost only one dollar apiece. Would you care to see any of them?"

"Why not?" I said. "As long as I'm here, anyway. What sort of colors are they?"

"I'll show them to you. To tell you the truth," he said with

220

a confidential smirk, "I'm saving some of them especially for my friends."

This, of course, instantly alarmed me, because I was quite sure that any friend of his was bound to be a leaping faggot, but just the same I decided to take a look. He pulled a box off the shelf, removed the lid, and exposed about two dozen crepe-de-Chine ties, all of them pink.

"Not a very great selection," I said. "How much are they, did you say?"

"A dollar apiece," he said. "They cost us more than that wholesale."

Now, then, who really knows what dark and sinister impulses are crouched and coiled in the recesses of man's unconscious? Who can guess what terrible unfulfilled longings in a man's heart are just waiting for the right word, or the right moment, to spring into instant, demoniacal action, for the sake of a long-deferred secret appeasement?

In short, I bought six of those pink crepe-de-Chine neckties, and, believe it or not, I even had a certain feeling of high accomplishment out of this demented proceeding. It was as if I'd pulled a particularly cute caper, not just on Sulka and Company, but on all the goddamned expensive shops up and down Fifth Avenue.

And that's how it happened that I came to wear a pink tie to work the next day. I labored, at the time, in the tower of the old Pulitzer Building, down on Park Row, and, when I first took off my coat, the screams, the whistles, the yowls and the yodelings all around me stopped all human activity on that floor for the next ten minutes.

But, since I was seventeen years old and a man of my convictions, I ignored this racket and quietly went about my business. My business was to make some black-and-white line sketches for the Sunday magazine section, and so I was able, for a while at least, to bend zealously over my drawing board, without having to meet anybody's eye. This was certainly a help, but even so it was hard for me to ignore the mad cavortings of the office boys and the various younger staff members, who made it their pleasure to pass my desk forty times an hour in that special mincing gait which has ever been the immemorial hallmark of the camping fairy.

I don't know how I lived through that first morning. At any rate, right before lunch I took off my tie and hung it in a metal closet where I usually kept only a pair of torn rubbers. When I got ready to quit work that evening, I had a shocking surprise waiting for me. Somebody on that floor had dipped my tie in a large glue vat that was permanently stationed near the fire exit. The glue had completely dried up and left the tie with a texture like a smoked kipper; but since

221

I knew that a lot of furtive eyes were certainly watching me at that moment, I just dropped my violated neckpiece casually into the garbage can and went home.

Fools! I thought. Just a pack of crude, conventional fools. Ah, well, they believed I was routed, did they? They thought they had me down for the count, eh? Well, they'd soon learn different. Damned soon, too! I'd show those mushheads a thing or two—or even five, if it came to that, because, as you perfectly well know, I still had five more of those ties hanging at home in my closet, ready and waiting to be launched whenever the spirit moved me.

I was determined to teach all those dopes a lesson, to teach them to respect a man's right to wear whatever the hell he goddamned well pleased. And so the battle lines were drawn, and no mercy was given or expected.

I wore my pink ties every day from then on, and, do you know, as the tense weeks went by a very funny thing happened. In about a month or so, I couldn't help but notice that slowly, ever so slowly, the fury and the clamor were beginning to die down. In fact, by the time I'd gotten around to wearing the third of my ties, somebody from the business office, who had never before seen my colorful haberdashery and was just about to launch himself into the gibbering state of epilepsy that the occasion seemed to call for, was stupefied into silence when a few of my nearby colleagues told him to shut his trap and to mind his own goddamned business.

You see, the young journalists on my floor had not only become used to my pink ties, they had developed a certain comradely state of tolerance toward my special eccentricity. They had come to consider it *their* peculiar privilege to razz me for acting out of line, but they all stood defensively by me if any unlicensed outsider ever decided to put me down.

In short, after six months of nothing but pink ties, nobody around me seemed any longer to notice that I was wearing anything out of the ordinary at all.

And then came a real crisis. I gave five of my ties away to be cleaned, in a store on West Eighth Street, and when I came back a few days later to reclaim them, I found to my horror that the place had been completely gutted by fire.

It was a real calamity for me, as you can plainly understand. Those pink ties were the symbols of my individuality, weren't they? And, to a certain extent, they had even become the tangible pennants that I had tremblingly fluttered before a hostile world, to announce my freedom of choice. I just couldn't let myself down now. I simply couldn't make my appearance at the office wearing some dark, practical colors, not after all I'd already been through, could I? If I did, all would be lost again.

Oh, yes, I could just see all those blubberheads on the paper saying, "Well, you've finally got yourself straightened out! Decided to rejoin the human race again, eh? Good for you, boy!"

No, no, no! It was out of the question. Eternal vigilance was the price of freedom! That was the basic rule of the game, and I damn well knew it.

And so, in this frightening emergency, I quickly hustled up to B. Altman's on Thirty-fourth Street, and bought myself three yards of candy-pink crepe-de-Chine material. Afterward I consulted a classified phone directory and found that the Acme Tie Company, right nearby, on Thirty-sixth Street, was prepared to make neckties in small quantities to private order.

I had myself quite a time finding that goddamned tie place, too, because it was located in one of those depressing blocks between Eighth and Ninth avenues, where there weren't even any drugstores or lunchrooms to break up the solid façade of grim wholesale manufacturing. I did find it at last, and it was, literally, just a very small hole in a very thick and forbidding wall.

Mr. Aron Buxbaum, the owner, turned out to be a neat little bearded elderly Jew who wore a black skullcap and satin sleeve garters, and who showed no surprise whatever at the unusual color of my material.

"I'm in a terrible hurry about these ties," I told him as I unwrapped the stuff. "How soon can I possibly have them?"

"Day after tomorrow," said Mr. Buxbaum. "We generally like to have more time, but, if it's an emergency, we'll just do the best we can."

"Fine," I said. "I'll pick them up around lunchtime on Friday."

When I returned, two days later, Mr. Buxbaum handed me a pretty good sized package, and a bill for fifteen dollars.

I nearly fainted. "How come, fifteen dollars?" I said. "You're charging me a fortune. After all, I supplied the material, didn't I?"

Mr. Buxbaum looked hurt. "We do very fine work here," he said. "You just take a look at those ties, and you'll see what you're getting for your money. You're getting a big bargain."

"Never mind," I said. "I haven't got time now, I have to get back to work. I don't get through until four o'clock."

Luckily, because it was payday, I had a twenty-dollar bill on me, and so I was able to square myself.

"Wear them in good health!" said Mr. Buxbaum, when I finally stood in the open doorway.

"Thanks," I said. "By the way, how many ties did you manage to get out of that material, anyway?"

"Exactly sixty-two," he said. "If you had bought just a quarter of a yard more, you could have had sixty-five."

And that's how it was.

Ties, I later learned, are cut on the bias and really require very little material. And so, at one stroke, I had added to my wardrobe a matter of more than five dozen pink ties.

They lasted for quite a while, too, and when they finally wore out I just bought some more material and had a new batch made up for myself over at Buxbaum's. And that's how it happened that I came to march through the ages as a peculiarly necktied man.

And then, sometime in 1947, all of my luggage was lost by one of the airlines, and I arrived in New York with only one pink necktie to my name, the one that I was wearing. Well, I naturally went straight up to Altman's to get myself three and a quarter yards of fresh pink crepe de Chine. I'd made these trips and these purchases quite often during the past thirty years, and I no longer had the slightest difficulty in locating the Acme Tie Company on West Thirty-sixth Street.

But when I finally got there, old man Buxbaum wasn't anywhere in sight. Instead, a sort of young and beardless caricature of him was sitting against the back wall and making entries in a huge ledger.

"You're Mr. Buxbaum's son, aren't you?" I said.

"Yes," he said. "I'm George Buxbaum. And you, I believe, must be Mr. King."

"I am," I said. "But how in the world did you know that?"

"Because," said George Buxbaum, "my father is now dead, and you used to be his only customer."

"What?" I said. "You mean that I alone have kept his whole enterprise going?"

"If you want to put it that way," he said. "Actually, the matter is a little more complicated than that. You see, my brothers and I are probably the largest wholesale tie manufacturers in America. In fact, we own this building, which houses one of our four factories."

"And what about this store?" I said.

"Ah, well, that was all my father's wish," he said. "You see, he came to this country as an immigrant and started to sell ties out of a cigar box, on Orchard Street. My mother used to make those ties on a foot-pedal sewing machine at home. Later on he got a pushcart, and by the time my brothers and I were going to high school he'd managed to get himself a nice little store on Second Avenue near Twelfth Street. Well, to make a long story short, we all of us somehow or other got into the necktie business, and we did so well in it that after a while the whole family kept pleading with my father to retire, to take it easy, or at least to take some kind of an executive position in one of our plants. But, for some reason or another, he just never had any real confidence in our success. It was all too big and much too vague for him. Everything was done by bank drafts and checks, and in our places of business he never saw any real money changing hands; and so, every time we expanded, or opened a new factory, he just got more worried about us.

"Finally, one day he pleaded with us to fix him up this little retail place right here, where he at least could go on making a real visible dollar across the counter. I think he felt that he was prepared to save the family from absolute ruin, when we had all smashed up with our grand and highfalutin notions. So we built this store for him, and for a while he even had a couple of dozen customers that used to trade here steadily. But for the last eight or ten years, the only jobs that came his way were your pink ties.

"And that brings me to still another point," he said. "You see, Mr. King, the whole family always gets together for dinner in my mother's house on Friday nights, and my father and my brothers and I, we would spend hours and hours, wondering and speculating what could possibly be the meaning of all those pink ties. Some of us thought it must be the emblem of some secret society. Others had the idea that maybe it had a certain religious significance, or something. But my father—you must excuse me for telling you this—my father was convinced that you were an artist, and that you painted naked girls on those ties, and that you sold them at stag parties."

"Your father overestimated my talents," I said. "No. I had those ties made for other good and sufficient reasons." And then I told young Buxbaum, briefly, the gist of my story.

"Well," he said, "I'm very glad you've explained it at last, because if my father's spirit is anywhere at all, it certainly must be hovering around this little store where he spent so many years of his life."

He opened a small desk file, and I could see that it contained only one single card. George Buxbaum showed me what his father had written on it. It was in Yiddish.

KING, ALEXANDER
PINK TIES.
*ONLY* PINK TIES.
WHY?

The children think he is some kind of a bolshevik, but I'm sure he only makes a few harmless dirty pictures.

He is a good and steady customer. May God preserve him from mischief. And from the police.

On the bottom of this card young Buxbaum now wrote *Account Closed*.

"So you are finally giving up the store," I said.

"Yes," he said. "By the end of next week the door and window will be walled up, and the premises will have been absorbed by the rest of the building. But don't worry, for old time's sake we'll make you this last batch of ties from the material you just brought. You'll just have to call for them on the seventh floor."

And that was the end of the Acme Tie Company, and that was the last of my pink ties, too, because I never had the heart to take my business to anybody else.

# CHAPTER TWENTY-THREE

HOWEVER, NOT EVERYTHING in my life proceeded from accident. No. I made some damned elaborate plans in my time, and a few of them even worked. One of my plans, which I made in close collaboration with Donald Friede, was to corner Eugene O'Neill, some day, somewhere, and to show him a few examples of my work. You see, I wanted very much to illustrate *The Emperor Jones,* and, since I'd been to Africa and brought back whole suitcases filled with sketches of Negroes, I really felt myself peculiarly qualified to do this job.

And then, in February of 1927, O'Neill wrote a letter to Horace Liveright in which he said that he planned to be in New York on March 14, and that he expected to drop into the office on that very date.

Now, I wasn't particularly friendly with Horace at that time, and, as far as I can remember, neither was Donald, but some secretary or office employee who seemed, for some reason or other, devoted to us, told us about the impending O'Neill visit. So we made our plans accordingly. I had already done three illustrations for *The Emperor Jones,* in oil, and I now moved these straight into Donald Friede's office. I also put about fifty black-and-white sketches into a nice handy folder and brought them up there, too. You see, Liveright was definitely planning to bring out the O'Neill plays

226

in individual illustrated editions, and so far, at least, nobody had been picked to do the job.

I'm not going to torture myself by trying to describe to you how miserably slowly the time crawled along for me until it finally got to be March 14. At any rate, I knew that O'Neill was due to arrive at Liveright's office at two o'clock in the afternoon, and you can be sure that I had been sitting in that goddamned waiting room of theirs since a quarter of one. I had to sit in the waiting room because Donald wasn't in his office. He'd gone out to a book auction somewhere, and his secretary told me that he'd said he'd be back at one-thirty.

Of course he wasn't back at one-thirty, or at a quarter of two, or at two sharp, when O'Neill suddenly walked into the waiting room. I recognized him at once, from his photographs—that large forehead molded with bumps of ominous forebodings, those baleful eyes, the sallow complexion, and the dark, carefully shaped mustache on his long Irish lip.

The situation was now so highly critical that I felt myself positively shaking with alternating waves of feverish heat and cold. I realized only too well that once he went into Horace's office, which was right next door to the waiting room, he was certainly lost to me forever, because, as I told you, Horace wasn't too keen about me just then; besides, they were surely going to go out to eat a long lunch somewhere together, and God only knew when I'd have another chance to get O'Neill that close to my pictures again.

Oh, damn Donald and his stinking book auctions, I thought.

I was such a battleground of conflicting emotions at that moment, that I hardly knew what I was doing; but before O'Neill had even had a chance to sit down, I quickly crossed the room and addressed him loudly by name.

He looked at me with the reserve of a man who has often in the past been bothered by persistent autograph collectors and who just goes on quietly hoping that they will all drop dead of ink poisoning some day.

"My name is Alex King," I said breathlessly, "and I've just recently returned from Africa, where I made thousands and thousands of drawings of Negroes. You see, Mr. O'Neill, I'd give both my ears for a chance to illustrate *The Emperor Jones*, and Donald Friede promised to introduce me to you. But God only knows where he is right now, and I'm so desperately anxious to show you some of my work that I hope you'll forgive me for accosting you in this ridiculous fashion. Please, please, forgive me!"

I couldn't say any more than that, and I just stood there, gasping and panting like a winded beagle.

And then he smiled. He was a rare, but a very sweet, smiler. "And where are these drawings of yours?" he asked.

"They're upstairs in Donald's office," I said. "If you wouldn't mind . . . ?"

"I'll be glad to look at them," he said. "To tell you the truth, I'm not at all sure that I particularly want any of those plays illustrated. Horace thinks it would be a good idea. . . . Well, let's go on up and see what you've done."

My paintings were all standing around the floor of Don's office; they were quite large, too, 20 by 30 or thereabouts, and—I can say this without vanity—like most of my work, they certainly had some of my frenzy boiling in them. I could see immediately that O'Neill was at least startled at the sight of them.

"I think they're very striking," he said. "And I'm glad to see that you understand that Negroes are not just white people with blackened up faces, that their humor, their dignity and their sorrows have all been conditioned by their present tragic status in this world of ours."

He looked at those pictures slowly and seriously, one after the other, and I was just about to show him some of my drawings from the folder, when the door was suddenly thrust open, and Horace Liveright stormed into the room.

"What's this?" he screamed. "What's going on here anyway? Why didn't you come straight to my office, Gene? Come on, let's go to lunch. I've got a table reserved for us and we're ten minutes late, already!"

He looked exactly like an impassioned cockatoo, with his flying white hair, and his hyperthyroid eyes popping dangerously out of his head. It goes without saying that he behaved exactly as if I weren't even in the same building with them, let alone in the same room.

He took O'Neill by the elbow and started at once to tow him purposefully toward the door. But O'Neill quietly and deliberately released himslf from his grip, and, as he did this, I must say I noticed that he looked at Horace with something very much like affection.

"Just a minute," said O'Neill. "I'm sorry, Horace, but I was looking at some of this young man's work just now, and I can tell you I find it quite fascinating."

"Oh!" said Horace, spinning around on his heel, and putting an impulsive, comradely arm around my shoulder. "This boy is going to be America's greatest book illustrator," he shouted. "I haven't the slightest doubt about it. Of course, some of his stuff is still pretty extreme. Like that one, over there, for instance."

"Well," said O'Neill, "it happens to illustrate a pretty extreme moment in the play, doesn't it?"

228

"It certainly does!" said Horace. "Well, what do you say, Gene, do you think we should entrust him with doing *The Emperor Jones*? How do *you* feel about it? We're all friends here, aren't we?"

"And we're going to stay friends," said O'Neill, shaking hands with me. "Maybe you'd like to bring some of your drawings over to my hotel later in the afternoon," he said. "I'm staying at the Wentworth Patterson, right in the next block. Suppose we make it around four-thirty. Is that all right for you?"

"I'll be enchanted," I said. And, believe me, I meant it with all my heart.

And at that moment Donald Friede finally tumbled into his office and gave all of us that gum-baring, catatonic grin of the man who is invariably late in an emergency. He was perspiring dreadfully, his arms were loaded down with books, and I do believe no one could possibly have looked more superfluous in that room than he did.

It stands to reason that Horace had taken complete charge of the situation by then. He proceeded at once most carefully to explain to Donald that there was no longer any need to look for other artists to do the illustrations for *The Emperor Jones*.

"King is the man!" he said sternly. "He's got the right feeling for the play, and Gene and he see eye to eye about the whole project. We don't have to look any further. Come on, Gene, let's go to lunch!"

Eugene O'Neill eventually became not only my good friend, but even my protector from the unpredictable vagaries of Horace Liveright. One of O'Neill's current biographers has recently shown me photostatic copies of letters in which O'Neill protested vehemently to Horace against hiring other artists to do the rest of his plays, after *The Emperor Jones* had already been published with my illustrations. O'Neill, who, as far as I know, never wrote a preface for anybody in his life, sent a two-word telegram in answer to a request by George Macy to write a foreword for a proposed bibliography of books I had illustrated. He wired back, "Glad to!"

And I suppose you must wonder how I felt about Donald Friede's performance on that memorable March afternoon when I first met Eugene O'Neill. Well, to tell you the truth, it didn't really make the slightest difference between us. Remember, I was no longer a tender package. I was already twenty-six years old, and I had learned to accept the palpable truism that most of mankind is permanently preoccupied with its own immediate concerns. These concerns may seem quite petty to us, merely because we ourselves are probably occupied with some all-consuming interests of our own that may, in turn, appear quite trivial to others.

In short, everybody in this world seems to be busy with his own goddamned business, and only a scattering of saints, and a few artists, have ever seemed to have any time left over for anybody else. I know that they do exist, though, these holy ones, because I myself have encountered a few of them during my own lifetime.

I met the last one in 1954, down at the narcotics farm in Lexington, Kentucky.

Just a few days before Christmas, I had a letter from my wife, in New York, telling me that she planned to come down and visit with me over the holidays. Let me tell you that I looked forward to this visit with a degree of eagerness that seemed hard to match with any other anticipation of my whole past life. Although I'd arrived in Lexington a full six weeks before, I was still in rather poor shape physically and was walking around the place dressed only in my pajamas and a bathrobe. So you can just imagine my joy over the good news of her early arrival.

And, then, suddenly, during one of my sleepless nights, a terrible thought came to me. My wife was going to land in Lexington on the twenty-fourth of December and I'd be allowed to see her for about two hours in the afternoon. But the twenty-fourth was Christmas Eve, and where, in heaven's name, was she going to spend Christmas Eve? At the Phoenix Hotel, downtown, or eating dinner alone at the Golden Horseshoe across the way, or what? It was all too horrible to think about. You can imagine that I barely lived till morning, in my sweat and my agony over these terrible conjectures.

Well, one hour after breakfast I marched up to the top floor of the hospital, where the psychiatrists and the psychologists all roosted, and I stopped off right at the first door, next to the stairway. There was a neat little sign on it which said: *Dr. Colbaugh (By Appointment Only)*.

I decided he would do.

So I knocked and, without waiting for a response, entered a well-lit, good-sized office, where two men, both in uniform, appeared to be conferring very seriously together. On of them, the older one, was quite bald, rather stocky, and seemed not at all inclined to be amiable over the interruption. The younger one, of whom I got just a glimpse, looked like the conventional college athlete, but a lot handsomer than most of them. In fact, he looked like the sort of football hero that the Leyendeckers used to paint for the cover of the *Saturday Evening Post*.

At any rate, the bald-headed man, who had three stripes on his sleeve, and who eventually turned out to be Dr. Colbaugh, stopped in the middle of a sentence and glowered disapprovingly at me. I must tell you that I was particularly well dressed for the occasion. Over my white pajamas I wore a loose corduroy bathrobe of deep purple, which I had wangled especially that morning by judiciously distributing a carton of cigarettes among the inmate assistants in the clothing room.

"Yes?" said Dr. Colbaugh, and it clearly meant "No!" to whatever the hell I was going to tell him. I realized, of course, that I'd have to say something pretty engaging, to tear these two characters out of their indignant mood of violated privacy.

And do you know what I said? I said, "I suppose it is a terrible mistake, and probably very tactless, too, for anybody to barge in on a psychiatrist when one is in trouble, isn't it?"

And then Dr. Colbaugh gave me a very tiny smile and pointed to a chair for me to sit down on.

"Well, what seems to be your trouble?" he said.

"To tell you the truth," I said, "I hardly sleep at all, anyway, but now I have an altogether new and hideous anxiety on my mind that makes my life completely unbearable. You see, it has to do with my wife's impending visit down here."

"Why? what's wrong? Don't you want her to come here?" said Dr. Colbaugh.

"Oh, no! I just live for the moment when I'll see her precious face again," I said. "It is simply that she's going to arrive here on the afternoon of the twenty-fourth, and that means she'll have to spend Christmas Eve alone in some ghastly hotel room, or eat dinner by herself in a restaurant with a lot of horse portraits on the walls."

"I see," said Dr. Colbaugh. "Well, it certainly presents a knotty problem. How old is your wife, by the way?"

"She's going to be twenty-one," I said.

"Oh!"

It was obviously a stumper for him. He'd probably thought that maybe I was married to somebody ten or fifteen years older than myself, and, since I was certainly in my fifties, that would have made my wife a helpless little old lady, lost in the blue-grass wilds of Kentucky. Twenty-one! Well, that made it a problem of a different wave length altogether.

"You see," I said, "she's originally from a very small town in Nebraska, and, although she's been to Paris and to Rome, to study for a year, she's always been with people who were related to her and who loved her very dearly. And the idea that this festive evening, an evening which seems particularly dedicated to family affections, should be passed by her, alone, among strange surroundings, is almost more than I can bear."

231

And then the other man in the room spoke up. "I think I have the solution to the whole problem," he said. "Why don't you just arrange for your wife to spend Christmas Eve with my wife, who will, anyway, he entertaining my parents, who are also coming down for the holidays. I have two small children, and so it will be a real family evening for everybody. And, what's more, since I'm on hospital duty that evening, you, if you like, can take Christmas dinner with me."

"What is your name?" I asked.

"I'm Dr. De Witt Montgomery," he said.

"Well, Dr. Montgomery," I said, "you've just moved into a very exalted hierarchy, indeed. You see, I'm about to make a niche ready for you among the major saints in my not particularly sanctified life. You can be sure I shall always remember you in my prayers."

"You must include Dr. Colbaugh in your prayers, too," he said. "You see, he is my superior officer here, and I couldn't possibly go through with my offer of hospitality to you if he hadn't, at one point of your talk, given me a very encouraging nod."

"I shall remember both of you in my prayers," I said. "And if heaven is kind to me and gives me back a little measure of health, I shall start painting again, and, what's more, I shall make each of you a really fine picture in memory of this occasion. This is a solemn promise, made with a heart filled with gratitude," I said, "and may my right hand lose its cunning if I should fail to keep it."

And so it came to pass that the dear wayfaring stranger spent a most gracious Christmas Eve at the home of the Montgomerys, while I had my turkey and Amphojel in company with the doctor at the narcotics hospital. A blessed, blessed holiday that brought six successive visits from my wife to me and was an occasion of kindness from the world, to both of us, which I shall always remember.

You know that I did finally emerge, cured, from my last visit to Lexington, four years ago, and it certainly behooves me to recall every man and woman who gave me a hand, or even waved encouragingly to me, along the way. Believe me, nobody can ever hope to climb out of a drug addiction unassisted and alone. That is why the percentage of cures is so infinitesimal.

Unless you have a De Witt Montgomery or his human equivalent standing by while you're still inside, and a Margie, with a heart full of love, waiting on the doorstep when you at last get out, you just can't make it, son. You can't possibly make it.

Of course there were other people in Lexington who were kind to me, too, particularly Mr. Morgan, the educational director, who possessed gifts of imagination rarely to be met with anywhere. I once told him how depressing it was to see the same dreary, collapsed, dope-addict faces all around me, month after month, and how I longed for the sight of someone who was quite uncontaminated by the institution.

The following Saturday, Mr. Morgan brought his two young children to visit with me, and I had the pleasure of passing a few enjoyable hours with these extraterrestrial beings, telling them stories and drawing a lot of pictures for their special amusement. It was a kindness that Mr. Morgan repeated several times during my stay, and I can tell you that those two children affected me like the sight of sudden spring flowers in a horrible cinder pile.

Some two or three nurses, still very young and therefore not yet "institutionalized," were also very considerate and thoughtful in their ministrations. I recall with particular pleasure the youngest of them, Virginia Maartens, who was obviously of Dutch ancestry and who still had the fair skin, the fair hair, and the pale, candid blue eyes that her forebears had originally imported from Holland, many years ago. She was a real darling. As matter of fact, as far as I could see, Virginia Maartens had only one major fault in her character, she was hopelessly movie-struck. To put it bluntly, she was at that time president of the Lexington chapter of the Greer Garson Fan Club, and, since she knew that I'd been to Hollywood several times, she just loved to talk to me about her celluloid enthusiasms.

Every sort of hero worship among grownups has always tended to depress me, but I had a special reason to feel embarrassed by Virginia's particular form of adulation, because I had once witnessed a remarkable and unexpected denouement to just such a worshiping orgy, which had upset me for quite a while afterward.

It was in the winter of 1939 and I was still working on *Life*, when I happened to run into Stanley Walker at the Hotel Algonquin one afternoon. Stanley had been city editor of the New York *Herald Tribune* and was at that time an editorial writer. I found him very interesting because I knew that he was always mixed up in a lot of extracurricular activities, too. So, after we'd swapped the usual Anglo-Saxon social banalities, I asked him whether he knew of any special stories which we on *Life* might be able to render more explicit through photography; I meant stories not particularly suited for his paper.

"I know only one subject that might interest you," he said, "and since I'm never going to do it, anyway, I'll give you whatever dope I have on it, and you're welcome to it."

"What's the story?" I asked.

"Autograph collectors," he said. "Now, don't make a face. You obviously know nothing about it. Believe me, it involves millions of people throughout the country, and these people wield an absolutely staggering power in the movie industry. Their letters and their enthusiasms worry and influence everybody, from Louis B. Mayer down to the pimpliest busboy in the Brown Derby. There are kids all around New York, for instance, who have watches from Tiffany's on their wrists, which were personally handed to them by some of the biggest stars in Hollywood. These kids know everything, and I mean *everything*! They even know which of the stars are Lesbians, and they know exactly who and where their girls friends are, and when and how they're going to visit them. One kid fell off a running board in the Holland Tunnel the other day. She was a stowaway on Katharine Hepburn's car, when Katie had come secretly to town, just for the day, and was on her way to visit some obscure relative of hers out in Jersey. I tell you, the subject is fantastic and I'm surprised you haven't stumbled on it before."

"I don't see any photo angles in it," I said. "Do these nitwits meet anywhere, or what?"

"Sure they do," he said. "Most of the free-lance kids meet in draughty subway stations or midtown hotel lobbies, but the autograph-hunting elite meet regularly in the lounge of the Loew's Lexington Theater. Why don't you go up there, next Thursday, and take a look?"

So I called the house manager, made the necessary arrangements, and, the following Thursday evening, went up to that movie house accompanied by a young staff photographer.

When we arrived at the theater, around eight-fifteen, the meeting of the Manhattan chapter of the Joan Crawford Fan Club was already in full session. The fans were all gathered in the lounge, which, in such movie houses, is just the dimly lit antechamber to the powder room and the ball room. Between these two comfort stations about fifty collapsible chairs had been set up by the accommodating management, and seated on those chairs was the surprise of my life.

You see, I'd always associated autograph collecting with a lot of dizzy kids with bad teeth and bad skin who had dandruff on their eyelashes. But here, assembled in this deadly anteroom to the two *pissoirs*, were a lot of sober-looking middle-aged and even quite elderly people. There were about a dozen and a half youngsters around, too, but, by and large, the group seemed like a cross section of any part of any middle-class American neighborhood.

It floored me. They weren't particularly well dressed or anything, but they certainly weren't on the bum, either. Very few people in America ever are, for long. Some of the women wore sweaters, but quite a few of them had hats on; not Lilly Daché or Mr. John type hats, but at least they wore head-pieces, instead of just hair nets. The men were the usual vacant-faced city dwellers who haven't any handicraft or other specialized occupation sufficiently differentiated to put its stamp on them.

One of them, sitting right on the aisle, where I couldn't help but see him, had somehow smuggled his fat little dog into this meeting. I noticed at once that both he and his pooch were chronic "blowers." In case you don't know what a blower is, it is a man who, when he's just sitting still or not doing anything special, fills his cheeks with great gobs of air; and then, when he slowly emits the air through his puckered lips, he gives off a slightly hissing sound. It can make you terribly nervous.

Well, this man had me completely bulldozed with his blowing, because I noticed right away that his dog was doing exactly the same thing. I just couldn't keep my eyes off them. I couldn't help wondering which one of them had gotten the habit first. Did the dog originate the blowing? Did the master? Who had influenced whom? It was a real teaser.

Watching those two lulus, I missed some of the proceedings down front, where the secretary was reading the minutes of the previous meeting. Well, when I finally began to pay a little more attention to the chair, it became quite obvious that the leading spirit of this organization was the officiating president, an unusually homely girl called Vera Zimmerman. Vera's hair seemed to have the exact texture of Brillo, and, although she couldn't have been more than fifteen, she already had the beginnings of a very promising mustache. Her other accomplishments I'm going to skip for the moment.

After the reading of the minutes, Vera cleared her throat so thoroughly that it took quite a sizable batch of Kleenex to take care of this transaction; then, after she'd downed two paper cups full of water, she made a truly stupendous announcement.

"I want to tell you confidentially," she said, "that Miss Joan Crawford is in town, right now. She is here incognito, so none of us is supposed to know anything about it."

I don't have to tell you that the room absolutely simmered with suppressed excitement. Even the blower permitted himself to be stunned out of his established rhythm and shot the air out of his wide-open trap, in one single puff. His dog took an uneasy gander at him and blinked incredulously. Joan Crawford enthusiasts of all sizes and ages had stopped fidgeting and scratching themselves and now looked at each other sideways, in wild surmise. It was a tense moment in our lives.

"I just want to tell you," Vera continued, "that, because

Miss Crawford is such a close friend of mine, and I kept begging her and begging her for about an hour—as I said, because she's such a close friend, she agreed to drop in on this meeting for a few minutes tonight."

The audience sat frozen in an absolute ecstasy of delight and stupefied anticipation. I could hear the horns growing all around me.

"She's going to the theater tonight," said Vera, "and I expect she'll be by here in about ten minutes from now. She's planning to just drop by, like any other member of our chapter, see? She'll go to the back of the room and participate in the meeting, like any other member, and she made me promise, on my solemn word, that everybody will just go on with the business of this meeting, just as if she wasn't here at all. Remember, she's anonymous! And I gave my solemn word to her, or she wouldn't drop in at all. Now, it's up to us to act like it was just an ordinary Thursday night and nobody special had dropped in at all."

Well, you can just imagine that the meeting was a complete shambles after that. Elderly matrons started tittering like schoolgirls; the younger people had to relieve their feelings by going, en masse, to the toilets; the blower shifted his dog to the other arm, and the secretary, whose name was Weaver Killian, once more began to read the minutes of the last meeting.

But it was all right by me, because now it looked as if we might get some real pictures. Meanwhile, everybody in that crazy room was shaking with acute autograph jitters. It was certainly tough for them to just go on living until their idol would really, finally, appear among them in the flesh.

Funny, I thought to myself, nothing ever changes very much in the human character. The gods of the Greek Areopagus came down from Olympus and visited, and sometimes even cohabited with, ordinary mortals. And now Joan Crawford was about to descend from her heights to shed a moment's beneficent luster on common mankind.

"How about some pictures? my photographer asked me.

"Well," I said, "we can't take any without permission. It's a ticklish situation right at this moment. We're liable to queer Vera and all the rest of them, because it will look as if she'd notified us. So hold it for a little while. Who knows what the hell is liable to happen."

Well, the next thing that happened was that Joan Crawford's golden evening slippers appeared at the top of the staircase, to be instantly followed by a white cascade of snarling foxes. A few seconds later, the staring, wild mask of her face became visible, and let me confess that even I had grown quite excited in the atmosphere of frantic suspense that pervaded the premises.

She looked surprisingly like a badly animated puppet, and, as she was covered from her ears to her ankles by dozens of limp skins, the impression of lifelessness was almost complete. She was accompanied by a tall, frozen-jawed Englishman, whose type was very much in vogue as an escort during that particular season.

Well, Joan and her Johnnie walked, or rather, drifted, to the back of the room and sat down on the two folding chairs that had obviously been prepared especially for them. My photographer and I happened to be sitting almost alongside them, and I tell you that it seemed to me that Joan was, for some mysterious reason, almost as excited at that moment as everybody else in the place. She had a tough time breathing with any sort of regularity, and I finally even noticed a handful of bloody fingernails come out of that bundle of fur and settle convulsively in the general region of her heart.

Down front, the officers of the club attempted to proceed about their business with some semblance of purpose and order. Weaver Killian read the minutes of last week's meeting for the third time. When he had finished, there was a moment of indecisive silence, and it was during this moment that I was suddenly assailed by the eeriest feeling. It seemed to me that I was witnessing some sort of staggering biological phenomenon, something like an atavistic reversion on an unprecedented scale. You see, I was convinced that the people sitting there in front of me were all starting to grow eyes in the backs of their heads.

They were so feverishly, intensely alert, that I could see the blood clearly pulsating in their ears, and I felt with growing certainty that all this suppressed tension was bound to end in some sort of explosion. I tell you, it was beginning to get insupportable.

And then Vera Zimmerman spoke up. She talked very strangely, like someone under a strong hypnotic compulsion, and it was clear to me that the words were absolutely wrung out of her, almost as if against her own real wishes.

"I gave my solemn word," she said. "I gave my solemn word to Miss Crawford—to Joan, I mean, she's asked me to call her Joan—and I just want to say that I told everybody here that she's here incognito. But, now that Miss Crawford, Joan, is really here amongst us, I hope she'll forgive me if I ask her to address just a few words to this meeting."

Poor Vera raised her stricken face and looked towards the back of the room so appealingly, that I was just on the verge of saying, "Hear! hear!" when Joan Crawford slowly got up and, in a trancelike condition just like Vera's, started to float down to the small dais.

And now that they were all officially absolved by their chairman's breach of contract, everyone in the place automatically swiveled in the direction of Joan's progress. The poor bewildered Englishman had also gotten to his feet, of course, and glided aimlessly in her wake toward the front end of the room.

Joan at last very abstractedly stepped onto the platform and looked down at the lot of us, as if she were suffering from an acute attack of amnesia. I'm telling you, she looked as if she was positively bewildered by all those goddamned staring faces in front of her.

It made no sense. After all, she was certainly used to mass adulation, wasn't she? So what the hell had suddenly gotten into the dame?

And then her arms slowly emerged out of that fur tent and she opened them wide, in the conventional gesture of the religious revivalist who is asking for volunteers to come up to the penitents' bench. She stood like that, silently, for about thirty seconds, and then, suddenly, unbelievably, she lowered her head and started to cry. But I mean cry! She bawled like a six-year-old kid whose first Didy-Doll has just dropped into the family well. She simply leaked with sorrow and shook with shameless, uncontrollable sobs. And then, when she started to wipe her face, she smeared mascara all over her white fox furs, all over her arms and hands, and believe me, she certainly didn't give the slightest damn what she looked like at that moment.

The Englishman kept fluttering around her, like a torn kite that's been caught in an updraft, but, despite his ineffectual appearance, he somehow managed to slip her a handkerchief, and he finally even got her down off that platform. In an emergency he turned out to be a real man, after all. In the end, I saw him firmly putting his arm around her shoulders and purposefully piloting her up the stairs, out into the night again.

But the rest of us remained. I'm wondering if anybody is really fit to describe the condition of that audience, which had been so completely stunned out of its not too abundant wits and now sat openmouthed and perspiring in the dim light of that gruesome meeting room.

A goddess had wept; had wept completely, and shamelessly, as any heartbroken human drab might weep. No wonder all their eyes were cast down, and not a single voice was to be heard; for the room had certainly been hexed and turned suddenly into a dwelling place of unnamable sorrow and ambiguous contrition.

238

As I looked at that assembly of white-faced, frightened people, it came to me that they were like a conclave of innocent communicants who had just been accused of activities terribly dangerous to the public safety. I watched them move slowly and reluctantly toward the exit, as if they expected an enormous police wagon to cart them all off to some unimaginable place of grim retribution. Let me tell you, it was a bitter Thursday night.

"What the hell was this all about?" said my photographer. "What the hell was wrong with the daffy doll, anyway?"

"It's obvious," I said.

Of course there was nothing obvious about it at all.

"She's a dame who was awful poor once herself," I said, "and I suppose, when she stood up there and looked at all those adoring schlemiels staring worshipfully up at her, it suddenly hit her, that there, but for the grace of God, was herself. Maybe it's been quite a long time since she's been face to face, and that close up to her own boring, mediocre past; it suddenly must have walloped her where it hurt her pretty bad."

I was making up this whole rigmarole, just for the benefit of a younger man who liked to have neat answers to everything. He was never satisfied merely to see Vesuvius erupting and covering the whole neighborhood with boiling water and hot ashes; he wanted to hear all the appropriate statistics relating to such an outburst, and, also, to know the meaning of the thermal-dynamics involved and to have it all properly arranged and classified for future reference. So I had just quickly improvised the sort of answer that would send him home peaceably and in a state of reasonable contentment.

Still, when I finally got home, I couldn't help but wonder whether I hadn't, by the merest accident, just happened to hit on the only right and sensible solution.

For, after all, why in hell did she suddenly bust out bawling the way she did?

Anyway, we got no pictures that night, and we never even had a story—until now.

## CHAPTER TWENTY-FOUR

YESTERDAY I REREAD everything I have written in this book up until now, and I came to the baffling conclusion that the only thing that has so far escaped these pages

239

is an actual, well-rounded account of my life. Maybe it can't ever really be done at all. I doubt that anyone has ever succeeded in giving us his life fully and comprehensively. No. I'm sure they all failed in different ways to do justice to their subjects, and I think that often they even overlooked the basic, motivating essentials which gave their existence its dynamic direction.

Indeed, it seems to me that the writers who weren't so determinedly autobiographical sometimes managed to tell us a good deal more about themselves by approaching their elusive identities obliquely, or even peripherally.

Well, I have this certainty about myself, for instance, that I could start writing an altogether new and faithful account of my life right this minute, without repeating a single episode contained in this present manuscript.

Because, as the Chinese poet, Rihaku, said, twelve hundred years ago.

It is like the flowers falling at spring's end
    Confused, whirled in a tangle.
What is the use of talking, and there is no end of talking,
    There is no end of the things in the heart.

Let me repeat, just in case you've been inattentive.

What is the use of talking, and there is no end of talking,
    *There is no end of the things in the heart.*

And that's the real hang-up. There is no end of the things in the heart that one might tell about completely. That's why, with the best intention in the world, I can offer you only this fragment, this perhaps misleading synopsis of a life in which the majority of days were recognized, as they happened, as gracious, unexpected gifts to my gluttonous appetite for awareness. I can only try not to overlook the circumstances and, particularly, the people who really deeply affected my thoughts and my emotions. I mustn't forget the many obscure heroes and saints who gave me thrilling glimpses of human benevolence, fortitude and courage in some of the darkest and dankest corners of the world.

And I certainly mustn't forget Nathan Garfein, because he helped me to understand the momentous problems of tact and protocol that may sometimes seriously affect the pride, the dignity and even the lives of very humble people.

Nathan Garfein was himself of rather small account in the community that employed him as a *shames*. That is to say, he was the sexton of a synagogue on Forsythe Street, and, for some reason, that particular profession has always had certain humorous connotations among Jews. Even American gentiles have freely adopted the word *shames* to serve as a slang synonym for detective, and in some parts of the country it has, incongruously, come to mean a croupier at a gambling table.

Old man Garfein, the *shames,* was a devout member of a very orthodox community over on New York's East Side. I originally came to know him through his son Morris, who went to grade school with me. Let me confess that I knew hardly anything at all about religious Jews at that time of my life, and I was even a little leery of most of them; I mean the bearded ones who wore the traditional earlocks and the long black coats, and who never learned to speak English properly.

This prejudice was first broken by old man Garfein, when his son Morris and I happened to find a woman's fur neck piece in the middle of Manhattan Bridge one Sunday afternoon. Morris and I had spotted it almost simultaneously, but, by the merest accident, I happened to be the one who actually picked it up. It looked like a very nice piece of fur, too, and so we both felt a little sheepish about who should enjoy exclusive property rights over it.

"I'll tell you what," said Morris. "Let's ask my father about it."

I laughed. I laughed because his father, whom I'd seen about a dozen times at their house, had never once during my visits raised his eyes even for a moment from the large prayer book that he always seemed to be holding in his hands.

"You think your father will want to bother himself with such things?" I asked.

"Oh sure," said Morris. "And he's very fair about judging things, and people. As a matter of fact, I think he'll get a kick out of our asking him."

Morris proved to be quite right.

When he presented our problem to his father and showed him the fur piece, the old man seemed extremely pleased.

"Hand me down the third book on the left side of that shelf," he said in Yiddish. "We'll find out in a minute what should be done about it."

Morris handed him the book he had asked for, obviously some section of the Talmud, and the old man began to hum a little, into his beard, as he started riffling the pages.

I couldn't understand it. The whole thing made no sense to me at all.

"You mean," I said to Morris, "that the Bible, or whatever it is he's looking up, tells you what to do with a fur piece that two people found on a Sunday afternoon on Manhattan Bridge?"

The old man had obviously understood my question, for he suddenly paused in his search and looked at me very seriously.

"These books," he said, "contain everything. Everything that a man needs to know. They may not say anything about a fur piece on Manhattan Bridge, that is true, but I'm quite sure they will have something that applies to this case. Something, maybe, about a lamb that strayed and was lost, long, long ago in Samaria, and was finally found by two people, who were just as puzzled about the rightful ownership then, as the two of you are puzzled now. You understand?"

As he talked to me, I suddenly realized how handsome he was. His eyes were the eyes of Rembrandt's famous rabbi, which I had seen in Amsterdam when we'd stopped off there for a couple of days on our way to the United States. Although I was still a very young man, I felt almost intuitively that his constant preoccupation with God and God's words had purified his brow and his complexion to an almost translucent spirituality. Here, in this vulgar East Side tenement, he seemed like a visitor from another planet, and I trusted him implicitly to judge fairly between us, even though one of the claimants in the case happened to be his son.

And he certainly didn't let us down. He finally managed to discover, as he had predicted he would, a similar case, relating to a valuable cloak which had been found, under almost identical circumstances, many centuries ago in Spain.

"The judgment at that time was," said Mr. Garfein, "that the two finders should sell the cloak and divide the proceeds equally between them."

And that's what Morris and I did, the very next day; it was a satisfactory solution all around. But what really made that Sunday afternoon important in my life was that I had suddenly seen a human being behind the forbidding traditional façade; the black velour hat, the dark clothes and the alien beard were no longer able to conceal a remarkable man called Nathan Garfein. He didn't read Keats or T. S. Eliot, but he certainly spent his time reading something more soul-sustaining than the funnies in the New York *Journal*.

Well, anyway, as time went on, I eventually lost touch with Morris Garfein—and naturally I didn't see his father, either—for about twelve years or so; and then one day, up in Bryant Park, of all places, right in back of the Public Library, I suddenly ran into the old man again. I'm glad to say he still remembered me, and, since we hadn't met for such a long time, I even persuaded him to sit down on a bench with me for a few minutes. Fortunately, in the intervening years I had learned to speak a proper sort of Yiddish, and so I was able to talk to him with complete ease.

"You're 'way out of your neighborhood," I said to him. "How is it you happened to stray so far among the gentiles, anyway?"

"You are right," he said. "It's the first time in my whole life that I've been above Fourteenth Street. But it's a special occasion. It's a kind of holiday for me."

"Your birthday?" I asked.

"Oh, no! A man my age doesn't make holidays out of his birthdays," he said. "He tries not to notice them. No. I saw somebody off on a ship this afternoon, and when I left the docks I seem to have turned in the wrong direction and landed here."

"Well, it brought us together," I said, "and so I'm very glad that you lost your way."

"That's true," he said. "I suppose I was excited by the ship, and by the crowd of people who came to see my friend off. And my feelings were all mixed up too, because, although I felt sorry that my friend is gone, I'm also very happy that he is at last on his way."

"Is it anybody from the family?" I said.

"No, no," he said. "It is a strange story, and I don't want to bore you with it, but some day, when God brings us together again, and you have a little time . . ."

"Nonsense!" I said. "I have all the time in the world right now, and you couldn't possibly bore me, no matter how hard you tried. So why don't you ease your heart and tell me all about it?"

I know that in English all this sounds like pretty fancy talk, "ease your heart" and all that stuff, but in Yiddish it didn't sound strange at all. Remember, the Jews were originally an Eastern people, and, all through the centuries of their exile, they've always had a taste for somewhat flamboyant turns of speech.

"Well," said Mr. Garfein, "if it isn't presuming on your kindness, I would, as a matter of fact, very much like to tell you this little story."

"Please," I said, "I'm only too anxious to hear it. Would you like a cigarette, maybe?"

"No, thanks," he said. "I have a pipe here in my pocket, and it is even filled with tobacco."

He took out a pipe and proceeded to light it by means of some large, sulphurous kitchen matches. I didn't even know that they still made matches that stank like that.

Incidentally, this pipe of his didn't seem to function properly at all, and I finally decided that it hadn't ever been meant to function; that, in fact, it was just a stylistic device by which Mr. Garfein created certain critical pauses in his talk—a sort of incendiary punctuation. Later, when we got up from our seats, we were both of us almost ankle deep in burnt-out matches.

"Well, Mr. Garfein," I said, "I'm certainly anxious to hear

all about your friend who sailed to Europe today. Was he a member of your congregation?"

"It all started in our synagogue," he said. "You see, just seven years ago this coming Passover, our old rabbi, may his soul rest in peace, died on the second night of the Seder. It was a terrible calamity for our congregation, and for quite a while after we buried him we had no rabbi at all. You understand, it isn't simple for people like us to find a rabbi. After all, we're all elderly people, set in our ways, and we couldn't just go and get some youngster fresh out of Yeshiva College to come and sit over us, could we? It was a real problem, a bitter problem, too, because it certainly didn't look as if it was going to be solved so easily. And then God granted us a piece of great good fortune. A member of our congregation, a Mr. Mitteldorf, who originally came from Russian Poland, had a letter from the old country, telling him that the synagogue in his home town had been destroyed by vandals and that the rabbi of that community was willing to come to America if a suitable congregation could be found for him."

"Wonderful!" I said. "So you sent for him, of course!"

"It wasn't quite so simple," said Mr. Garfein, thoughtfully.

"Why not?" I said. "A man your own age, I should think everybody would have been anxious to have him."

"Yes, it would seem like that," said Mr. Garfein, "but a few of the members were worried about him. They were afraid he might turn out too much of a foreigner. You hear? There isn't a single man in my congregation who can say an English sentence of five words without mixing in three words of Yiddish, and yet some of them had a feeling that he might be too much of a greenhorn! Well, even they were finally won over, because we had letters from various people in Europe who knew him and who assured us that he was one of the rare chosen ones and that the *Shechina* of God surely rested upon him."

"And so he came over," I said.

"He came, and he was received at the boat with torchlights by the whole congregation, and after he had been installed he delivered an oration in which he gave thanks to God, and to us, for the mercy and the goodness that had been showered on him. Believe me, I've heard quite a few rabbis in my day, but the words that came that night out of the mouth of Rabbi Eliezer were like the pure golden threads which form the Star of David on the curtains of the Torah. I blessed the Almighty for the privilege of having been permitted to sit in the shadow of such a learned man. The whole community was in ecstasy."

"Great!" I said. "I'm glad to hear that some things in this world do work out just the way they were planned."

"Yes, it worked out just as we had planned, for about three months—or three and a half months, maybe."

"Why, what happened?" I said. "Didn't the rabbi like it here?"

"The rabbi never complained," said Mr. Garfein. "It had nothing to do with the rabbi; it was the congregation—or, at least, some members of the congregation that started all the trouble."

"Why, what did they want?" I asked.

"I will tell you what they wanted," he said. "You see, the rabbi caught a cold shortly after he arrived in this country, and so he sometimes had to stay away from services. Not often, about two or three times a month. Believe me, it didn't matter at all, because when he did show up he spoke to us with so much burning eloquence, in words of such beauty and meaning, that it was better to have him present once a year than have a lesser man every single day."

"I understand," I said. "But they were worried about his health because they'd just lost the other rabbi, I suppose, is that it?"

"That's what they *said*, that's what they *pretended*, but the truth—the truth was somewhere else altogether."

"And what was the truth?" I asked.

"The truth was," said Mr. Garfein, "that the members of our congregation are just very little people—little butchers, little grocers, little bakers and hardware dealers—and so when they come to the synagogue, after working hard in their shops and stores all week, they don't need a synagogue, they don't want a synagogue at all. What they really want is a social club, you understand? The truth is that the rabbi's high and precious words were a constant reproach to them for their week-long niggling and haggling; the truth is that the pure flame that was shining in him was burning much too brightly for the dim twilight of their little souls."

Mr. Garfein's beautiful eyes were moist with the passion of his convictions. He may have been only the sexton of that congregation over on Forsythe Street, but at that moment he was certainly the personification of its accusing conscience.

"And so," I said, "what did they finally do about it?"

Mr. Garfein gave a profound sigh before he answered me. "They did what they always do when something unpleasant has to be done—they ordered me to do it. After all, I'm just like an errand boy in their eyes."

"And what exactly did they expect you to do?" I asked.

"They expected me to fire him," said Mr. Garfein. "That's all they expected."

"So what did you do?"

"I went to bed," said Mr. Garfein. "I simply lay down in

bed on Friday afternoon, and I got up the following Tuesday."

I had just recently finished reading Sigmund Freud, and so I couldn't help remembering what he had said about such curious behavior. Freud would have diagnosed Mr. Garfein's temporary hibernation as a manifestation of his desire to get back into his mother's womb, where everything was peaceful and orderly, and where there weren't any rabbis to be fired. Of course I didn't mention any of this to Mr. Garfein, because the chances were he wouldn't have cared for it.

"Well," I said, "you finally had to get out of bed on Tuesday, so what happened then?"

"I washed myself, and then, after I had prayed, I went to call on the rabbi. It wasn't very far from my house, it was right across the street from the synagogue, in fact. The members of the congregation had rented two small rooms for him on a parlor floor, and they had also hired a Polak from the neighborhood to do some chores around the house for him, particularly on the Sabbath. Well, I knocked on the rabbi's door, and, believe me, he might really have heard me coming a long way off, just by the loud beating of my heart. It was, of course, obvious that Reb Eliezer was a little surprised by my visit. After all, though he had always treated me with kindness and consideration, I was just a *shames* and no special bosom friend of his. However, despite his momentary puzzlement, he was very courteous in receiving me. He asked me to sit down, and he told the Polak to make me a glass of tea.

"I can't tell you what my feelings were as I sat there looking at him. First of all, that room of his had an unearthly stillness, as if it weren't in New York at all. I don't know how it happened, but a wonderful quiet suddenly settled even on my troubled heart. I suppose the presence of true greatness always does that to a man. I tell you, there were no calendars in that room, and no alarm clocks, either. There was only goodness, and wisdom, and serenity . . . and the fine smell of lemons and apples. There was a bowl full of them on the table, and when the rabbi noticed me looking at them he said, 'I always kept flowers in the house, back home in Poldishi, but in the winter when there were no flowers, it was a good thing for the eyes and for the heart to see fruit on the table.'

"'Yes,' I said, 'it is always a good thing to see God's wonderful handiwork about one. I'm going to pick up some lemons and apples myself, on my way home.' At any rate, I can't repeat to you everything we said to each other that Tuesday afternoon, but when it was nearly dark and I had to go to *shul* for the evening prayers, the rabbi and I had talked over all the past and present sorrows of Israel, and we had even speculated endlessly on all of its promised glories to come."

246

"But you didn't *fire* him!" I said.

"You talk exactly like the leaders of my congregation," said Mr. Garfein. "They were waiting for me at the very gates of the synagogue and wanted to know, at once, when the rabbi was planning to leave. 'Just a minute!' I said to them. 'We are talking here about a learned man, aren't we? We are talking about a rabbi, and not about a bookkeeper! A little respect, if you please! I will tell him that you no longer want him to be part of this community, when the time is ripe. Don't worry, I'm employed by you and I will certainly carry out your orders to the letter. But one thing I insist on—respect for his office, and respect for the man!'"

"So, what did they say to that?" I asked.

"What did they say? They were dissatisfied, of course. But at the same time they did realize that you can't just go up to a rabbi and tell him to pack up his bundle and get out. And so on the following Thursday I again dropped in on Reb Eliezer, and this time he acted almost as if he'd been expecting me. We had tea together again and he told me a good deal about his past in Poldishi and how good and sweet life had sometimes been in the years when his wife was still with him. I could see his heart was heavy about the loss of his synagogue in the old country, and also because he was no longer able to visit and to pray at his wife's grave. They had had no children, but although a Jew may, according to our law, divorce his wife for her failure to bear him offspring, I'm sure Reb Eliezer had never even thought about such a thing. As they grew older, they had clung more and more to each other, and his only consolation was that she had, mercifully, died before his synagogue had been destroyed. Well, the rabbi and I talked away the whole afternoon that way, until it was again time to go and say the evening prayers. The congregation didn't wait for me on the front steps, this time, they just gave me a lot of dark and reproachful looks, which I pretended not to notice.

"And so, to make a long story short, I went back again to Reb Eliezer's the following Tuesday, and now, on my third visit, he already greeted me like an old friend. Unfortunately, the friendlier we grew, the harder it became for me to tell him about my terrible errand. It just got so that after a while I couldn't even imagine myself speaking to him about it. I tell you every Tuesday and Thursday that I dropped in on him brought us closer and closer together. To bring up the real subject for my calling became altogether an impossibility. It was awful! And of course the congregation was after me all the time, worse than ever. They were getting tired of the way I was handling the situation, and a few of the more unpleasant members were sometimes even pretty sarcastic with me."

"What a terrible ordeal for you!" I said.

"But now," said Mr. Garfein, "let me tell you about a still greater complication that happened, a complication so serious than I went right back to bed again, for another three days. You see, one evening, right after services, a strange Jew stopped me on the corner of my block and called me by name. I had never seen him before and, to tell you the truth, I didn't care very much for his looks. He had a neat little scissor-trimmed beard on him, like the ones the reformed Jews often wear, and his clothes looked just a little too fancy for an ordinary weekday. But he introduced himself to me very politely and, after telling me that his name was Reb Shmul Gershon, he stretched out his hand to me. Well, when a Jew stretches out his hand to you, you've just got to shake it, don't you?

"And then, right there on that windy corner, Shmul Gershon told me right off why he had come, and why he had stopped me. He told me he was the *shames* of a very rich congregation over in Brooklyn, and that the members of that congregation had, for the longest time, been after our rabbi to quit his position with us and to come to officiate out at their synagogue. They had notified Reb Eliezer that if he would accept the rabbinate in their community they were prepared to pay him five times the salary that we were paying him.

" 'And, what's more,' said Reb Gershon, 'I'm prepared to give you, Mr. Garfein, a hundred dollars in cash, which I have right here in my pocket, if you will talk Reb Eliezer into taking that job with us."

"I tell you, as that Jew was talking to me I got so shaky, I had to lean up against a lamppost, just to steady myself. 'Just a minute,' I said to him, 'did you already approach our rabbi in person about all this?'

" 'Certainly!' he said. 'But he's a true saint, and although he would like to earn more money—because he sends every penny he gets right back to Poldishi, to help rebuild his old synagogue—he says that he can't possibly leave your congregation, because your spiritual needs are very serious and very great, and that he couldn't abandon you now, steeped as you are in darkness and in error.' 'Holy father in heaven!' I thought. While I was trying to get up my courage to tell him we no longer wanted him, he, in his turn, had letters in his pocket from this rich congregation in Brooklyn, and he couldn't ever get around to telling me about his troubles, either. As I said before, I went straight home and went instantly to bed."

"And when you finally got up?" I said.

"You can just imagine," he said. "The next time I called on Reb Eliezer and looked into his eyes, and realized how ungrateful we had been to him, and what a shameful mission had fallen to my lot, I nearly burst into tears. I don't know how I survived it all. Sometimes a man can be stronger than iron."

"And how long, in heaven's name, did all this go on?" I said.

"It went on for six years," said Mr. Garfein.

"What?" I said. "Six years!"

"Yes," he said, "and those petty, nasty naggers in my congregation were after me every minute of that time, too."

"But, just the same," I said, "you must admit they did let it drag on for six whole years, didn't they?"

"So what?" said Mr. Garfein. "Remember we are talking about a learned man, a great scholar. We are talking about a rabbi, not a bookkeeper."

"True," I said, "and how did it finally end?"

"It finally ended today, on that steamship that is taking Reb Eliezer back to Poldishi. You understand, he had sent home enough money, over the years, to rebuild his old synagogue. The whole congregation came down to see him off this afternoon, but you know what happened? You see, through all those visits which I had paid him twice a week for six whole years, he and I had finally come to be really very close to each other. And then this afternoon, in front of the whole assembled community, and before this whole proud-stomached city, Reb Eliezer pressed only me close to his heart and called me his beloved friend. We mingled our tears in sorrow, but in joy, too, because neither one of us had ever had to disclose the sordid, worldly secrets that had so long and so bitterly burdened our hearts."

## CHAPTER TWENTY-FIVE

I SUPPOSE THAT all through the writing of these pages there trembled in my heart a sort of submerged hope that the story of my life would finally come to form a meaningful pattern, a signpost, if not exactly a guide, for some of my more alert progeny. Well, I'm happy to say I've found it, all right, the moral and the meaning, too, even if you can't always see it too plainly.

The moral is that it behooves a man to act at all times like a testicled animal, and to accept the gifts and the burdens of his peculiar identity without regret, and without too much fear.

If you examine the various characters whom I have written about, from the scholarly Julian Griefer, who stoically banished himself to Oswego because his girl was giving him a raw deal, to the shrewdly cosmopolitan Alexander Ince, who risked and lost his life's savings just to publish a magazine that he believed in, you can see that most of these people were real men. What's more, they all quietly accepted that there was no possible form of insurance against the deepest sorrows and the greatest tragedies that fall upon mankind, and so they decided to live bravely, in a world where everything was destined for eventual extinction anyhow.

Only two weeks ago, the son of a friend of mine was offered a fine job by the General Electric Company. He still hasn't made up his mind, because he wants to make sure that they guarantee him the most satisfactory retirement fund available in today's labor market. He's going to be twenty-two years old next December.

I have nothing to say in disparagement of such an attitude; it just doesn't interest me. It never did. I know all the reasons for playing it safe; who should know better than I? But if you have read my story with even the most superficial sort of attention, you must have come to realize that the great joys and the true ecstasies in my life came from surprises and achievements which were the results of certain risks that I was willing to take. Heaven knows, I have perpetrated some terrible errors in my day, and I have even committed some shameful and unnecessary crimes, but I have never settled for just a full crib of corn in a warm, rainproof stable. Not I!

Which brings me to another important point—namely, that all people, even the worst dullards, like to dream themselves out of their torpid routines; but, believe me, most of them, even if they had the chance to alter things, would only change over to another sort of torpid routine.

In fact, you will do well to remember this, too: It may be most helpful to you in life if you'll somehow manage to acquire a little housebroken system for shocking people; just shaking them into giving you a little useful attention, maybe. You see, this stodgy world of ours really adores excitement and melodrama, but you must learn to evolve a suitable technique whereby you can administer the required electrifying charge in socially acceptable dosages. You probably have already discovered that certain people absolutely have to have all sorts of exaggerated testimonials or demonstrations, just to bring them up to a reasonable standard of decent human responsiveness.

Let's suppose, for instance, that your girl has been stringing

250

you along for quite a while, and you've finally gotten to the very end of your patience and composure. Well, then, it is obviously no further use for you to just go on telling her that you love her and that you're feeling very serious about her. But just suppose that, while you *are* telling her all this, you also, at the same time, slash yourself straight across the wrist with a fragment of a broken gin bottle. You know perfectly well that at the very moment when you start bleeding all over her carpet she automatically stops being lethargic and pre-occupied.

Of course, I'm giving you an extreme example of getting somebody's undivided attention. What I'm trying to make clear is that she can't just go on coquetting with her adorable image in the surrounding mirrors, while you're shpritzing beet juice all over her landscape. She'll have to bandage you up with her petticoat, or call a doctor, or something; but she'll certainly undergo a salutary catharsis about you, one way or another, and you'll either *have* her or be *rid* of her for good. Anyway it will be the end of her unresponsiveness. Get it?

I have never, myself, had occasion to do anything quite so drastic to achieve a desired result, but there were many times in my life when a sudden, unexpected action or even a shocking statement managed to put a finish to some pretty insupportable situations.

Let me give you a rather trivial example which has just come to my mind.

One Saturday afternoon some years ago, I was picked up for speeding somewhere just outside of Pleasantville, New York. Now, Pleasantville was a notorious speed trap, and if I'd had my wits about me I certainly would have remembered it. At any rate, the traffic cop had clocked me at seventy miles an hour, and since the court generally charged ten dollars for every mile above forty-five it is plain to see that I was going to be out exactly two hundred and fifty dollars. An additional piece of nuisance was the fact that you weren't taken before their judge immediately upon being pinched, you had to come back four days later. It was a real drag.

So, the following Wednesday, I took two hundred and fifty dollars out of the bank and I hied myself up to the court, twenty-five miles outside of New York City. All the way driving up there, I was in an absolute stew of indignation about this whole stinking deal, but I really didn't see what the hell I could do about it. I had asked a couple of lawyer friends for some possible way out, but they had advised me to take along the dough, and to write it all off to experience.

When I finally got to the courthouse the place was jammed, mostly with other New Yorkers, both men and women, whom the smugly smiling, fat-legged cops had nailed, just like me, on the previous Saturday.

His Honor turned out to be an ancient ostrich-head with corrugated wattles; the only hair that still grew on this monster was sprouting from his nose and his ears. In less than a minute I heard him sock two speed violators for three hundred and fifty dollars.

Then it was my turn.

"Guilty with an explanation!" I said.

"Eh? What's your explanation?"

"Because it was Saturday," I said. "My doctor only stays in his office till one o'clock. I phoned him and begged him to wait for me another half hour, Your Honor, because a terrible emergency had happened."

"What emergency?" croaked the ostrich.

"I had blood in my urine," I said.

"*What? What? What?* Sh! . . . What's the matter with you anyway? Come on up here, and don't say another word!" He was absolutely apoplectic with horror, that I'd mentioned urine in his courtroom, aloud, in front of a lot of ladies, too.

When I was just three inches away from him, he cupped both his hands around his mouth and said, "What was wrong?"

"Well, to tell you the truth—"

"Sh!" he said. "Come closer, and don't shout."

I moved in on him another inch. "I've never had a venereal disease in my life, You Honor, and so, you can imagine how shocked and frightened I was."

"Has nothing to do with venereal disease," said His Honor. "Nothing!"

"No," I said. "It proved to be gravel in my kidneys."

"Of course," he said. "Had it myself once. Terrible pain! Terrible! The most terrible!"

Out of the corner of my eye I could see the leather leggings of my traffic cop shifting about uneasily. He couldn't hear what we were saying to each other, but he was alarmed just the same. The judge was an old man. Sickness of any kind, even in other people, had probably fascinated him before, and, to tell you the truth, it was exactly his horribly collapsed looks that had inspired me to bring up this experience of mine. —which had really happened to me about two years before.

At any rate, the judge hastily scribbled something on a piece of paper, and handed it to me. It read: *Dr. Justin Frankfort, G.U. Specialist, Mt. Sinai Hospital. Recommended by Judge Lincoln Perterkin, Pleasantville, N.Y.*

"The best man in the business," he said. "He'll get that gravel to pass right out of you, and you'll be as good as new. Or better!"

We solemnly shook hands.

252

"Sentence suspended!" he said to the court at large.

Just when I was about to get into my car to drive back to New York, a fat, smartly dressed little man came puffing up to me and put a hand on my arm.

"I'll give you fifty dollars," he said, "in fact, I'll give you a hundred if you tell me what you said to that old scarecrow."

"It won't do you any good," I said. "In cases like that, it's the sudden shock value that counts, and that, I'm afraid, is now pretty well dissipated. No, to get any consideration out of him now, you'd have to spring an active lung hemorrhage right across his desk, and even then I don't think it would help you. You see, I don't believe he's ever had trouble with his lungs. I was just plain lucky. He's an old gravel pit—and so he just happened to feel sympathetic toward a young sandbank like myself. Sorry!"

You would probably never have guessed it, but now that my little saga is about to come to an end, certain small misgivings have recently started to assail me. It suddenly seems to me that I may, perhaps, have been a little severe on a few of the people I have written about. Henry R. Luce, for instance. I'm afraid I've given a rather one-sided impression of him. After all, on occasion I've found him capable of very agreeable human foibles, and sometimes I have known him to be activated by almost whimsical impulses, and he is certainly not the completely stuffed shirt that I have made him out to be. I should like, however tardily, to correct this false impression, and perhaps I still can.

Well, one night, after I'd taken dinner with the Luces up at Westport, suddenly, a little after midnight I felt quite hungry, and, since I was spending the weekend with them, I simply got up out of bed, put on my bathrobe, and went downstairs to hunt myself up some grub. This proved less easy than it sounds because it was a large house and I didn't seem to have any luck in finding the kitchen. At last, after about fifteen or twenty minutes, I landed in some sort of pantry, the servants' pantry, I'm sure, because the food that I discovered here was infinitely superior to anything we had been served at the dinner table.

At any rate, I picked up some odds and ends, like breast of turkey, lobster salad, pecan pie, and a glass of milk, and went into the living room to eat some of this stuff at my leisure. And then, just as I was settling myself comfortably, I heard footsteps coming down the spiral glass staircase. When I looked up, there was Harry Luce, in his bathrobe, and I could see he was greatly puzzled by my strange midnight behavior.

"What's wrong?" he asked. "Anybody wake you?"

"Just my stomach," I said. "I was hungry, so I got myself a snack. Wanna join me?"

I could see that he was in a real quandary. As a good host, he couldn't help but encourage me to go on eating. All the same, there was something unorthodox and almost rowdy in my behavior, and by the time he'd finally come abreast of me and my spread I don't think he cared too much about these nocturnal proceedings.

"It's all right, Harry," I said. "Raiding the refrigerator is the ancient prerogative of American males. Norman Rockwell even made a cover for the *Post* showing an old codger in his nightshirt lifting a drumstick out of the icebox. What's more, his little grandson is standing right there beside him,"

Luce's face visibly brightened. He was no longer at a loss. The matter had obviously some sort of popular sanction and had further been ratified and, one might say, almost hallowed in the public prints.

"Where did you get all this stuff?" he asked me.

"In the servants' pantry," I said. "Your help certainly doesn't suffer here. Come on, I'll show you."

I led him to the loaded refrigerator and he also cheerfully helped himself to some pie and a glass of milk.

I've eaten with the Luces at many festive tables and at fiendishly expensive, fashionable restaurants, but the most companionable meal I ever had with Harry was that midnight snack up at Westport.

Of course, the next morning he couldn't quite resist boasting a little to Clare about it. "Raided the icebox last night," he said. "Had some first-rate pie for a change, too. I haven't had a good piece of pastry like that since we moved into this house. You know where it came from? From the servants' pantry. You must tell the cook not to stint us, and to do at least as well by us as she does by the hired help. At any rate, I must say it was a real pick-me-up!"

You see? Just a regular guy.

Another regular guy I once raided an icebox with was William Faulkner, but that was a hell of a long time ago, 'way back in 1927. We were sleeping over at Harrison Smith's, right here in New York, for some reason or another, and we wandered into his kitchen in the middle of the night, also to look for some likely provender. I remember I felt particularly sorry for Faulkner at the time because that very afternoon I'd happened to eavesdrop on a most revealing conversation about him, down at Harcourt, Brace, his publishers.

Harrison Smith was an editor for Harcourt, Brace at the time. I had dropped into Hal's office that afternoon to show him some of my illustrations for *The Magic Island*. Hal was

254

*out of the room when I arrived, but I could hear him talking*
to Alf Harcourt right next door.

They had obviously been discussing Bill Faulkner and his work, because I heard Hal saying, "He's a very gifted guy, Alf, and I think he'll be a tremendous asset to us. You'll see."

"Oh, well," said Harcourt, "you can't ever be sure about that, not at this stage of the game, anyway."

"You're wrong," said Hal. "I think *The Sound and the Fury* will raise a violent critical storm, and, what's more, I think it definitely launches an important new talent in American letters."

"Well," said Mr. Harcourt, "that may well be so. But somehow, I still don't feel at ease about him."

"Why?" said Hal. "What did he do to rub you the wrong way? Come on, suppose you tell me what it is that makes you so leery about him."

"All right," said Harcourt, "I'll tell you what's bothering me. You know, this Faulkner person looks to me like the type of guy, who . . . well . . . who might come to *hang around* quite a lot. You understand?"

Hal understood, of course, and so did I. Faulkner, who was practically unknown at the time and had very few friends in New York, had probably fallen into the habit of dropping in at the Harcourt, Brace offices a couple of times a week. Well, poor Faulkner couldn't possibly have known that the last thing a successful publisher wants hanging around his office is an author. It makes everybody uneasy, because he looms like the most incongruous of intruders in a business that it seems possible to run so marvelously well without him.

Every sober, sensible, and right-minded person can appreciate and understand *that* much.

# CHAPTER TWENTY-SIX

AND WHAT CAN I say in summation? What have I overlooked?

Well, I forgot to speak of my dear son, Mervin, and his wonderful wife, Betts, and I suppose I ought to explain why I have hardly mentioned the endless numbers of very famous people whom I have come to know in the course of my life. They don't appear in this book simply because I don't see any particular reason why I should try to aggrandize myself at the expense of their distinguished reputations.

Many of them have been unbelievably kind to me, and most of them are actually having a hell of a bad time of it. A lot worse than I ever had.

You see, I can look anybody in the eye, because all I ever owed anybody was just *money!*

I don't owe the world a Hit Play every year, or a Smash Television Contract each season, or even a Successful Off-Broadway Opening in some flea bag on the East Side.

I've never yoiked my griefs into the ears of greedy, sick psychiatrists, because most of my miseries could easily be settled by just applying a little convenient cash. Dig?

As my dear father once said to me, "If you have a few dollars in the bank, you can laugh indefinitely."

And, unlike Henry IV, I'm not a bit sore at the people who didn't bother to give me a friendly hand when I was in my most desperate jam. Remember what this king said after the Battle of Arques to his comrade at arms, Crillon, who had failed to arrive in time to help him? "Hang yourself, brave Crillon, we fought at Arques, and you were not there!"

I have no such rancorous feelings.

Not a bit of it.

I'm full of good will and salt-free baby food. You can see that I'm gradually falling into the benign and harmless pattern of a second childhood, and I only hope that it will prove as full of raptures, and even heartbreaking surprises, as the first one was.